When You Lie Down & When You Rise Up

Daily Readings in B'resheet - Genesis

Rabbi Jonathan Allen

Preface by Dr Daniel Juster

When You Lie Down & When You Rise Up
Daily Readings in B'resheet - Genesis
ISBN 1-901917-09-6
Copyright © 2011 Jonathan Peter Allen

Cover Design by Naomi Allen

Typeset in Times New Roman, Viner Hand, Aquaduct, Briner Pro

Where Scripture quotations are unattributed, they are the author's own translation. Otherwise they are attributed and taken from:

CJB — Complete Jewish Bible, Copyright © 1998 by David H. Stern. Published by Jewish New Testament Publications, Inc., Clarksville, Maryland, U.S.A. www.messianicjewish.net/jntp Used and adapted with permission.

ESV — The Holy Bible, English Standard Version, Copyright © 2001 by Crossway Books, a division of Good News Publishers. www.gnpcb.org Used by permission. All rights reserved.

GWT — GOD'S WORD Translation. Copyright © 1995 God's Word to the Nations. Used by permission. www.godsword.org All rights reserved.

JPS — Tanakh - The Holy Scriptures, Copyright © 1985 by The Jewish Publication Society. www.jewishpub.org All rights reserved.

Living Torah — The Living Torah, by Rabbi Aryeh Kaplan, Copyright © 1981, Maznaim Publishing Corporation, New York

Message — The Message by Eugene H. Peterson, Copyright © 1993-96, 2001-02. Used by permission of Navpress Publishing Group. www.navpress.com All rights reserved.

NASB — New American Standard Bible, Copyright ©1960, 1962, 1963, 1968, 1971, 1972, 1973, 1975, 1977 by The Lockman Foundation. www.Lockman.org Used by permission.

NIV — Holy Bible, New International Version, Copyright © 1973,1978,1984 by International Bible Society. Used by permission of Zondervan. www.zondervanbibles.com All rights reserved.

NKJV — New King James Version, Copyright © 1982 by Thomas Nelson, Inc. www.thomasnelson.com/consumer Used by permission. All rights reserved.

NLT — Holy Bible, New Living Translation, Copyright © 1996. Used by permission of Tyndale House Publishers, Inc., Wheaton, Illinois. All rights reserved.

NRSV — Holy Bible, New Revised Standard Version, Copyright © 1989, 1995. Division of Christian Education of the National Council of the Churches in Christ in the United States of America

RSV — Holy Bible, Revised Standard Version, Copyright © 1952, 1971. Division of Christian Education of the National Council of the Churches in Christ in the United States of America

Published by Elisheva Publishing Ltd.
www.elishevapublishing.co.uk

Contents

Preface

Depth in Scripture requires more than just reading. Scholarship alone does not provide the depth we desire, though it does provide us with greater interpretive context. Depth requires interaction with the text, a waiting on the Spirit for insight, and conversation with others who have wrestled with the meaning of the text. It also requires practical application and may well bring change in the interpreter.

Jonathan Allen is one of those who deals with the text in all of the above stated ways. He approaches the text with a mind renewed by the Spirit according to New Covenant teaching. While Mr. Allen's comments are quite accessible to an ordinary reader, there is great weight behind the commentary. If one knows Mr. Allen, one will not be surprised. He is a person who approaches life with a deep commitment to Yeshua and a seriousness of purpose that is reflected in his approach to the text.

His interpretation is devotional without at all engaging in the fanciful fluff that sometimes passes for devotional interpretation. How the *Torah* applies to our lives today, in a practical way, is a subject of great import. A book such as this will bring much gain to us, for it answers the need for that very subject to be dealt with with sensitivity and skill.

I trust that the reader will greatly benefit from time spent in careful consideration on these writings. This is material to be read with due deliberation, in contrast to the manner of our contemporary period where quick responses and limited time dominate our lives. Savor the biblical text and Jonathan Allen's reflections on it, reflections in interaction with others who have reflected, and then add your own thoughts to the conversation.

Daniel Juster, Th. D., Director Tikkun International

Introduction

Genesis - the Book of Beginnings - starts not only the *Torah* but the whole Bible. It is filled with stories and narratives that stretch back to people and places of long ago, but still teach us critical lessons today about God: what He has done, what He is like, how He interacts with people. More importantly, they provide a foundation upon which to base the rest of the Hebrew and Greek Scriptures: the initial revelation.

The *Torah* does not mince its words as it describes sibling rivalry, dubious interpersonal relationships, obedience and disobedience and the call of one family to be God's representative people on the earth. Join in the conversations that have been going on about and within the text for almost as long as the text itself has existed.

These commentaries on the weekly *Torah* portion have been written over the course of seven years: one per portion, per year. They have grown as we have grown; they have developed as our knowledge and understanding of the Hebrew texts, the classic and modern commentators has also developed. Like us, they are themselves a work-in-progress. They step in turn through the seven readings or *aliyot* into which the weekly portion is divided, to offer seven commentaries in each portion. You can read one at a time for each day of the week, or dip into them on an *ad hoc* basis.

This work is, in a sense, "old hat" in that they have been published week by week on our website: *http://www.messianictrust.org.uk* and, indeed, new commentaries continue to be published each week. Please do visit the website or sign up for the weekly e-mail to join in the ongoing conversation and have your say on the thoughts presented.

We have resisted the temptation to rewrite or enlarge the earlier commentaries, believing that their value lies in what - we trust - God has been saying, rather than in the cleverness (or otherwise) of the words or the number of citations. We have nevertheless taken the opportunity to remove some spelling mistakes and typographical issues, hopefully without inserting a fresh collection during the collation and editing phase.

It is true to say that the body of Messiah outside the Messianic Jewish world has largely ignored and rejected the work of the Jewish rabbis in discussing and processing - often at great length - the words of *Torah*, God's foundational revelation to the patriarchs and the people of Israel. This has been a significant loss to the body, as many early insights into the multiple layers of meaning and nuance within the text have essentially been denied to the believing community. One of the aims of these commentaries has been to share some of the insights, commonly held among Jewish people from Second Temple times - the times of Yeshua's (Jesus')own earthly ministry -

and successive generations, with the wider body of Messiah. In particular, it is our desire and - we believe - calling, to encourage our own people to re-discover the riches of the rabbinic writings and hear the ancient voices and conversations afresh in the light of our faith in Yeshua, the Jewish Messiah.

Technicalities

We usually follow the Ashkenazic division of the *parasha* into the seven readings in which the text is read during the *Torah* service on *Shabbat*, but on occasion we have used the Sephardic divisions. Where this is done, it is clearly marked on the *parasha* page.

As this is a work based upon the Hebrew Bible, we have followed a number of conventions of the Jewish world that may need some explanation:

a. names: we use Hebrew names for Yeshua (Jesus), Rav Sha'ul (the Apostle Paul), the patriarchs, Moshe and Aharon, the books of the *Torah* and the individual *parasha* names; this is of no doctrinal significance, but is part of our culture as Messianic Jews

Avraham	Abraham	B'resheet	Genesis
Yitz'khak	Isaac	Shemot	Exodus
Ya'akov	Jacob	Vayikra	Leviticus
Moshe	Moses	B'Midbar	Numbers
Aharon	Aaron	D'varim	Deuteronomy

b. the chapter and verse numbering of the traditional Hebrew text: this is occasionally different from the conventional English numbering and most often only varies by one or two verses; we usually follow the numbering of the Bible version from which we are quoting

There is one commentary for each of the seven *aliyot*; seven commentaries in each portion. These can be read one at a time for each day of the week, or dipped into on an *ad hoc* basis. Each commentary contains a short Hebrew text, its transliteration into an English character set and an English translation, followed by a commentary based upon the text, some verses or passages for further study and some application suggestions.

Citations from the ancient Jewish writings - the Mishnah, the Talmuds and the Midrash Rabbah are accompanied by their appropriate references. The prefix "*m.*" means Mishnah, "*y.*" the Jerusalem Talmud, "*b.*" the Babylonian Talmud. Each part of Midrash Rabbah is given its Hebrew name, for example B'resheet Rabbah. Talmud references give the page (or folio) number in normal type, while the side *a* or *b* in italic.

References to the classic commentators show their names in the

Aquaduct font; there are brief biographical details listed for each named source in the Biography section at the end of the book. These are intended to provide a frame or context from which the commentator speaks. Author and book names also share the Aquaduct font and can be found in the Bibliography section, at the end of the book.

Terms and expressions in an italic typeface are explained in the Glossary section at the end of the book. This provides definitions of some of the other documents, languages and factual information that are referenced in the commentaries, or explain some of the terms that maybe unfamiliar to modern readers or those from a less Jewish-friendly background.

Quotations from the Scriptures themselves are shown in Brinar Pro font so that they are distinct from the commentary text.

One particular Jewish convention is used with such frequency that although it has glossary entries, we felt that we should explain it here as well. It is Jewish custom not to use or pronounce the tetragrammaton covenant name of God in an inappropriate or irreverent way in order to fulfill the commandment not to take God's name in vain. Jewish custom is therefore to use one of two allusions to allow the name of God to be use and referred to in a "safe" way. Obviously, the tetragrammaton appears many times in the Hebrew biblical text. When formally read or used in a worship context, the word is pronounced *Adonai*; on other occasions it is pronounced *HaShem*, which literally means "The Name". You will find these words used in many places in the commentaries.

Every book that includes transliteration of Hebrew words into an English alphabet has its own particular style. The purpose of the transliteration is provide a pronunciation that also reflects the different letters where possible. We denote the Hebrew letter *chaf* by 'ch', *khet* by 'kh' and *kof* by 'k'. A *chaf* with a *dagesh* (a dot in the middle of the letter) is also shown as 'k'. We represent both *sin* and *samech* by 's' and *tzadi* by 'tz'. Dipthongs are usually shown by adding an 'i' or 'y' to the ordinary vowel letter. We generally follow modern Israeli pronunciation, so *vav* has a 'v' sound and *tav* and *tet* are both always 't'. In particular we do not follow the Ashkenazic custom of pronouncing a *tav* without a dagesh as 's'.

We do not take account in this book of *Rosh Chodesh* or the "special" *shabbaton* during the year, such as *Shabbat Shekalim* or *Shabbat Shuva*, when some of the ordinary readings may be replaced by an otherwise out-of-sequence reading.

בְּרֵאשִׁית

B'resheet - In The Beginning

B'resheet / Genesis 1:1 - 6:8

רִאשׁוֹן	Aliyah One	B'resheet/Genesis 1:1 - 2:3
שֵׁנִי	Aliyah Two	B'resheet/Genesis 2:4 - 19
שְׁלִישִׁי	Aliyah Three	B'resheet/Genesis 2:20 - 3:21
רְבִיעִי	Aliyah Four	B'resheet/Genesis 3:22 - 4:18
חֲמִשִׁי	Aliyah Five	B'resheet/Genesis 4:19 - 26
שִׁשִׁי	Aliyah Six	B'resheet /Genesis 5:1 - 24
שְׁבִיעִי	Aliyah Seven	B'resheet/Genesis 5:25 - 6:8

The division of this *parasha* into *aliyot* follows the Sephardic tradition

בְּרֵאשִׁית א'

B'resheet - In The Beginning - 1

B'resheet / Genesis 1:1 - 2:3

B'resheet/Genesis 1:1 In the beginning, God created the heavens and the earth

וְאֵת הַשָּׁמַיִם אֵת אֱלֹהִים בָּרָא בְּרֵאשִׁית
v'et   ha'shamayim   eyt   Elohim   bara   b'resheet

הָאָרֶץ:
ha'aretz

    Rashi tells us that Rav Yitz'khak suggested that the *Torah* could have begun with the commandment to observe the New Moon as it is the first commandment given to the Jewish people as a nation and instituted the Jewish Calendar. "This month shall be the beginning of months for you; it is to be the first month of the year to you" (Shemot 12:2, NASB). Rashi then goes on to connect our verse to Psalm 111:6 where the Psalmist tells us that "He has made known to His people the power of His works, to give them the heritage of the nations" (NASB). He then adds the comment that since God created the world, He also has the right to give it to whomsoever He pleases (Jeremiah 27:5). It can be difficult to accept God's gifts and those to whom He chooses to give, them without knowing that He has that right as the Creator of all things. Beginning with the creation can be foundational.

    The fact that the whole Bible starts at the beginning rather than some other part of history, however logical, teaches us two important things about life in *malchut ha'shamayim*, the Kingdom of God. The first thing we learn is that our relationship with Him must start at the beginning; we cannot jump in part-way through to suit ourselves. As believers in Messiah Yeshua, we have to come to Him first and enter the kingdom through the narrow gate. Until we have made *t'shuvah*, repented of our sin, there is a barrier between us and God. The second thing we learn is that as we go through our lives, God desires to fashion the likeness of His Son in us and in order to do this, He builds certain character traits and habits while removing others. In each of these operations there is a beginning and He has to take us there for

3

the work to start.

If we want to know Him and receive the heritage of the nations, we have first to see and acknowledge Him as the Creator and Authority in both the universe and our lives; then we have to allow Him to make new beginnings in our lives.

Further Study: John 1:1-3, Colossians 1:14-17

Application: Is there an area of your life today that God is drawing to your attention, so that He may make a new beginning? Look out for God showing you the power of His works so that He may share with you the heritage of the nations.

בְּרֵאשִׁית ב׳

B'resheet - In The Beginning - 2

B'resheet / Genesis 2:4 - 19

B'resheet/Genesis 2:4 This is the account of the heavens and the earth

אֵלֶּה תוֹלְדוֹת הַשָּׁמַיִם וְהָאָרֶץ
v'ha'aretz ha'shamayim   tol'dot   Eyleh

The word תּוֹלְדוֹת - variously translated account, chronicles, history or story in different English versions - is also the name of a complete *sidra* further on in the book of Genesis (25:19-28:9) where the text tells the story of Yitz'khak when he takes over from his father Avraham as head of the family and Patriarch living in the Land. It comes from a root verb יָלַד, which means to bring forth and speaks of family history and origins. Our family history, together with our physical appearance, tells people who we are and, more importantly, where we come from and who is responsible for us.

In the Psalms, the Bible tells us that "The heavens declare the glory of God, the dome of the sky speaks the works of His hands. Every day it utters speech, every night it reveals knowledge. Without speech, without a word, without their voices being heard, their line goes out through all the earth and their words to the end of the world" (Psalm 19:1-4, CJB). In the book of Acts, we find Rav Sha'ul and Barnabas telling the crowds at Lystra that God "did not leave Himself without witness, in that He did good and gave you rain from heaven and fruitful seasons, satisfying your hearts with food and gladness" (Acts 14:17, NASB).

Everything that God does is for a purpose, for a testimony to bear witness to who He is and the fact that He exists. We are a part of that witness to the world by our actions and by our words, by the choices we take and the attitudes that we demonstrate - often sub-consciously - as we go about our daily lives. Yeshua told the disciples, "You are the light of the world. A city set on a hill cannot be hidden" (Matthew 5:14, NASB), and Peter wrote to the believers in the *Diaspora* that they should "live such good lives among the pagans that even though they now speak against you as evil-doers, they will, as a result of seeing your good actions, give glory to to God on the day of His coming" (1 Peter 2:12, CJB).

Whether we like it or not, whether we are aware of it or not, everything that we do or say tells a story of who we are, where we come from and who is responsible for us. The question is: what story do we tell?

Further Study: James 3:4-12, Matthew 12:37

Application: Try and observe yourself during today and see what message you are sending out to those who are watching you. As well as listening to your words, what else is coming from the tone of your voice and from your body language? Are you a good witness for God?

בְּרֵאשִׁית ג'

B'resheet - In The Beginning - 3

B'resheet / Genesis 2:20 - 3:21

B'resheet/Genesis 2:20 ... but for Adam there was not found a helper suitable for him

וּלְאָדָם לֹא־מָצָא עֵזֶר כְּנֶגְדּוֹ
k'neg'do eyzer matza lo ool'Adam

Rabbi Akiva used to say, "Beloved is man, for he was created in God's image" (*m*. Pirke Avot 3.18). The Maharal asks, "More beloved than whom? More beloved than animals? Isn't that obvious? More beloved even than the angels." Man is the pinnacle and focal point of creation - more precious to God than any other creature, he was created in the image of his Maker (Tosafot Yom Tov).

Among all the creation there was found no suitable helper for Adam because man is unique - man alone is made in the image of God. The Psalmist asks the Lord, "What are mere mortals, that You concern Yourself with them; humans, that you watch over them with such care?" (Psalm 8:3, CJB). Yeshua reminds us, "Aren't sparrows sold for next to nothing, two for an assarion? Yet not one of them will fall to the ground without your Father's consent. As for you, every hair on your head has been counted. So do not be afraid, you are worth more than many sparrows" (Matthew 10:29-31, CJB).

Man is distinctively different from the animal kingdom because he has a soul, because he was created for relationship with God and because God desires relationship with him. While man often has relationship with animals - dogs, cats and horses being perhaps the most common - man is the master in the relationship, as the Psalmist goes on to say, "You had him rule what Your hands made ... sheep and oxen, all of them, also the animals in the wilds, the birds in the air, the fish in the sea" (Psalm 8:7-9, CJB). In the same way, Father God is the Master in our relationship with Him, and as a good and loving Master, He provides everything we need.

So when we are cast down, we need to remember that we are different from everything else in creation, for we were created for fellowship with our Master.

Further Study: Jeremiah 29:11-14; 1 Corinthians 9:9-10

Application: Do you feel just the same as everyone else? Are you one of those people who always seem to lead a dog's life? Does life seem humdrum and without purpose? Reach out to God today, because He cares for you as no other can. He has a plan and a purpose for your life.

בְּרֵשִׁית ד׳

B'resheet - In The Beginning - 4

B'resheet / Genesis 3:22 - 4:18

B'resheet/Genesis 4:1 ... [Eve] said, "With the help of the Lord I have brought forth a son."

וַתֹּאמֶר קָנִיתִי אִישׁ אֶת־יהוה
Adonai   et   iysh   kaniytiy   vat'omer

Jewish mysticism teaches that when a husband and wife come together [physically] with the proper intention, God's presence dwells between them (Zohar, Aharei Mot 59a). There is a team at work here: man, woman and God, acting together to create new life. This points us to a larger truth - that we are called to be God's workmen, as Rav Sha'ul tells us: "For we are God's co-workers" (1 Corinthians 3:9, CJB), co-labourers or fellow workers as other translations put it. Now this is a mystery if ever there was one: we are working alongside the Master of the Universe, working together with Him to bring about His desire for the world. God has, as Rabbi Abraham Joshua Heschel explains, limited Himself to working through human agency and is - in a certain way - constrained by what we allow Him to do in and through us.

This should not come as a surprise to us, for the idea of *tikkun ha'olam* has long been a part of Jewish understanding. Fixing up or repairing the world, restoring the earth or the universe, is seen as the duty of every Jew, to do his part to hasten the coming of Messiah. In recent years, the Lubavitch movement has majored on the keeping of the *mitzvot* and encouraged their followers to take on the observance of more and more *mitzvot* in order to tilt the balance and increase the world-wide level of obedience to God's commandments so that Messiah will be able to come soon.

As believers, we know that Yeshua is the Messiah, who has already come and is to return, when "every eye shall see Him" (Revelation 1:7). Rav Sha'ul points out that although we have been "saved by grace" (Ephesians 2:8), we are "His workmanship, created in Messiah Yeshua for good works, which God prepared beforehand, that we should walk in them" (v. 10, NASB). Our purpose for being here is to walk in His ways, do His works and be His

9

witnesses in this world.

But do we do this on our own? Do we have to take the strain of this on our own shoulders? Yeshua told His disciples, "Come to Me, all who are weary and heavy laden, and I will give you rest. Take My yoke upon you, and learn from Me, for I am gentle and humble in heart; and you shall find rest for your souls. For My yoke is easy, and My load is light" (Matthew 11:28-30, NASB). He will take the lead, He will take the strain, but we have to play our part and be prepared to labour in the Kingdom alongside our Lord and Master.

Further Study: Matthew 9:37-38; 2 Corinthians 1:23-24

Application: Where and how are you supposed to be working with the Lord? Ask the Master to show you what His purpose is for you today.

בְּרֵשִׁית 'ה

B'resheet - In The Beginning - 5

B'resheet / Genesis 4:19 - 26

B'resheet/Genesis 4:19 Lemekh took for himself two wives

וַיִּקַּח־לוֹ לֶמֶךְ שְׁתֵּי נָשִׁים

nashim   sh'tey Lemekh lo vayikakh

The *Midrash* tells us that in the generations before the flood, men would take two wives: one for bearing children, the other for pleasure. While the wife for pleasure was pampered and petted, the wife for children was scorned and treated more like a slave. This is hinted at in the names of Lemekh's wives: one is called 'Adah', which in Aramaic means 'removed', while the other is called 'Tzilah' which in Hebrew is related to the word 'tzeyl' meaning shadow, so the Rabbis taught that Tzilah always lived in Lemekh's shadow (B'resheet Rabbah 23:2).

Can you see a connection to some words that Yeshua spoke? "No servant can be slave to two masters, for he will either hate the first and love the second, or scorn the second and be loyal to the first" (Luke 16:13, CJB). While Yeshua goes on to apply that observation to 'God and money', the Scriptures show us that it applies very clearly to a husband that takes more than one wife. Look at the *tsuris* between Ya'akov's two wives, Leah and Rachel. Although the Talmud sanctions polygamy, "A man may marry as many wives as he pleases" (*b*. Yevamot 65*a*), generally it is recognised that a husband had only one wife, for example: "A man's home is his wife" (*m*. Yoma I.1), and polygamy was formally banned in a rabbinic decree issued by Rabbi Gershon in the early Middle Ages[1].

Yeshua's words warn us of the difficulties we will encounter if we have split or divided loyalties and in particular if we are divided between something and God. Anything that competes for our attention with God is an idol: something that sometimes, even if not often, comes before Him in our favour, time and devotion. Many people struggle with this issue; for some it is money, for others football or golf, for yet others some consuming hobby

---

1. Reportedly issued for Ashkenazi Jewry at a synod around 1000 CE under pressure from the church.

like stamp collecting or cross-stitching. Whenever we devote our time, energy, attention and money to anything other than the Lord, we run the risk of making it into an idol and it becoming a snare for us. Remember that "the Lord your God is a consuming fire, a jealous God" (D'varim 4:24, NASB). He will not share our affections.

Further Study: 2 Kings 18:1-4; 2 Timothy 2:14-18

Application: Look at your life today and see if there is something that is competing with God for your best attention and favour. Has some habit or pursuit eaten into your time and devotion to the Lord?

בְּרֵשִׁית ו׳

B'resheet - In The Beginning - 6

B'resheet / Genesis 5:1 - 24

B'resheet/Genesis 5:24 ... and he was no more, for God had taken him

וְאֵינֶנּוּ כִּי־לָקַח אֹתוֹ אֱלֹהִים
Elohim   oto   lakakh kiy v'eynenu

This intriguing piece of text has interested scholars in many generations and places, as they try to work out exactly what the words mean. *Targum Yonatan* paraphrases this to say, "he was not with the sojourners of the earth, for he was withdrawn and he ascended to heaven by the word of God." Rashi suggests that although Enoch was a righteous man, he was not firm enough in his convictions, so that he might have ended up committing sin had he stayed longer on this earth. Consequently, he was taken away from the world before that happened. It is clear that Enoch's departure was by the hand of God because the word לָקַח, 'took' is used in the same way in Ezekiel 24:16 when God tells Ezekiel that He is going to take his wife from him.

Whether we accept the Sages' suggestions about Enoch's character or not, the Scriptures are explicit that God knows the measure of man, "for God sees not as man sees, for man looks at the outward appearance, but the Lord looks at the heart" (1 Samuel 16:7, NASB), "for the Lord searches all hearts, and understands every intent of the thoughts" (1 Chronicles 28:9, NASB). Indeed, although many people saw Yeshua's signs and miracles and "believed in Him", He didn't commit Himself to them, "for He Himself knew what was in man" (John 2:25, NASB).

It is good that our God knows and remembers that we are "fearfully and wonderfully made" (Psalm 139:14, KJV). He values us and takes care that we are not placed in situations that we cannot, in His strength, handle; He does not set us up for failure. Rav Sha'ul speaks of this when he tells the believers at Corinth, "No temptation has seized you beyond what people normally experience, and God can be trusted not to allow you to be tempted beyond what you can bear. On the contrary, along with the temptation He will also provide the way out, so that you will be able to endure" (1 Corinthians

10:13, CJB).

This shouldn't be taken as an excuse, whenever the going gets a little rough, to cry 'Wolf!' and expect the Lord to pull us out of testing circumstances. Rav Sha'ul also writes about us having to take up the whole armour of God so "that you may be able to resist in the evil day, and having done everything, to stand firm" (Ephesians 6:13, NASB). But it does give us the assurance that whatever happens, in Him, we can withstand. "No, in all these things we are more than conquerors in through Him who loved us" (Romans 8:37, NRSV).

Further Study: 1 Peter 5:7; James 4:7

Application: When we get into difficulties, we often shout for help and expect the Lord to wave a 'magic wand' and make things better. Do you have any areas in your life where you are trying to bail out and avoid having to stand and deal with the issues?

בְּרֵשִׁית ז׳

B'resheet - In The Beginning - 7

B'resheet / Genesis 5:25 - 6:8

B'resheet/Genesis 6:4 The N'filim were in the earth in those days

הַנְּפִלִים הָיוּ בָאָרֶץ בַּיָּמִים הָהֵם
ha'heym bayamiym va'aretz hayu han'filim

Who were the N'filim? Jewish tradition has many answers but no conclusive proofs. By all accounts, they were giants. Rashi points out that their name comes from the root נָפַל, meaning to fall, and connects this to several ancient sources that claim they were fallen angels. Ibn Ezra, on the other hand, suggests that they were so called because the hearts of those who saw them fell in amazement. The Gur Aryeh says that by their sinfulness they caused the world to fall in wickedness in the generation of the flood. The name reappears in B'Midbar 13:33 to describe the "giants in the land", the descendants of Anak, that the twelve spies saw when they were scouting out the Land of Israel. Since only Noah's family survived the flood, that text cannot refer to the same people as here. What conclusions can we draw? Only that no-one knows for sure.

Does it matter if we do not know exactly who the N'filim were? To some, this might be a troubling question and one of the reasons that there are so many suggested answers. But Moshe tells us that "Things which are hidden belong to Adonai our God. But the things that have been revealed belong to us and our children forever" (D'varim 29:28, CJB). Or, in other words, some things God has revealed and some He has not. Some things we do not even know the existence of, some things are hinted at, some - such as Higg's Boson[2] - are theorised but unproven, and others are clearly revealed. Some things change from being hidden, or just hinted at, to being revealed by God, as Daniel told the king: "However, there is a God in heaven who reveals mysteries, and He has made known to King Nebuchadnezzar what will take place in the latter days" (Daniel 2:28, NASB).

Of course, the greatest mystery that has been revealed to mankind is

---

2. A hypothetical elementary particle predicted to exist to resolve inconsistencies in theoretical physics but never observed.

"the mystery which has been hidden from the past ages and generations; but has now been manifested to His saints ... which is Messiah in you, the hope of glory" (Colossians 1:26-27, NASB). Yeshua has been revealed to us as the Messiah for whom we have been waiting; and not only for us, but for all those among the nations who would receive Him as their Lord and Saviour. Yeshua told His disciples, "To you the secret [or mystery] of the Kingdom of God has been given" (Mark 4:11, CJB). He has revealed to us, by His Spirit, the saving knowledge of who He is and the means for entering the in Him.

As we look around the world today and once more we see giants in the land: the giants of financial instability, unemployment, the housing market, the myth of global warming, famine in Africa, the Middle-East peace process and many other looming disasters that are completely beyond our control, we are tempted to feel hopeless and quake in our boots. Instead, we should speak out against uncertainty and falsehood where it exists and share the truth that we have been given. We know a Man who not only knows about, understands and has defeated all these giants, but has promised to be with us and preserve us through these last days. He sums it up for us: "And just as it happened in the days of Noah, so it shall be also in the days of the Son of Man" (Luke 17:26, NASB).

Further Study: Ephesians 3:3-12; Hebrews 1:1-3

Application: Has God revealed to you the hope of glory in your life? If not, seek Him today for a fresh revelation by His Spirit, that you may share in the fullness of the .

נֹחַ

Noakh - Noah

B'resheet / Genesis 6:9 - 11:32

רִאשׁוֹן	Aliyah One	B'resheet/Genesis 6:9 - 22
שֵׁנִי	Aliyah Two	B'resheet/Genesis 7:1 - 16
שְׁלִישִׁי	Aliyah Three	B'resheet/Genesis 7:17 - 8:14
רְבִיעִי	Aliyah Four	B'resheet/Genesis 8:15 - 9:7
חֲמִשִׁי	Aliyah Five	B'resheet/Genesis 9:8 - 17
שִׁשִׁי	Aliyah Six	B'resheet /Genesis 9:18 - 10:32
שְׁבִיעִי	Aliyah Seven	B'resheet/Genesis 11:1 - 32

Noakh - Noah - 1

B'resheet / Genesis 6:9 - 22

B'resheet/Genesis 6:9 These are the generations of Noah. Noah was a righteous man.

אֵלֶּה תּוֹלְדֹת נֹחַ נֹחַ אִישׁ צַדִּיק
tzadiyk iysh Noakh Noakh toldot eyleh

Proverbs 10:7 tells us that "the memory of the righteous will be for a blessing" (CJB), so immediately after setting the context for this week's *parasha* - the days of Noah and his children - the *Torah* tells us that Noah was a righteous man. The *Midrash* says that this commendation of Noah comes before the list of Noah's sons in order to teach that the main offspring of the righteous are good deeds (B'resheet Rabbah 30:6).

While we know that it is "by grace you have been saved through faith ... not as a result of works" (Ephesians 2:8-9, NASB), Rav Sha'ul goes on to tell us that we are God's workmanship, "created in union with the Messiah Yeshua for a life of good actions already prepared by God for us to do" (Ephesians 2:10, CJB). Should we be asking ourselves what it is that will mark us out in our generation as men and women of God?

Peter wrote to the believers living in the *Diaspora* to, "live such good lives among the pagans that even though they now speak against you as evildoers, they will, as a result of seeing your good actions, give glory to God on the Day of His coming" (1 Peter 2:12, NASB). It is a question of witness: how we are seen and perceived by those around us, by those with whom we live and work. If we are to be a blessing to those with whom we are in daily contact, we must be good and consistent witnesses for the Kingdom of God.

Whilst Rav Sha'ul told Timothy to be "ready in season and out of season" (2 Tim 4:2, NASB), there is nothing worse than the bore who cannot seem to open their mouth without cramming the gospel down everyone's throat, whether it is appropriate or not. As far as the gospel is concerned, words are often one of the last steps required. Advertising executives tell us that it takes seven successful contacts to persuade someone to buy a product, and a direct appeal to buy is nearly always rejected before the final step. Although there is no documented record, St. Francis of Assissi is said to have sent out his disciples to share the gospel with everyone they met in all possible ways, concluding his instructions by saying that the disciples could even use words if necessary.

Further Study: James 2:14-26

Application: If you went home to be with the Lord today, what would you want people to write in your obituary? How do you think people would remember you? In your generation, are you a righteous person?

נֹחַ ב׳

Noakh - Noah - 2

B'resheet / Genesis 7:1 - 16

B'resheet/Genesis 7:1 "... for you I have seen as righteous before Me in this generation."

כִּי-אֹתְךָ רָאִיתִי צַדִּיק לְפָנַי בַּדֹּור הַזֶּה׃

hazeh   bador   l'fanay   tzaddik   ra'iytiy   ot'cha kiy

Comparing this verse to 6:9, Rabbi Jeremiah ben Eleazar said, "Only a part of a man's praise may be said in his presence, but all of it in his absence" (*b*. Eruvin 18*b*). God is able to speak to Noah because he is righteous; that is, he acknowledges and seeks to please God. God describes him as "righteous and wholehearted" (B'resheet 6:9, CJB). By the time that God calls Noah to "come ... into the ark" (7:1), He has seen that only Noah is righteous. Even Noah's sons are a mixed bunch, as the story of Ham is later to show.

The word 'generation' is often used by the Bible to describe all the people living at a particular time or period rather than just one family. So we see Yeshua speaking to those who pestered Him for proof that He was Messiah when He said, "A wicked and adulterous generation asks for a sign?" (Matthew 12:39, CJB). Again, as in the days of Noah, the people of the time were showing themselves not to be righteous, not to be prepared to engage with God on His terms but only on their own.

Now, again, in our generation we see the people and leaders of the world intent on pursuing their own affairs without reference to God. The picture painted by Ezekiel the Prophet seems to be appearing before our eyes: the leaders "are like wolves tearing the prey, by shedding blood and destroying lives in order to get dishonest gain ... the people of the land have practised oppression and committed robbery, and they have wronged the poor and needy and have oppressed the sojourner without justice" (Ezekiel 22:27,29, NASB).

Today, the voice of God is still calling, "I searched for a man among them who should build up the wall and stand in the gap before Me for the land, that I should not destroy it" (Ezekiel 22:30, NASB). God is still seeking His people in this generation who will be righteous, who will not compromise, who will stand before Him and intercede for the land that He should not destroy it. It is a tough call and a demanding role - are you up to it?

Further Study: 1 Timothy 2:1-3, 2 Peter 3:8-11

Application: Ask God how you can 'stand in the gap' for those whom you come into contact with today. Whether praying, helping, leading or serving, we must engage with and for the world.

Noakh ~ Noah ~ 3

B'resheet / Genesis 7:17 - 8:14

B'resheet/Genesis 7:17 And the flood was forty days upon the earth

וַיְהִי הַמַּבּוּל אַרְבָּעִים יוֹם עַל־הָאָרֶץ
ha'aretz al yom ar'ba'iym hamabul vay'hiy

The word אַרְבָּעִים, forty, is the plural of the word אַרְבָּע, meaning 'four', which in turn comes from the rarely used root רְבַע, to be four-sided or four-square. Grammarians argue over whether the verb, which is found only in *Qal* or *Pu'el* participle forms, comes from the number or vice-versa. Be that as it may, the number forty is a significant Biblical number, occurring many times throughout both the Hebrew and Greek Scriptures. In the immediate context of this week's *parasha*, starting at 7:4, this is the first time the number forty is introduced; here as days, but also often as years.

Hirsch points out that our Sages comment that forty days is the same period as that required for the formation of the human foetus, so that the duration of the flood/catastrophe could in itself be taken as showing the destruction to be, in a deeper meaning, also the formation of a new future.

Another noticeable 'forty' is the forty days that the spies spent investigating the Land when our people reached Kadesh Barnea for the first time, and the forty years our people then spent in the wilderness as a result of disobeying God and refusing to enter the Land at that time. Again, we can see the motif of both the forty days and the forty years being the equivalent of formation or gestation periods: the forty days for the bad report that ten of the twelve spies brought of the Land (B'midbar 13:31-33); the forty years for the destruction of the complete generation who had accepted the bad report and by so doing, rejected God and His promises, but at the same time, the formation of the next generation who experienced God's miraculous provision (food, water, indestructible clothes and shoes) and then entered and took the Land under Joshua's leadership.

We can find two 'forty day' periods in Yeshua's earthly life: His forty days of fasting and testing at the start of His ministry (Luke 4:1-2), and the forty days He spent with the disciples between His resurrection and ascension (Acts 1:3). The first followed His baptism and the descent of the *Ruach HaKodesh* and was clearly a time of formation and consolidation before the three critical years of ministry to the people, calling out and training the disciples who were to be His witnesses and proclaim Him to the world, culminating in His greatest work on the execution stake. The second was also a time of formation: following the depression of witnessing the arrest, trial and crucifixion of their Master, then the euphoria of the Resurrection and seeing Yeshua alive again amongst them, the disciples needed a crash course in interpreting Biblical prophecy, consolidation to see all the pieces fitted together, and to be moulded into a team of witnesses ready to await their empowerment ten days later at *Shavuot*. God uses times of apparent destruction, withdrawal, formation and consolidation to bring forth new things in our lives.

Further Study: 1 Kings 19:7-8; Ezekiel 29:9-16

Application: Do you feel that you are in set-aside mode at this time? Is God doing a work of cleansing and reforming in your life so that you will be equipped to serve Him in a new and enhanced capacity? Be encouraged, for this is God's way and pattern for His servants.

Noakh - Noah - 4

B'resheet / Genesis 8:15 - 9:7

B'resheet/Genesis 8:16 Go out from the ark, you and your wife, your sons and the wives of your sons with you

צֵא מִן־הַתֵּבָה אַתָּה וְאִשְׁתְּךָ וּבָנֶיךָ

oovaneycha v'ish't'cha atah hateyvah min tzey

וּנְשֵׁי־בָנֶיךָ אִתָּךְ:

itach vaneycha oonshey

The word starting the verse, צֵא, is the *Qal* imperative form from the root יָצָא, meaning "to go out" or "to leave". *HaShem* is actively telling Noah to leave the Ark. Though it has been a place of safety for him, his family and the animals, it is now time to move on. *HaShem* is not giving Noah the option of using the Ark as a base and making occasional sorties while he gets himself ready for going out; God knows that Noah must go and must go now or perhaps he will never let go of the security that the Ark provided during the flood. The animals must be released so that they can disperse to their natural territories; Noah and his family must come out, have children, found the nations and move forward to fulfill God's command to "fill the earth, subdue it and take dominion" (B'resheet 1:28).

Rashi points to the resumption of normal life by highlighting the difference between the instructions to enter the Ark (6:18) where God says, "you, your sons, your wife and your son's wives" and these instructions to leave the Ark. He suggests that in the former, there is an implied gender segregation upon entry, whereas in the latter the couples are united again as they leave the Ark. Rashi therefore deduces that God forbade Noah and his sons from having relations with their respective wives for the duration of the time in the Ark, perhaps as if they needed all their resources and energies to focus on the immediate task in front of them. Rav Sha'ul addresses the same issue in his letter to the Corinthians: "Do not deprive each other, except for a limited time, by mutual agreement, and then only so as to have extra time for prayer; but afterwards, come together again" (1 Corinthians 7:5, CJB).

25

Each of us goes through seasons of security and seasons of insecurity; places where we feel comfortable and safe and those where we feel the need to be careful; people and relationships that are open and trusting, where we can share our feelings freely, and those that are less so and we need to be more guarded. God calls us to move between the cycles in our lives as we grow and develop, as we are ministered to by others and as we - in our turn - minister to others; sometimes we are receiving love and security, at other times we are providing it for others, be they family, friends, work colleagues or members of our congregation or fellowship. The transitions between these phases can often be difficult for us, because we naturally prefer to remain in the place of comfort and security, stability and continuity. But although we may be making progress and growing in those times, God will call us to move through other cycles of relative insecurity, giving out to others more than we receive, difficult and challenging relationships, even times when our faith and love may be snubbed or ridiculed - our very relationship with God being attacked. These are the times when we grow the most, when we are stretched - almost, as it were, to breaking point - when the blacksmith builds strength and character by the heat of the fire, the blows of the hammer on the anvil, and the cold of the water that quenches and tempers the iron.

How do we know, like Noah, that God is calling us to move on and into a time of challenge and growth? Simply that He goes before us and calls us. Yeshua said, "[The shepherd] calls his own sheep, each one by name, and leads them out. After taking out all that are his own, he goes on ahead of them; and the sheep follow him because they recognise his voice" (John 10:3-4, CJB). That is how we know to move forward - because Yeshua calls us and we know His voice.

Further Study: Joshua 3:14-17; Daniel 3:24-26; Acts 16:35-40

Application: Are you in that place where you know that you have heard God calling you to move forward, to move on and follow Him? Perhaps you don't want to leave the people or place where you are, but you can't ignore or put down that voice that is calling you? Take courage, take godly counsel and take that step of faith today, without delay, and He will be with you!

Noakh - Noah - 5

B'resheet / Genesis 9:8 - 17

B'resheet/Genesis 9:9 And I - look! I Myself - am establishing My covenant with you and your seed after you

וַאֲנִי הִנְנִי מֵקִים אֶת־בְּרִיתִי אִתְּכֶם
itchem   b'riytiy   et   maykiym hin'niy v'aniy

וְאֶת־זַרְעֲכֶם אַחֲרֵיכֶם:
akhareychem zar'achem v'et

It is at this critical point - after Noah and his family have come out of the ark, and the first round of blessings and sacrifices have taken place - that God takes the initiative and moves to assure Noah there really is a long-term future for mankind on the earth.

Rashi expresses doubts in Noah's mind as to the future: should Noah really be prepared to invest his time and energy into building a permanent position, in encouraging his family to spread out and re-populate the earth, developing cities, nations and civilisations, or would God feel obliged to step in and destroy everything again if it got out of hand? According to Rashi's picture, Noah is sitting on his hands, unwilling to move forward or commit to anything until God - almost reluctantly it would seem - gives him a promise that He won't destroy the earth and all the people again. This could be seen in the almost patronising tone of our text: "I - look, I Myself, it really is Me - I will establish My covenant with you and your seed".

Taking a larger view, Richard Elliot Friedman sees this passage in a more positive light as the first in a series of "major covenants that provide the structure in which nearly all of the Bible is framed." Friedman counts four: Noah (B'resheet 9) - the security of the cosmos, Avraham (B'resheet 15, 17) - the Land and relationship with Avraham's descendants, Moshe (Shemot 20, 34; D'varim 5, 7:12-15) - well-being and a way of life in the Land, David (2 Samuel 7; Psalm 89, 132) - kingship over Jerusalem and Judea. As believers, we logically extend the count to five by including the renewed covenant (Jeremiah 31:31-34; Luke 22:20) in Messiah Yeshua.

These all show that time and again it is God who takes the initiative in the human-divine relationship and offers covenant - a legal, binding, permanent, committed relationship - to man; it is God who sets the terms, provides the surety and offers all the benefits. History shows that it is also God who alone is faithful to the covenant, God who renews the covenant and constantly calls His people back to the covenant, God who will not let His people go but keeps their feet to the fire whenever they turn away from Him.

Three times every day we proclaim the faithfulness of God in the first stanza of the *Amidah*: "Blessed are You, O Lord, our God and the God of our forefathers, God of Avraham, God of Yitz'khak and God of Ya'akov; the great, mighty and awesome God, the most high God, who bestows acts of loving kindness and creates everything, who remembers the loving kindness of the patriarchs and brings a redeemer to their children's children for the sake of His name in love." This speaks of the consistency and constancy of God and His covenant relationship with us, His people. He has been in covenant with us, in spite of our many failures and abandonments over the years, since the days of the patriarchs, and He is still bringing a redeemer - Messiah Yeshua - to us every day so that we may turn to Him and find rest for our souls (Matthew 11:28).

So God's basic nature is that He is a maker and a keeper of covenant; not only has He made them, but He has paid the penalty for our non-keeping of the covenant through the body of Yeshua on the stake so that His covenant-keeping might become ours in Him (2 Corinthians 5:21). We are made in the image or likeness of God (B'resheet 1:26-27) and are called to be like Him; in particular, we are called to be faithful in the covenants that we make: marriage as a primary example, but also in business and other relationships. The divorce rate in both the church and the wider Jewish community is pretty much equal to that of the non-believing world, suggesting that we're not too clever on that front, and it is difficult to open the pages of the Jewish Chronicle without reading of some court case, bankruptcy hearings or financial misconduct that is either between or includes Jews.

Yeshua calls us to a higher standard in the Sermon on the Mount. First, in the area of marriage relationships He tells us: "I tell you that anyone who divorces his wife, except on the ground of fornication, makes her an adulteress; and that anyone who marries a divorcee commits adultery" (Matthew 5:32, CJB). Marriage is to be a permanent covenant, made and kept before God as a model to the world of His covenant faithfulness toward us. Yeshua goes on, "let your 'Yes' be a simple 'Yes' and your 'No' be a simple 'No'" (v. 37, CJB). We are not to compound our commitments to each other with complicated or fearsome sounding oaths as if our words are meaningless unless we invoke some dire calamity upon our heads; we are to be people of our basic word, who can be trusted simply on the basis of what we say. This is indeed a challenge in our day, but God has set us the example: "See, I am establishing My covenant with you and your seed after you".

Further Study: Isaiah 54:9-10; Matthew 23:16-22

Application: How do you rate on the covenant keeping scale today? Can people trust you and rely upon what you say? Remember that God knows how to keep covenants and can help you to do the same. He wants you to be a good reflection of His character, so why not get Him on your case today!

נֹחַ 'ו

Noakh - Noah - 6

B'resheet / Genesis 9:18 - 10:32

B'resheet/Genesis 9:19 These three were the sons of Noah, and from these the whole world dispersed.

שְׁלֹשָׁה אֵלֶּה בְּנֵי־נֹחַ וּמֵאֵלֶּה נָפְצָה

naph'tsah oomey'eyleh Noach b'ney eyleh   sh'loshah

כָּל־הָאָרֶץ׃

ha'aretz chol

The second half of this verse obeys the normal Hebrew word order: the subject - כָּל־הָאָרֶץ, "all the earth" or "the whole earth" - following the verb - נָפְצָה, a *Qal* affix 3fs form to agree with its subject. The root is נָפַץ, "to break, dash in pieces, to disperse or scatter, to disperse themselves" (Davidson) and is essentially an active verb; it was the peoples who dispersed themselves, who spread out from the place where the ark came to rest and Noah their father settled and planted a vineyard.

Targum Onkelos, on the other hand, uses the Aramaic *itpa'al* stem to switch the voice of the verb from active to passive: אִתְבַּדַּרוּ כָּח אָרְעָאthey were dispersed over the whole earth. Instead of the whole earth dispersing from them, they are dispersed over all the earth; the focus changes from the people to God who disperses them and takes the active role to ensure the population of the whole earth.

The Sforno comments that although Ham - the wicked son, because he had humiliated his father - was among them, yet because they were all sons of Noah, and all had been blessed by God when they came out of the ark: "Be fruitful and multiply and fill the land" (9:1), the result was that all three sons experienced the spreading out, the blessing of progeny, the increase to fill the world. Because God had already given the blessing, its fulfillment was not dependent on the behaviour of the individual sons; as a group the blessing was still worked out. So it has always been with our people; both in biblical times, as the Bible's narrative shows, and in the two millenia since, that despite our mixed behaviour and obedience to God - consider the secular Jews, the humanist Jews and even the Buddhist Jews - still God blesses us as a people, still the Jewish people are a blessing to the nations, still the Jewish people are overweight in the world ranks of scientists, doctors, lawyers, human rights activists, the arts and the caring professions. It is not of ourselves, but of God, who fulfills His promises through us and sometimes despite us!

Hirsch points out that the verb נָפַץ is also the root for the noun מַפֵּץ, a hammer, an object that breaks into pieces. A hammer is a tool that can be used for beating out metal to spread it out thinly, to make a covering and effect a design. In the context of the first communities of believers, this illustrates God's purposeful dispersion of the people around the Land so that they had to move away from their natural centre in Jerusalem. The book of Acts records that, "starting with that day, there arose intense persecution against the Messianic community in Jerusalem; all but the emissaries were scattered throughout the regions of Y'hudah and Shomron" (Acts 8:1, CJB). This was the way that God caused the gospel to spread throughout the Land of Israel - He used the persecution as a hammer to break the holy huddle into pieces and to spread it out over all the villages and towns so that all the Jewish people - where Yeshua Himself had been ministering and proclaiming the Kingdom of God in recent years - would have an opportunity to hear and respond to the good news. The narrative tells us that, "those who were scattered announced the Good News of the Word wherever they went" (Acts 8:4, CJB). A little later on, we can see how far the dispersion had reached: "Now those who had been scattered because of the persecution which had arisen over Stephen went as far as Phoenicia, Cyprus and Antioch; they spoke God's word, but only to Jews. However, some of them, men from Cyprus and Cyrene, when they arrived at Antioch, began speaking to the Greeks too, proclaiming the Good News of the Lord Yeshua. The hand of the Lord was with them, and a great number of people trusted and turned to the Lord" (Acts 11:19-21, CJB). Not only were physical boundaries crossed, but religious and spiritual boundaries were also crossed as the message was spread out to the Gentiles.

The Scripture uses two contrasting pictures to describe God's word and the effects that it has. One, hinted at already, is that of fire and a hammer: "'Isn't My word like fire,' asks Adonai, 'like a hammer shattering rocks?'" (Jeremiah 23:29, CJB); the other is of water: "For just as rain and snow fall from the sky ... so is My word that goes out from My mouth" (Isaiah 55:10-11, CJB). Both fire and water are devastatingly powerful forces in nature, destroying and demolishing families, homes, businesses; every facet of life can be swept away and disrupted. At the same time, the water picture also speaks of a gentle encouraging or nurturing action: "watering the earth, causing it to bud and produce, giving seed to the sower and bread to the eater"

(Isaiah 55:10, CJB), as God provides the means for life and growth. So it is with our lives: sometimes God needs to break us up and scatter us further afield in order to increase our effectiveness, to reach more people, to stop us becoming inward-looking; but once dispersed, we need the means of growth so that we may bring forth a crop for the Kingdom. Cycles, then, of growth and change should be expected in our lives, but behind it all the steady plan and purpose of God, moving us on and growing both us and others "until we all arrive at the unity implied by trusting and knowing the Son of God, at full manhood, at the standard of maturity set by the Messiah's perfection" (Ephesians 4:13, CJB).

Further Study: Matthew 10:23; 1 Thessalonians 2:1-2

Application: Are you in a dispersal phase or a growth and consolidation phase? Either way, know that the hand of God is upon you, moving and shaping your life according to His good will and purpose. Be aware of His hand upon you today and ask Him to show you where you are and how you can co-operate with Him to accomplish the best in your life.

Noakh - Noah - 7

B'resheet / Genesis 11:1 - 32

B'resheet/Genesis 11:1 And all the earth was [of] one lip and [of] one words

וַיְהִי כָל־הָאָרֶץ שָׂפָה אֶחָת וּדְבָרִים אֲחָדִים׃

akhadiym   ood'variym   ekhat   sapha   ha'aretz chol vayhiy

The literal translation of this verse reads strangely in English; a more readable translation might say, "used the same language and the same words" (NASB). By so doing, however, the reader may conclude that the text here is talking solely about vocabulary, when perhaps more is being conveyed by the Hebrew text.

Rashi comments that the phrase שָׂפָה אֶחָת - "one lip, one language" - means that everyone in those days spoke Hebrew. He alludes to the ancient commentators (*Midrash Tanchuma* 19, *Targum Jonathan* and *y*. Megillah 1:9) who say that all other languages other than the Holy Tongue, by which God created the world, are hybrids, developing and borrowing from each other. Latin and Greek words, for example, occur in all the European languages as well as English. Latin itself is heavily based upon Greek which is, in turn, based upon an ancient predecessor. The rabbis claim that only Hebrew - biblical Hebrew - is pure of foreign traces and so can be called the Holy Tongue. Rashi is supported by the Ba'al HaTurim who uses *gematria* to make this phrase into a proof text; the *gematria* of the two words שָׂפָה אֶחָת (794) is considered equivalent to that of לְשׁוֹן הַקֹּדֶשׁ - the Holy Tongue (795).

The second phrase וּדְבָרִים אֲחָדִים - "and one words" - has what is to English speakers an odd clash; the word for 'one' אֶחָד has a masculine plural ending so that it agrees with the noun it is qualifying: words. Although the Hebrew is quite comfortable, the commentators leap in to offer an explanation of this apparent anomaly. *Targum Onkelos* translates the phrase "one way of speaking", while Ibn Ezra proposes that "they had only a restricted set of words", a very limited vocabulary. In almost the opposite direction, the Ba'al HaTurim points out a *masoretic* note to the word וּדְבָרִים that it only appears twice in the Hebrew scriptures, the other time being in the phrase וַהֲבָלִים וּדְבָרִים הַרְבֵּה "and vanities and many words" (Ecclesiastes 5:6). From this, he deduces that the conversation of the people in those days was full of empty and vain words.

Rashi sees a deeper meaning, however. His comment reads: "They came with one plan of action and they said, 'God does not have the right to select for Himself the higher realms. We will go up to the firmament and wage war with Him'". The people were unified in rebelling against God; they were defiant and together planned to declare themselves equal to God. Without going quite so far, Hirsch agrees with Rashi's idea: "the sameness of the formation of words and sentences which is brought about by spiritual and mental agreement in the way that things and their relations are looked at." The people all used the same words because they were expressing the same thoughts; they looked at their situation and reached the same conclusions because they saw things the same way, in the same light. They were united together by a set of common values and expressions; therefore they could all work together towards the same goal.

The Hebrew scriptures speak again of unity in the words of the *Sh'ma*: "Hear, O Israel: the Lord our God, the Lord is One" (D'varim 6:4), words that are recited several times in each of the three daily prayer services and are to be said on rising and going to sleep each day. As Jews, we are saturated with this expression of God's oneness and unity. Yet the prophets speak of a day when "the Lord will be One and His name One" (Zechariah 14:9); another verse that finds an echo in the daily prayers. How are we to understand this text - that *HaShem* is somehow not one now? Only inasmuch that all men do not acknowledge Him as Lord and all men do not call upon His name alone. In that day they will do both; then not only will He be one, as He always has been, but He will be universally proclaimed and acknowledged as the One True God. The whole of mankind will abandon all the other religions and their false gods to worship the King and serve Him alone.

Yeshua spoke of the unity that we were to have as disciples. At the conclusion of His last meal with the twelve He prayed for them "The glory which You have given to Me, I have given to them; so that they may be one, just as We are one - I united with them and You with Me, so that they may be completely one, and the world thus realize that You sent Me, and that You have loved them just as You have loved Me" (John 17:22-23, CJB). This is an amazing picture: all the believers in Yeshua being as closely one as the Father and the Son are One! Wow - can you imagine that? It seems an impossible goal, given all the differences in doctrine, interpretation and practice that are to be seen between just the dozen or so major denominations around the world, let alone all the thousands of smaller groupings. Yet Rav Sha'ul is insistent: "there is neither Jew nor Gentile, neither slave nor freeman, neither male nor female; for in union with the Messiah Yeshua, you are all one" (Galatians 3:28, CJB). Without blurring the differences of biology, calling and function within the body of Messiah, it is clear that we are to be one.

How are we to bring this about? How is He to bring it about? The ecumenical movement is not the answer. Ecumenism has the reputation of reducing everything to the lowest common terms and not talking about the rest. People come together on the smallest slivers of common ground, the few fragments of the gospels that all parties can affirm without dispute or too many reservations, and agree not to talk about all the other particularities that each of the parties hold dear. Of course, this is a caricature of the truth - there are large areas of common agreement between believers - but differences about issues such as the exact meaning and practice of communion, the gifts of the Spirit, the place and ministry of women, and many others, threaten to derail meaningful engagement between the parts of the body. How can we address this? Not by pretending that we don't have differences, but by mature and serious engagement to acknowledge the differences, explore them together and work with them rather than despite them. Rav Sha'ul again: "I, therefore, the prisoner of the Lord, entreat you to walk in a manner worthy of the calling with which you have been called, with all humility and gentleness, with patience, showing forbearance to one another in love, being diligent to preserve the unity of the Spirit in the bond of peace" (Ephesians 4:3, NASB). This isn't a matter of choice; we are commanded to work together so that we may be one.

As we see the world gathering forces, coming together to agree against Israel and against the body of Messiah - inspired and driven, of course, by the Accuser and enemy of our souls - we need to recognise the unity that is being forged among the nations, the activist groups and the false religions against God and His Messiah. In that respect, it will not necessarily be too long before all the world is once again of one speech and one manner of speaking. Just as in the days of the Tower of Babel, they will be asserting their right to deny God and make a name for themselves. We too, as the Kingdom of God on earth, need to be united and strong in His strength to preserve a witness for God in these last days. Fragmented, we can easily be isolated and picked off; as Yeshua said: "If a kingdom is divided against itself, that kingdom can't survive; and if a household is divided against itself, that household can't survive" (Mark 3:24-25, CJB). We need to get real with God, get real with ourselves and - while preserving our differences in function and calling within the body of Messiah - start acting like a body.

Further Study: Ephesians 4:13; Colossians 3:14

Application: What can you do to build unity in the body of Messiah where you live? Do you pray with and for other believers from different traditions than your own? Why not ask the Lord what He would like you to do today!

Lech L'cha - Go for yourself

B'resheet / Genesis 12:1 - 17:27

רִאשׁוֹן	Aliyah One	B'resheet/Genesis 12:1 - 13
שֵׁנִי	Aliyah Two	B'resheet/Genesis 12:14 - 13:4
שְׁלִישִׁי	Aliyah Three	B'resheet/Genesis 13:5 - 18
רְבִיעִי	Aliyah Four	B'resheet/Genesis 14:1 - 20
חֲמִשִׁי	Aliyah Five	B'resheet/Genesis 14:21 - 15:6
שִׁשִׁי	Aliyah Six	B'resheet /Genesis 15:7 - 17:6
שְׁבִיעִי	Aliyah Seven	B'resheet/Genesis 17:7 - 27

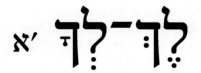

Lech L'cha - Go for yourself - 1

B'resheet / Genesis 12:1 - 13

B'resheet/Genesis 12:1 "Get yourself out of your country, away from your kinsmen and away from your father's house..."

לֶךְ־לְךָ מֵאַרְצְךָ וּמִמּוֹלַדְתְּךָ וּמִבֵּית אָבִיךָ
aviy'cha oomibeyt oomimolad't'cha mey'artz'cha l'cha lech

This is the moment when God speaks to Avram and challenges him to pick up the call on his life and set out to prove God and to prove himself. As we know, Avram is obedient to God's call and after arranging his affairs, travels from Haran to the land of Canaan, taking his wife, his nephew and all their possessions and servants.

The first two words of our reading, undistinguishable in the consonantal text לך לך, tell us something quite critical. The first לך comes from the verb הָלַךְ, in the imperative, and means "Go!"; the second is the prefix preposition לְ combined with the 2nd person singular pronoun ending ךָ and means literally "to/for you". So God is telling Avram, "Go, for yourself!" In other words, God is telling Avram that he must leave home because he, Avram, needs to, for his own sake.

Rashi suggests that Avram is told to go "for your pleasure and your benefit", almost as if both words meant "for you". Many things that we do in this life are either pleasurable or beneficial, but not both, while some are neither. But this leaving home is both necessary and appropriate: a moving on, a moving into blessing.

Right back in the garden, God told Adam, "A man shall leave his father and mother and shall cleave to his wife; and they shall become one flesh" (B'resheet 2:24, NASB). Yeshua echoed that when He was questioned about divorce in Matthew 19.

But leaving home is not necessarily an easy thing to do, as God pointed out to Avram: "leave your country, your family and your father's house". Obeying God is often something that appears to have a significant cost attached as Avram is about to find out. He has to leave his familiar surroundings and environment to be a stranger, a foreigner; he has to leave the extended family network to do everything himself; he has to leave his position of authority as the heir in the family hierarchy and establish his own authority as head of his own household.

Yeshua challenges us in the same way when He says, "The foxes have holes, and the birds flying about have nests, but the Son of Man has no home of His own" (Luke 9:58, CJB). There comes a time in each of our lives when we simply have to abandon everything in order to follow Yeshua; we just have to get up and go!

Further Study: Luke 9:23-25

Application: Is God speaking to you about something in your life at the moment? Is He calling you to put something down and move on with Him? Ask God to confirm it to you once more and then delay no further.

Lech L'cha - Go for yourself - 2

B'resheet / Genesis 12:14 - 13:4

B'resheet/Genesis 12:14 And the Egyptians saw the woman, that she was beautiful, very!

וַיִּרְאוּ הַמִּצְרִים אֶת־הָאִשָּׁה כִּי־יָפָה הִוא
hiv   yafah kiy   ha'ishah   et   hamitz'riym   vayir'u

מְאֹד
m'od

The woman in question was Sarai, the wife of Avram. An early *midrash*, elaborating on Avram's fear of being killed so that Sarai would be 'available' for some Egyptian man because of her beauty, tells the story that Avram hid her in a box so that she would not be seen. However, the border guards, zealous to collect customs duties, insisted upon the box being opened so that, at the very point of their entry into Egypt, Sarai was seen and her beauty noted and praised to Pharaoh (B'resheet Rabbah 40:5). One cannot help being reminded of Yeshua's words when He said, "There is nothing hidden that will not revealed. There is nothing secret that will not come to light" (Luke 8:17, GWT). Avram had hidden Sarai, his wife, to protect his own life and keep her for himself; and his very act of hiding her drew attention to her beauty, very!

On the other hand, the Psalmist also confesses to hiding things: "I have hidden Your word in my heart that I might not sin against You" (Psalm 119:11, NIV). Notice the difference in motive here - the writer has hidden God's word in his heart so that he might not sin against God. By having God's word, His sayings, hidden - and the Hebrew word צָפַן used here can also mean 'treasure' or 'store up' as well as 'hide' - it is available at all times "for teaching, for reproof, for correction, for training in righteousness, that the man of God may be adequate, equipped for every good work" (2 Timothy 3:16-17, NASB). Again, Yeshua's words bring this into focus: "Every scribe who has become a disciple of the Kingdom of Heaven is like a head of a household, who brings forth out of his treasure things new and old" (Matthew

43

13:52, NASB).

So hiding things away, treasuring them up for a rainy day or preserving them for the future is not necessarily a good or bad thing, depending on what you intend to do with them. If you are acting for selfish purposes, then disclosure and possible forfeiture are certain; if for sharing and enriching the lives of others, then blessing will follow. Not surprisingly, Yeshua spoke about this too: "Stop storing up treasures for yourselves on earth, where moths and rust destroy and thieves break in and steal. Instead, store up treasures for yourselves in heaven, where moths and rust don't destroy and thieves don't break in and steal. Your heart will be where your treasure is" (Matthew 6:19-21, GWT).

Further Study: Luke 12:15-21; Mark 10:17-22

Application: What is the purpose of storing things up in your life? Do you rent storage space to store more stuff than you can get in your house? Only storage in and for the Kingdom of God will endure the ravages of time.

לֶךְ־לְךָ ג׳

Lech L'cha - Go for yourself - 3

B'resheet / Genesis 13:5 - 18

B'resheet/Genesis 13:5 And also to Lot, who travelled with Avram, there was flock, herd and tents.

וְגַם־לְלוֹט הַהֹלֵךְ אֶת־אַבְרָם הָיָה צֹאן־וּבָקָר
oovakar tzon hayah Avram et ha'holeych l'Lot v'gam

וְאֹהָלִים:
v'ohaliym

At the start of the chapter, the text has already told us that Lot was travelling with his uncle, Avram: "And Avram went up from Egypt ... and Lot with him" (13:1), so why does the *Torah* tell us again, only four verses further on, that Lot was travelling with Avram?

Rashi comments on this phrase, "What caused him to have this? His going with Avram." The Sages of the *Midrash* (B'resheet Rabbah 41:3) and the Talmud (*b*. Bava Kamma 93*a*) tell us that the apparently redundant phrase is to indicate that is was precisely because he went with Avram that he had come into possession of many sheep, cattle and tents. Perhaps this is the first example of the blessing *HaShem* gave Avram when He called him to leave Haran at the start of this *parasha*: "I will bless those who bless you, but I will curse anyone who curses you; and by you all the families of the earth will be blessed" (B'resheet 12:3, CJB). Already, association with Avram brought blessing and prosperity.

Solomon tells us, "He who walks with the wise will become wise, but the companion of fools will suffer" (Proverbs 13:20, CJB) and Rav Sha'ul writes to the Corinthians, "Bad company corrupts good morals" (1 Corinthians 15:33, NASB). These teach us not only that we learn from those we spend time with, but that that learning - be it language, behaviour, dress - is obvious to others.

The *Torah* relates that when Moshe had been with God, "Moshe did not know that the skin of his face shone because of his speaking with Him" (Shemot 34:29, NASB), Moshe had to wear a veil over his face when he was not speaking to God because even Aharon his brother and the elders were afraid to come near him. In Mark's account of the arrest and trial of Yeshua, we read how Peter was identified and challenged: "One of the Chief Priest's servant girls came in and seeing Peter warming himself there, looked hard at him and said, 'You were with the Nazarene, Yeshua' ... The girl spotted him and began telling the people standing around, 'He's one of them' ... After a little while, the bystanders brought it up again, 'You've just got to be one of them. You've got "Galillean" written all over you'" (Mark 14:66-67, 69-70, Message). People could tell that Peter had been spending time with Yeshua.

So from Lot, who was blessed materially because he travelled with his uncle Avram and whose blessing stopped when they separated and Lot went down to the cities of the Plain, to the wise and foolish people of King Solomon's time who became like the people they spent time with, to Moshe who didn't even know that he was glowing in the dark because of being face to face with God, to Peter who couldn't hide the fact that he was a disciple of Yeshua, the Scripture tells us that we become like those we spend time with and sound like those we talk to.

Further Study: Proverbs 2:20-22; Hebrews 6:11-12

Application: Do you spend enough time with Yeshua that people cannot help knowing that you have spent time with Him? If not, then now is the time to start: set aside special time to be with Him and become like Him each day.

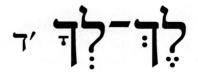

Lech L'cha - Go for yourself - 4

B'resheet / Genesis 14:1 - 20

B'resheet/Genesis 14:13 And the one who escaped came to Avram the Hebrew

וַיָּבֹא הַפָּלִיט וַיַּגֵּד לְאַבְרָם הָעִבְרִי

ha'Ivri   l'Avram   vayageyd   hapaliyt   vayavo

Nahum Sarna describes the factors that contribute to the uniqueness of Genesis chapter 14. According to modern scholars, the section of text is separated from the text before and after in many ways: linguistic, style, vocabulary and even content. In a word, scholars tell us that these verses do not belong in this place, having been inserted by some ancient editor, and probably come from an even older documentary source that has been spliced into the main narrative text at this point. The passage is the only occasion when we see Avram/Avraham acting in such a definite and military way; it offers the few potentially dateable sets of names and events which could locate the larger Genesis narrative in a wider historical context and it provides an example of the volatility of ancient Middle East kingdoms, city states and power struggles.

Notwithstanding the differences, the story is clearly linked to the surrounding texts: Avram risks his own life to rescue his nephew Lot, from whom he had separated in the previous chapter when Lot chose to occupy the fertile Jordan valley; after Avram has been renamed Avraham (17:5) he finds himself bargaining with *HaShem* over the judgement of S'dom and Amorah (18:16-32) where Lot returned to live after this episode, and Lot then escapes from the destruction of the two cities (ch. 19).

Moreover, we see two important things coming from this story. Firstly, this is the only occasion when Avram/Avraham is given the title 'The Hebrew'; coming from the root עָבַר, to pass or cross over, it affirms that Avraham had crossed over - not just the fertile crescent to come to the Land of Canaan, but from the world of pagan religions into a faith relationship with the One True God. The *Midrash* comments that "all the world was on one side and he was on the other" (B'resheet Rabbah 42:13). Yeshua uses the same vocabulary when He says, "I tell you that whoever hears what I am saying and trusts the One who sent Me has eternal life - that is, he will not come up for judgement but has already crossed over from death to life" (John 5:24, CJB) and Rav Sha'ul completes the picture by adding, "Therefore, be sure that it is those who are of faith who are sons of Abraham" (Galatians 3:7, NASB).

Secondly, Melchizedek, the priest of God Most High (an unusual name for God, found only here and in Psalm 78:35) appears with bread and wine to pronounce a blessing on Avraham and on God. Melchizedek, a priest without beginning and end - for there is no record either of his genealogy or his appointment to the priesthood - is the type for the eternal priesthood of Yeshua, prophesied of the Messiah by David: "You are a cohen forever, to be compared with Melki-Tzedek" (Psalm 110:4, CJB), who although He was a descendant of David and therefore from the tribe of Judah and not a son of Aharon from the tribe of Levi, was nevertheless a priest forever because He Himself is without beginning and without end and serves as our *Cohen Gadol* - High Priest - in the heavenly tabernacle (Hebrews 8:2), interceding for us before the Throne of Grace (Hebrews 7:25).

Whatever the exact provenance of Genesis 14, then, we can see that the *Ruach HaKodesh* - as Editor-in-Chief of the Scriptures (2 Peter 1:20-21) - made sure that key pieces of our tradition, faith and heritage were preserved and included in God's revelation for us: "For everything written in the past was written to teach us, so that with the encouragement of the Tanakh we might patiently hold on to our hope" (Romans 15:4, CJB).

Further Study: Hebrews 7:1-7; 1 John 5:11-13

Application: Is your faith shaken by the various pronouncements of so-called scholars or pundits concerning the reliability of the Scriptures? Do you wonder, as in "The Da Vinci Code", whether there is some elaborate hoax being played out through history, that makes it impossible for you to be secure in your faith? If so, then use this opportunity to realise that the prophetic word is sure (2 Peter 1:19) and that God has already provided all the answers in His word, which is sure and can be trusted completely.

Lech L'cha - Go for yourself - 5

B'resheet / Genesis 14:21 - 15:6

B'resheet/Genesis 14:21 Give me the people and take the spoil for yourself.

תֶּן־לִי הַנֶּפֶשׁ וְהָרְכֻשׁ קַח־לָךְ׃

lach kakh   v'harchush hanefesh   liy   ten

On the face of it, this doesn't seem like an unreasonable request. The king of Sodom is offering Avraham all the money while relieving him of the responsibility of providing for any of the people that he has rescued from the five kings that had raided Sodom and the other local city-states. Nechama Leibowitz points out, however, that "the *Torah* does not describe the character of its figures by direct psychological analysis, but only indirectly, through their utterances, actions and even lack of action." This is a possible reason why this verse follows the three previous verses - the intriguing mention of Melchizedek, king of Salem and priest of God Most High, to whom Avraham gave a tithe - rather than following on directly from verse 17. The *Torah* wishes to draw a contrast between the characters of Avraham and the king of Sodom.

Abravanel explains that the text intends to throw into relief the cunning of the king of Sodom. After he had been rescued from defeat - possibly even death - and the loss of his kingdom, he would never have had the *chutzpah* to ask Avraham to give him anything since, according to the custom of the time, all that the victor rescued from the enemy was his. But when he saw Avraham's generosity in giving a tenth to Melchizedek the priest, he immediately took advantage and asked for something for himself. Or Hahayyim comments: "The interpolation regarding Melchizedek is introduced to reflect credit on the righteous and show the difference between them and the wicked. The king of Sodom went forth to welcome Avraham empty-handed though he was under obligation to repay him generously. The wicked went empty-handed, whereas Melchizedek the righteous with no obligation behaved generously and welcomed him with bread and wine."

The Psalmist describes God as a rescuer of captives: "He leads out the prisoners into prosperity" (Psalm 68:6, NASB) and the prophet Isaiah speaks of the Messiah when he says, "The Spirit of the Lord God is upon me, because the Lord has anointed me to bring good news to the afflicted; He has sent me to bind up the broken-hearted; to proclaim liberty to captives and freedom to prisoners" (Isaiah 61:1, NASB). The Hebrew Scriptures look to a time when God will intervene in the affairs of men to release people from bondage and captivity and bring them into freedom and comfort.

Yeshua Himself claimed the fulfillment of the Isaiah passage when He read from the scroll in the synagogue at the start of His ministry: "The Spirit of Adonai is upon Me; therefore He has anointed Me to announce the Good News to the poor; He has sent Me to proclaim freedom for the imprisoned ..." (Luke 4:18, CJB) and Rav Sha'ul applied the passage from the Psalms to Yeshua when he wrote, "When He ascended on high He led captive a host of captives" (Ephesians 4:8, NASB). Yeshua routed the enemy of our souls in the same way as Avraham defeated the kings who were attacking Sodom: "stripping the rulers and authorities of their power, He made a public spectacle of them, triumphing over them by means of the stake" (Colossians 2:15, CJB). By custom and convention, all the victor wrested from the enemy belonged to him, so by defeating the enemy, He rescued all our souls and we now belong to Him.

More than that, as Avraham rejected the king of Sodom's offer, refusing to accept anything from him lest he should be able to say that he made Avraham rich, so Yeshua responded when challenged by the devil. After a period of fasting in the wilderness, Yeshua was tempted three times by the devil to take matters into His own hands. The last of these three trials took place when "the devil took Him to a very high mountain and showed Him all the kingdoms of the world and their glory, and he said to Him, 'All these things I will give you, if you fall down and worship me'" (Matthew 4:8-9, NASB). Refusing the (false) offer to achieve His objectives by the wrong means - that is, by not submitting solely to the Father - Yeshua rebukes the devil and answers him from Scripture. In the same way, we should follow Yeshua's example and refuse any short-cuts or easy options that would take us out of the will of God; He has a plan for our lives and we must obey Him and stay within the limits He has set us.

Further Study: Jeremiah 39:18; 2 Corinthians 2:14; 1 Peter 3:18-22

Application: Are you tempted to take things into your own hands, take a short-cut or exploit forbidden information in order to speed things up or obtain a better position? Stand firm and resist the devil, for this is not God's way and order for you. "Resist the devil and he will flee from you" (James 4:7, NASB).

לֶךְ־לְךָ 'ו

Lech L'cha - Go for yourself - 6

B'resheet / Genesis 15:7 - 17:6

B'resheet/Genesis 15:7 I brought you out from Ur of Kasdim to give to you this land to possess her

הוֹצֵאתִיךָ מֵאוּר כַּשְׂדִּים לָתֶת לְךָ אֶת־הָאָרֶץ

ha'aretz   et   l'cha   latet   kasdiym   mey'ur   hotzeytiycha

הַזֹּאת לְרִשְׁתָּהּ׃

l'rishtah   hazot

     HaShem's statement here precipitates one of those "How could they say that?" moments. The chapter starts with *HaShem* encouraging Avram and promising him a reward. Not unreasonably, Avram responds by asking *HaShem* what use a reward will be to him since he is childless and as things currently stand, his steward would inherit all his household. *HaShem* then assures Avram that he will yet have a son of his own and that his descendants will be as many as the stars. Verse 6 brings Avram's statement of faith - "Then he believed in the Lord; and He reckoned it to him as righteousness" (B'resheet 15:6, NASB) - and the confirmation that righteousness comes from a faith relationship. *HaShem* continues the conversation with our text above: Why else did I bring you here if not to possess the land? At this point, as if having now crested the wave of faith, Avram appears to step backwards and asks, "O Lord God, how may I know that I shall possess it?" (v8, NASB). Centuries later, one of his descendants, a certain priest named Zechariah, was to ask a very similar question (Luke 1:18)!

     Ramban is definite that, "This is not similar to the question of Hezekiah, 'What shall be the sign that the Eternal will heal me?' (2 Kings 20:8)", simply asking for a sign; "but Avram desired to have definite knowledge that he would inherit the Land and that neither his sin nor that of his seed should withhold it from them. Or perhaps the Canaanites might repent ...". The **Ramban** is saying that Avram is trying to determine whether the promise is conditional - that is, in some way dependent on him

51

or his offspring - or absolute, dependant only on God. "The Holy One, blessed be He, made a covenant with him that he will inherit the land under all circumstances."

Hirsch, on the other hand, comments that while the wording of the first time this promise is given, "To you and your descendants I will give this land" (B'resheet 13:15) requires no co-operating action on the part of Avram or his descendants, the wording here "'to give you this land to take it into possession' has the idea of self-action so strongly that it is used with the meaning of conquering or capturing" in which Avram and his descendants have to participate with God to secure the promise in physical terms.

Davidson lists a number of related meanings for the root יָרַשׁ: 1. to take, seize upon; to take possession of; 2. to dispossess, to drive out; 3. to possess, hold in possession; 4. to inherit. So the Sforno comments, "**to give you this land** that you, yourself, should take possession of it through an act of acquisition; **to inherit it** so that your children will inherit it from you as an inheritance which is never ending." Avram has already been told (B'resheet 13:17) to walk the length and breadth of the Land, one of the methods of acquisition (*b*. Baba Batra 100*a*), so here, Avram is being reminded that it was God's intention that Avram should perform the acquisition so that he can transmit it to his children as an eternal inheritance.

Both of these ideas are found in one of Rav Sha'ul's more frequently quoted writings: "for by grace you have been saved through faith. And this is not your own doing; it is the gift of God, not a result of works, so that no one may boast. For we are His workmanship, created in Messiah Yeshua for good works, which God prepared beforehand, that we should walk in them" (Ephesians 2:8-10, ESV). The basic thrust is that salvation is from God, He provides it, we appropriate it by faith, but that faith in turn also comes from Him. It was always His intention that we should be believers, united with Messiah. At the same time, we have to participate in that process; firstly, by exercising the faith we have been given, by walking in faith and not in unbelief; and, secondly, by doing the "good works", deeds of righteousness, that He calls us to and has already prepared for us to do. James, the leader of the Jerusalem church famously comments that, "You see that a person is justified by works and not by faith alone" (James 2:24, ESV); it is a joint effort - the gift and intentionality of God, and the obedience and exercise of man.

This is why we find Rav Sha'ul saying, "Work out your own salvation with fear and trembling, for it is God who works in you, both to will and to work for His good pleasure" (Philippians 2:12-13, ESV). God has a plan for each of our lives, a way to bless and grow us while also advancing the Kingdom and reaching other people with His invitation to become a part of that Kingdom. God is not subject to random change, simply reacting to events as they happen on the ground; He acts according to a specific and deliberate purpose and plan, that all mankind may acknowledge Yeshua as the Messiah of Israel and the Saviour of the world, that "the earth shall be full of the knowledge of the Lord as the waters cover the sea" (Isaiah 11:9, ESV). Yet in spite of God's over-arching plan for the whole universe, we are not reduced to simply being nameless or faceless cogs in the machine. At the very same time as He is working on the master plan for history, God also has an individual plan for each of us and our generation; He says - originally to the captives in Babylon, but equally to us today - "'For I know the plans I have for you,' declares the Lord, 'plans for wholeness and not for evil, to give you a future and a hope'" (Jeremiah 29:11, ESV). This is why God brought us out of sin and death to give us a share in His Kingdom to possess and inherit.

Further Study: Job 23:8-14; Isaiah 58:8-12

Application: How are you co-operating with God to actualise your inheritance today? Are you aware of the moving of God in your life and the lives of those around you to bring about His purposes for you? How could you participate more fully with Him to make that happen? Why not ask Him these questions today so that together you can move forward as a team!

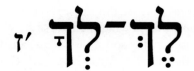

Lech L'cha - Go for yourself - 7

B'resheet / Genesis 17:7 - 27

B'resheet/Genesis 17:7 And I will establish My covenant between Me and you and your seed after you

וַהֲקִמֹתִי אֶת־בְּרִיתִי בֵּינִי וּבֵינֶךָ וּבֵין זַרְעֲךָ
zar'acha uveyn uveynecha beyniy   b'ritiy   et   vahakimotiy

אַחֲרֶיךָ
akhareycha

What is it that holds the Jewish people together? The old saying goes, "two Jews, three opinions" and we all love to argue and debate our points, sometimes with so much passion that we fall out with each other. Yet the Jewish people are unique in the history of the world as a people who have held together and who are still recognisable after two thousand years of exile from their own land and being scattered among the other nations. Just what is the secret of our longevity? The plain and simple answer lies in the first word of this verse: וַהֲקִמֹתִי, here translated "And I will establish". This is a *Hif'il* affix 1cs form of the root קוּם - to stand - in a *vav*-reversive construction to give it a future tense. The *Hif'il* stem has a causitive voice, so that the literal meaning of the word is "I will cause to stand" and hence "I will establish".

Who is speaking? This is the key: *HaShem* is speaking. As it happens, He is speaking to Avraham and confirming the covenant that He initially 'cut' with him a couple of chapters earlier when "he believed in the Lord and He credited it to him as righteousness" (B'resheet 15:6). Of course, this follows *HaShem's* call to Avram that starts this portion - לֶךְ־לְךָ "Go for yourself" (B'resheet 12:1) - when Avram is chosen and called to leave his land, family and father's house so that *HaShem* may raise up a people for Himself. This is the fundamental reason for our continued existence: "I will establish" - it is God who maintains and upholds the covenant between Himself and the Jewish people.

Rashi asks "And what is the covenant?" and then answers his own question from the second half of the verse: "To be God to you". Well of course that is the answer; that is what the text says. What is bothering Rashi that he asks a question with so obvious an answer? Rashi wants to emphasise which of the various promises that God has made is most important or might be uppermost in Avraham's mind. Is God going to confirm the promise of a son? Perhaps the promise of the land? Neither of those would be worth anything without a relationship with God, and neither of those would be permanent or guaranteed without God. Only when God is part of and upholding the covenant, when He is in His rightful place as God, do the other components of the promises make sense.

Obadiah Sforno adds an important comment on the verse, "To be God to you and to your offspring after you: I will associate My Name with yours without an intermediary, as I associate it with all that is eternal, as it says, 'For whatever God does, it shall be forever' (Ecclesiastes 3:14)". Sforno points out that when God does something, it is permanent or eternal; when God wishes to do something temporary, He uses a human intermediary, whose works are temporary. So God is establishing a personal relationship with Avraham and the Jewish people that will last for ever. At various times, the Philistines, the Assyrians, Nebuchanezzar and even the Romans were God's agents to punish, chasten or challenge His people; Cyrus was God's instrument to return the people to the land and rebuild the Temple, Herod glorified it as one of the seven wonders of the ancient world. All the human intermediaries have faded away while God's work and word remains. This is why Rav Sha'ul writes to Timothy: "there is only one mediator between God and mankind, Yeshua the Messiah, Himself a man" (1 Timothy 2:5). It is only Yeshua, who is both God and man, that can act as God's personal and permanent intermediary for all of mankind; God is doing it Himself.

Nahum Sarna points out that the expression "to you and your descendants after you" occurs five times in verses 7-10 and again in verse 20 of this chapter; it also appears in 35:12 and 48:4 in connection with the covenantal promises. Sarna explains that this is legal terminology: "The inclusion of the phrase in documents relating to the devolution of property upon the death of the owner assured that the real estate automatically passed on from generation to generation without restriction." The covenant that God gives the descendants of Avraham, Yitz'khak and Ya'akov is to be a permanent covenant, that He is going to establish and guarantee and it is to pass without restriction from generation to generation so that all the generations shall be a part of it and included it in. Hear Moshe's words when he confirms the covenant on the plains of Moab with the generation of Israelites who are about to enter the Land: "Now not with you alone am I making this covenant and this oath, but both with those who stand here with us today in the presence of the Lord our God and with those who are not with us here today" (D'varim 29:14-15, NASB); the covenant was not just for them, but for all the future generations who would - and do - continue to be God's sign people among the nations.

The biblical record tells us that, being human, the descendants of Ya'akov failed time and again to keep their side of the bargain, to uphold God's covenant with them. God, on the other hand, never gave up. Hirsch puts these moving words in God's mouth as He speaks to Avraham: "The realisation of this destiny which I have fixed for your descendants will be no easy task. It will meet with many obstacles and endure many struggles, but I will keep it established, I will form, guide, purify and educate your children after you until they become My children." Knowing the difficulties that were involved, God nevertheless promised that He would make sure that the covenant did endure from generation to generation; He would always be there to pick up the pieces and cajole the people back into relationship with Himself.

Yeshua spoke of the certainty His followers would have as they trusted in Him: "I give eternal life to them, and they shall never perish; and no-one shall snatch them out of My hand" (John 10:28, NASB). No-one can take us away from Yeshua or break our relationship with Him. Isn't that security! But how can Yeshua be so certain - is there something more? He goes on: "My Father, who has given them to Me, is greater than all; and no one is able to snatch them out of the Father's hand" (v. 29, NASB). The Father, who has sent the Son for this very purpose, stands behind Him. He has given His children to Yeshua and just as *HaShem* has never broken a covenant or reneged on a promise, He isn't going to start now; His fundamental character would not allow it. This is surely why Rav Sha'ul can write, "For I am convinced that neither death nor life, neither angels nor other heavenly rulers, neither what exists nor what is coming, neither powers above nor powers below, nor any other created thing will be able to separate us from the love of God which comes to us through the Messiah Yeshua, our Lord" (Romans 8:38-39, CJB).

Even though relationship with Yeshua is not inherited - each physical or spiritual generation has to enter that for themselves by confessing Yeshua as Lord - nevertheless, God promises that the spouses and children of believers will have a certain level of preparedness for taking that step: "For the unbelieving husband is sanctified through his wife, and the unbelieving wife is sanctified through her believing husband; for otherwise your children are unclean, but now they are holy" (1 Corinthians 7:14, NASB). As believers, we share our faith with those closest to us and, in the case of children, teach them about the Lord and how to pray; we encourage and prepare them to know Yeshua for themselves; we invite them to make that connection for themselves, just as Moshe encouraged the Israelites on the plains of Moab. And the wider circles of our acquaintance - our work colleagues, other parents at the school gate, people we meet on buses or in supermarket checkout queues - what about them? Does God have a plan for their lives? Absolutely; no matter where they are or what they have done, God still wants to rescue them from the wrath to come; the offer of relationship with Yeshua is available for them too. As the modern vernacular would have it: How cool is that!

Further Study: 2 Corinthians 4:13-14; 2 Timothy 1:12

Application: Do you know the certainty of God's covenant with you? Are you able to trust Him, no matter what may happen, to uphold the covenant He has made? Read and re-read those promises until the Spirit brings you His assurance; then you will know that you know that you know.

וַיֵּרָא

Vayera - And He appeared

B'resheet / Genesis 18:1 - 22:24

רִאשׁוֹן	Aliyah One	B'resheet/Genesis 18:1 - 14
שֵׁנִי	Aliyah Two	B'resheet/Genesis 18:15 - 33
שְׁלִישִׁי	Aliyah Three	B'resheet/Genesis 19:1 - 20
רְבִיעִי	Aliyah Four	B'resheet/Genesis 19:21 - 21:4
חֲמִשִׁי	Aliyah Five	B'resheet/Genesis 21:5 - 21
שִׁשִּׁי	Aliyah Six	B'resheet/Genesis 21:22 - 34
שְׁבִיעִי	Aliyah Seven	B'resheet/Genesis 22:1 - 24

וַיֵּרָא א׳

Vayera - And He appeared - 1

B'resheet / Genesis 18:1 - 14

B'resheet/Genesis 18:1 Adonai appeared to Avraham ... as he sat at the entrance to the tent during the heat of the day

וַיֵּרָא אֵלָיו יהוה ... וְהוּא יֹשֵׁב פֶּתַח־הָאֹהֶל

ha'ohel petakh yosheyv v'hu ... Adonai eylayv vayera

כְּהֹם הַיּוֹם:

hayom k'khom

The Talmud tells us that the Lord had come to visit the sick (*b*. Sotah 14*a*). According to Rabbi Chana, it was the third day since Avraham's circumcision and the Lord came to enquire about his welfare (*b*. Bava Metzia 86*b*). Whatever the historical accuracy of the tradition's additions to the written Biblical narrative, the story can teach us three things: firstly, God sought to comfort Avraham in his physical discomfort and distress; secondly, although Avraham's wound would still have been weeping, God set aside the cleanliness/purity laws that were later to be given to Moshe (Vayikra 15:1-15) in order to visit Avraham and share his hospitality; and thirdly, God appeared at an unexpected time - when travellers would normally be resting in the shade, as indeed Avraham himself was doing.

From this we can learn three important principles: firstly, God desires to comfort His people in their affliction. As the Psalmist wrote, "when I walk through the valley of the shadow of death ... Thou art with me" (Psalm 23:4, KJV); and Yeshua tells the *talmidim* as He is about to leave them, "Remember! I will be with you always, yes, even until the end of the age" (Matthew 28:20, CJB).

Secondly, although God will not tolerate or compromise with sin, He nevertheless reaches out to us in order to rescue us when we stumble. After all, Rav Sha'ul tells us that, "God demonstrates His own love toward us, in that while we were yet sinners, Christ died for us" (Romans 5:8, NASB). As in the Jewish tradition, all the *mitzvot* (save three[3]) can be suspended in order

---

3. The three commandments that cannot be set aside are the prohibitions against idolatry,

to save life, so God Himself will reach into our lives to gain relationship with us or re-open a blocked channel of communication.

Thirdly, even when we are not expecting Him, God breaks through into our lives. Whether He arrests us in a hidden sin that we thought He could not see; whether He speaks into our loneliness, depression or despair; or whether He breaks our silence of neglect or forgetfulness (or even busy-ness!) towards Him, God wants to be a part of our lives and to be there for us when no-one else can or will.

Further Study: Psalm 139:7-12, 2 Corinthians 5:21

Application: Have things between you and God been a little sticky lately? Have you lost touch in the pressures and pains of life? Then reach out to Him, for He is longing to visit you in the heat of the day.

---

sexual immorality and murder.

וַיֵּרָא ב׳

Vayera - And He appeared - 2

B'resheet / Genesis 18:15 - 33

B'resheet/Genesis 18:15 And Sarah lied, saying, "I did not laugh," for she was afraid.

וַתְּכַחֵשׁ שָׂרָה לֵאמֹר לֹא צָחַקְתִּי כִּי יָרֵאָה
yarey'ah kiy tzakhak'tiy lo leymor Sarah vat'chakheysh

In a moment of panic, having just heard *HaShem* Himself say that she was to bear a son within a twelve-month, Sarah finds herself trying to lie to God. Caught out laughing at God's prophetic word, Sarah attempts to deny that she was laughing. How could Sarah expect to get away with such a bare-faced lie, particularly to God Himself? Let's see if we can work out what is going on here.

The first possibility is that Sarah didn't know that the figure whose words she overheard, as she stood in the tent doorway behind her husband while he received the words of the stranger, was God. After all, it was and still is a middle-eastern custom to call down a blessing on those who have given you hospitality as you leave. Perhaps she thought that the stranger was simply making nice noises and offering traditional wishes without even being aware of Sarah's age.

The second possibility is that Sarah thought that her act of laughing was either not visible because she was hidden inside the doorway of the tent and that, as the Hebrew construction could be saying, she only laughed inside - to herself, as it were. In other words: she thought she could reasonably get away with it. She didn't allow for God's all-seeing knowledge and hoped that her moment of indiscretion or discourtesy would be able to pass unseen.

The third and most likely option is that given in the text itself: Sarah was afraid. Consider how she felt: she had never heard God speak to her before, she had just heard what seemed an impossible and potentially scary prophecy - that her old and withered body, long past the age of childbearing, would revive to bear a child - she had then laughed in incredulity at the enormity of the promise and finally, she was called on her lack of faith in a way that showed that God knew exactly what she was thinking. In sheer panic then, she attempted to deny the laughter; after all, either the coveted promise of a son might be withdrawn or worse things might befall Avraham and herself for laughing at God's words.

In any event, *HaShem* quietly points out what they all knew: she had laughed, and without saying anything else, walks away with Avraham and the other men (angels) with Him. In time, God's words are borne out: Sarah does indeed conceive and bear a son, Yitz'khak, the only one of the three patriarchs to be born, live and die entirely in *Eretz Yisrael* without ever leaving the Land that God promised to give to Avraham and his descendants for ever.

Further Study: 1 Kings 17:17-24; Luke 1:8-20

Application: How do we react when God speaks to us or lays His hand on our lives in a way that we don't expect? Do we respond in faith or is our first thought that we couldn't possibly have heard correctly, to laugh at ourselves for imagining things, or simply ignore the whole thing?

וַיֵּרָא 'ג

Vayera - And He appeared - 3

B'resheet / Genesis 19:1 - 20

B'resheet/Genesis 19:1 The two angels came to S'dom in the evening

וַיָּבֹאוּ שְׁנֵי הַמַּלְאָכִים סְדֹמָה בָּעֶרֶב

ba'erev S'domah hamalachiym sh'ney vayavo'u

Why did it take the two מַלְאָכִים, angels - also translated messengers, from the unused root לַאַךְ, to send or minister, from which we also have מְלָאכָה, work or labour - so long to get from Hevron to S'dom? Even allowing time for their meal, they were with Avraham at mid-day, yet did not get to S'dom until evening; this is an easy walk at human speed, but since these messengers were angels, they could presumably travel instantly.

Rashi asks the question and then answers it by saying, "They were angels of mercy, delaying in case Avraham would be able to mount a defence for the people of S'dom" (cf. B'resheet Rabbah 50:1). The commentator Mizrachi adds that as long as there was any possibility that the advocate could find some defence for his client, and the judge remained in the court to hear it, the hand of the prosecutor is stayed; but once the judge leaves and the advocate has done all that he can, then the prosecution proceeds to carry out the verdict of the court (cf. B'resheet Rabbah 49:14).

The voices of the prophets articulate clearly that there is a time to seek God. "Seek the Lord while He may be found; call upon Him while He is near. Let the wicked forsake his way, and the unrighteous his thoughts; and let him return to the Lord, and He will have compassion on him; and to our God, for He will abundantly pardon" (Isaiah 55:6-7, NASB). "For thus says the Lord to the house of Israel, 'Seek Me that you may live ... Seek the Lord that you may live, lest He break forth like a fire, O house of Joseph, and it consume with none to quench'" (Amos 5:4,6, NASB). Within the space of each man's life, God calls out to him, time and again, seeking repentance; we say these words three times each day in the *Amidah*: that God is the God who desires repentance. Peter the *shaliach* picks this theme up when he writes, "The Lord is not slow in keeping His promise, as some people think of slowness; on

65

the contrary, He is patient with you; for it is not His purpose that anyone should be destroyed, but that everyone should turn from his sins" (2 Peter 3:9, CJB).

Equally clear is that God's patience with each individual is finite. From the beginning of the Scriptures when *HaShem* says, "My Spirit will not continue to judge man forever, since he is nothing but flesh. His days shall be 120 years" (B'resheet 6:3, Living Torah), to "It is appointed for men to die once and after this comes judgement" (Hebrews 9:27, NASB), the Scriptures are consistent in stressing that men should call on God as soon as they can, during their time of life, because once dead, they will have no more opportunity. This is why the words of the prophet are quoted so eloquently by Rav Sha'ul when he says, "We also urge you not to receive the grace of God in vain ... behold, now is the accepted time; behold, now is the day of salvation" (2 Corinthians 6:1-2, NASB).

Further Study: Isaiah 49:8-13; Psalm 69:13-15

Application: Have you been holding out on God and not responding to His promptings? If so, now is your moment to recognise that He is speaking directly to you: He wants you to turn to Him, confess your sin and receive His forgiveness, that you may live and that your relationship with Him should be restored. Do it now - don't delay another moment!

וַיֵּרָא ד'

Vayera - And He appeared - 4

B'resheet / Genesis 19:21 - 21:4

B'resheet/Genesis 19:24 ... sulphur and fire, from Adonai, from heaven

גָּפְרִית וָאֵשׁ מֵאֵת יהוה מִן־הַשָּׁמָיִם:
hashamayim min Adonai meyeyt va'eysh gafriyt

The well known epithet "a fire and brimstone preacher" is based upon this verse as the two words גָּפְרִית וָאֵשׁ are translated by the King James version of the Bible. The word גָּפְרִית, brimstone or sulphur, is related to the word גֹּפֶר, which only occurs in B'resheet 6:14, the word used to describe the material used to build the ark; a wood that is heavy with resin so that it burns, cracks and spits, not just with the heat of the wood, but with the extra heat of the burning resin, like pitch or sulphur. The same phrase is found in Ezekiel 38:22: "a torrential rain, with hailstones, fire and brimstone" (NASB). גָּפְרִית also turns up again in the description of Hell found in Isaiah 30:33: כְּנַחַל גָּפְרִית, "like a torrent of brimstone" (NASB), "a stream of sulphur" (Artscroll).

Hirsch focuses on the second half of the text: "from Adonai, from heaven". He is concerned lest people should look at the geographic region of the Dead Sea, see what geologists would refer to as the volcanic nature of the district and explain the destruction of S'dom and Amorah as a completely natural occurrence. On the contrary, Hirsch sees the inclusion of the otherwise redundant phrase - for the verse starts by saying that "God rained upon S'dom and Amorah ..." - as an explicit corrective to ensure that we should know that this judgement was brought about specifically and deliberately by God Himself, because the sin of the cities had risen before Him, rather than as the inevitable result of the build-up of sin over generations and God simply allowing the natural geology to act for Him.

When we read *HaShem*'s warning to the Israelites: "You are therefore to keep all My statutes and all My ordinances and do them, so that the land to which I am bringing you to live will not spew you out" (Vayikra 20:22, NASB), it can be easy to see sin in the same way as food poisoning. Eat food that is contaminated with bacteria or toxin and the stomach reacts by vomiting the offending material out again; a God-given natural systemic response to protect against pathogens. Often the body system waits until the level of threat has reached a particular level or threshold before triggering the evacuation, the while attempting to contain the invasion by normal digestive means. This view is supported by God's comments to Avraham that, "in the fourth generation [your descendants] shall return here, for the iniquity of the Amorite is not yet complete" (B'resheet 15:16, NASB) and Peter's reminder that "The Lord is ... patient with you; for it is not His purpose that anyone should be destroyed, but that everyone should turn from his sins" (2 Peter 3:9, CJB).

While God's patience and forbearance give us all many opportunities to know Him in Messiah Yeshua, to forge a relationship with Him, to set our house in order, to be ready for the return of Yeshua, we should not let that blind us to the fact that God does sometimes act, in a completely unexpected and sovereign way - be that by natural or spiritual means - to bring judgement on an instant basis. Yeshua told the story of the rich man to whom God said, "You fool! This very night you will die! And the things that you have prepared - whose will they be?" (Luke 12:20, CJB) - natural means; while after Peter's rebuke, "On hearing these words, Ananias fell down dead; and everyone who heard about it was terrified" (Acts 5:5, CJB) - supernatural means.

As we are to be ready, "for the Son of Man will come when you are not expecting Him" (Matthew 24:44, CJB), remembering that "It will go well with that servant if he is found doing his job when his master comes" (v. 46, CJB), we should keep short accounts with the Lord, aware that we could be with Him tomorrow - by either natural or supernatural means, but either way at His express command.

Further Study: Psalm 11:1-7; Luke 17:26-30

Application: Many people find it difficult to stay connected to the reality of God's sovereignty in the natural phenomena that surround us every day. Take a moment to remember that our God, who loves and cares for His people, can also act in swift and awe-inspiring judgement among the sons of men. Do not be surprised or frightened, but make sure that you are ready for Him at any time.

וַיֵּ֫רָא 'ה

Vayera - And He appeared - 5

B'resheet / Genesis 21:5 - 21

B'resheet/Genesis 21:6 And Sarah said, "God has made laughter for me; everyone who hears will laugh for me."

וַתֹּ֣אמֶר שָׂרָה צְחֹק עָשָׂה לִי אֱלֹהִים
Elohim   liy   asah   tz'khok   Sarah   vatomer

כָּל־הַשֹּׁמֵעַ יִצְחַק־לִי׃
liy yitzakhak hashomeya kol

This verse contains two instances of the root צָחַק, to laugh: a noun צְחֹק, meaning laughter or ridicule, which is only used twice in the Hebrew Scriptures - here and in Ezekiel 23:32; and the verb יִצְחָק, *Qal* prefix 3ms, meaning "he will laugh". Normally, according to Davidson, when צָחַק is followed by the preposition לְ - as it is here in both cases - it takes on the meaning "to laugh at", so that would translate this verse as a lament: "God has laughed at me and so will everyone who hears" as if God is turning Sarah's laughter at Him when He told Sarah that she was to have a child in her old age (cf. B'resheet 18:9-15) back on her. None of the translations take it that way, however; the NASB chooses, "Everyone who hears will laugh with me" attaching a footnote: "Lit., 'for'". This follows *Targum Onkelos* where the Aramaic word יֶחְדֵי means "he will rejoice", giving the idea that whoever hears about Sarah will rejoice with or for her.

Commenting to this phrase, Rashi says, "Many infertile women were remembered along with her. Many sick people were cured on that day. Many prayers were answered along with hers. And there was much cheerfulness in the world." This comes from B'resheet Rabbah 53:8, where "Rabbi Berekiah, Rabbi Judah ben Rabbi Shimon and Rabbi Hanan said in the name of Rabbi Samuel ben Rabbi Isaac: when the matriarch Sarah was remembered [i.e., gave birth], many other barren women were remembered with her, many deaf gained their hearing, many blind had their eyes opened, many insane became sane." Why should this be? The sages connect this verse to Esther 2:18: "[the king, Ahasuerus] made a holiday for the provinces and gave gifts according to the king's bounty" (NASB) - where a gift is given, it is given to the whole world, so also in Sarah's case, as she was given a gift, God also gave similar gifts to others in the world. We might be tempted to dismiss this as simple rabbinic wishful thinking were it not for two passages in Matthew's gospel.

At the start of Yeshua's ministry, Matthew records a significant aspect of what Yeshua was doing. "Yeshua went all over the Galil teaching in their synagogues, proclaiming the Good News of the Kingdom of Heaven, and healing people from every kind of disease and sickness. Word of Him spread throughout all Syria, and people brought to Him all who were ill, suffering from various diseases and pains, and those held in the power of demons, and epileptics and paralytics; and He healed them" (Matthew 4:23-24, CJB). There is no record of Yeshua not being able to heal anyone who came to Him; on the contrary, the emphasis seems to be that anyone and everyone was healed - a sign of the proximity of the Kingdom as Yeshua said, "Turn from your sins to God; for the Kingdom of Heaven is near!" (Matthew 4:17, CJB). When God's power for healing was being poured out, it was poured out for everyone who was in the neighbourhood, all who needed and would receive it.

More significantly, in Matthew's account of the crucifixion we find: "At that moment, the parokhet in the Temple was ripped in two from top to bottom; and there was an earthquake, with rocks splitting apart. Also the graves were opened, and the bodies of many holy people who had died were raised to life; and after Yeshua rose, they came out of the graves and went into the holy city, where many people saw them" (Matthew 27:51-53, CJB). At the outpouring of energy at the cross and resurrection, other people were also affected that were in the vicinity and other bodies were raised from the dead - a foretaste of Isaiah's words: "Your dead will live; their corpses will rise. You who lie in the dust, awake and shout for joy, for your dew is as the dew of the dawn, and the earth will give birth to the departed spirits" (Isaiah 26:19, NASB).

When God's power and grace are being poured out, we should expect that many people will be affected. Jonathan Edwards reports that during the Great Awakening, people passing by a room or a house where a prayer meeting was in progress would be overcome by the presence of God. In these days, when the is again drawing near, breaking through into our every day world, we must cling on to God's coat-tails and watch to see what He will do. We dare not hold back or stifle the movement of the Spirit, for He is the very breath of God in us who wants to touch and impact our communities.

Further Study: Acts 19:11-12; Acts 5:12-16

Application: Where is the power of God in your area? Look for the signs of the Kingdom and follow Him. Don't be deceived by froth and bubbles, but where lives are being changed and the fruit of the Kingdom is shown, God is surely at work among His people!

וַיֵּרָא ו׳

Vayera - And He appeared - 6

B'resheet / Genesis 21:22 - 34

B'resheet/Genesis 21:22 God is with you in all that you do.

אֱלֹהִים עִמְּךָ בְּכֹל אֲשֶׁר־אַתָּה עֹשֶׂה:
oseh   atah   asher   b'chol   imcha   Elohiym

This statement is made by Abimelech, the king of Gerar, and Phicol, the commander of the king's armies, to Avraham. They come to him to ask if he will make a covenant with them not to deal falsely with them, plot against them, or - presumably - make war against them. Their motivation has attracted the attention of the commentators; Avraham may be rich and have a large household, but surely he wouldn't represent a threat to an established kingdom? Avraham was a nomad, a sojourner in tents - here today and, relatively speaking, gone tomorrow - while they are city dwellers with thick stone walls and city gates, rooted in the sand and bed-rock of the land; why should they be concerned about Avraham?

Rashi starts by telling us that "[Abimelech and Phicol] saw that he had left the vicinity of Sodom safe and sound, and that he had waged war against the kings and they fell into his hand, and that his wife was remembered by God in his old age." Avraham had come unscathed through the destruction of Sodom and Gomorrah, the report of his chasing the five kings the length of the country and rseturning all the captives was well known, and the miraculous birth of a son to a couple in their nineties had not escaped the notice of the King of Gerar. The Sforno dryly puts these words in Abimelech's mouth: "**God is with you** therefore I fear you and desire a treaty with you, not because of your might or wealth." In spite of Avraham's wealth, which was considerable, and his apparent might, which seemed beyond dispute, what really motivated the king of Gerar and the commander of his armies was that God was with Avraham. With divine favour, guidance, power and resources, Avraham would be more than a match for even the largest of armies and the thickest of city walls. Although *Targum Onkelos* - known for paraphrasing away anthropomorphisms from the Hebrew text - translates this as מֵימְרָא דַיְיָ בְּסַעֲדָךְ, "the Memra [Word or

Wisdom] of the Lord helps you", this only serves to emphasise the awe that Avraham must have had in the eyes of the king and his general; the creative power and force of God, His active word, was working alongside Avraham in everything he did.

Hirsch finds it difficult to accept that the men of Gerar were concerned about what Avraham himself would and could do. Avraham was, after all, only one man, quite old, and would not have the drive and determination of a younger man. No, Hirsch maintains, they were concerned about how he would inspire and teach the next generation: his son Yitz'khak! Abimelech and Phicol can see a more disturbing future for their country than Avraham; they trust his ability as a father to raise up and educate sons to follow him, they have confidence in his power to train and establish a dynasty that will maintain and walk in their father's values in future generations. They would rather have Avraham's progeny as a friend than an enemy so they offer him a covenant that gives him freedom of the land - a thing of no mean value - in order to gain a friendly relationship with him in a way that the future generations will also honour and keep.

Using one of the Hebrew names for Messiah, עִמָּנוּ אֵל - God with us, God gave the prophet Isaiah a warning for the surrounding nations who were eyeing Israel up covetously for conquest:

> God is with us! You may make an uproar, peoples; but you will be shattered. Listen, all of you from distant lands; arm yourselves, but you will be shattered; yes, arm yourselves, but you will be shattered; devise a plan, but it will come to nothing; say anything you like, but it won't happen; because God is with us. (Isaiah 8:8b-10, CJB)

Because God was with Israel, their plan to conquer and plunder Israel would not only come to naught, but they themselves would be shattered in the process. This rested entirely upon the promises and presence of God among His people, for they were already weak and were unable to defend themselves against the strong and well-armed nations who were poised to march in and take possession. 'Look,' God is saying to the nations, 'see things as they really are: I am with My people and you can't overcome Me!'

The Jewish leaders recognised the same quality in Yeshua. Nicodemus came to Yeshua at night and said, "Rabbi, we know it is from God that you have come as a teacher, for no-one can do these miracles You perform unless God is with him" (John 3:2, CJB). Later on, the man who has been blind from birth but was given sight by Yeshua tells the Jewish leaders, "In all history no-one has heard of someone's opening the eyes of a man born blind. If this man were not from God He couldn't do a thing!" (John 9:32-33, CJB). The following *Hanukkah* when Yeshua was again in Jerusalem, some of the leadership tried to stone Him for they thought He was blaspheming, but Yeshua told them "If I do not do the works of My Father, do not believe Me; but if I do them, though you do not believe Me, believe the works, that you may know and understand that the Father is in Me, and I in the Father" (John 10:37-38, NASB).

Rav Sha'ul understood what this meant in a very practical sense. He wrote, "What then shall we say to these things? If God is for us, who is against us?" (Romans 8:31, NASB). He saw the power of God at work in each believer, the in-dwelling of the Holy Spirit, that other people would see and want for themselves: "For it is God who is at work in you, both to will and to work for His good pleasure" (Philippians 2:13, NASB). We should expect the people around us to see God in our behaviour, to hear God in our words, to be questioning how and why we do what we do and the attitude of love that we show to them and each other. If not, then we need to ask why. It is not that God doesn't want that to be happening, for not only has He told us to be like that, but He wrote in His word that it would be so: "Thus says the Lord of Hosts, 'In those days the men from all the nations will grasp the garment of a Jew saying, "Let us go with you, for we have heard that God is with you"'" (Zechariah 8:23, NASB).

Further Study: Joshua 2:8-13; Hebrews 13:20-21

Application: How does your world view match against God's? Do you really expect that God will be revealed in your life? Perhaps it is time for a reality check, where we ask God to align our expectations with His word and then be ready and open for Him to show Himself in us. Then stand back and see what God will do!

וַיֵּרָא ז׳

Vayera - And He appeared - 7

B'resheet / Genesis 22:1 - 24

B'resheet/Genesis 22:2 And He said, "Take, please, your son ..."

וַיֹּאמֶר קַח־נָא אֶת־בִּנְךָ
bincha et na kakh vayomer

Nahum Sarna writes that "the particle נָא added to the imperative usually softens the command to an entreaty". The dictionaries offer two principle translations: 'now' or 'please', depending on the context. One clearly strengthens the imperative nature of the command, the other lessens the tone to little more than a plea or an invitation. The former can be seen when Moshe addresses the people in some anger before striking - rather than speaking to - a rock to bring forth water: שִׁמְעוּ־נָא הַמֹּרִים - "Listen now, you rebels ..." (B'Midbar 20:10, NASB); you can almost hear the air crackle! An example of the latter whispers through the lips of Samson after he has been blinded and chained up in the temple of the Philistines: זָכְרֵנִי נָא וְחַזְּקֵנִי נָא אַךְ הַפַּעַם הַזֶּה - "please remember me and strengthen me this once" (Judges 16:28).

The Sages project a conversation between *HaShem* and Avraham in the following words of this verse; the words in bold are the biblical text: "Said He to him: **Take, I pray thee** - I beg thee - **thy son**. 'Which son?' he asked. **Thine only son**, replied He. 'But each is the only one of his mother?' - **Whom thou lovest**. - 'Is there a limit to the affections?' **Even Yitz'khak**, said He" (B'resheet Rabbah 15:7 from *b*. Sanhedrin 89*b*). The conversation highlights the gentleness with which God makes the request of Avraham; this is no harsh command that must be obeyed without question, simply at God's whim because He demands it. This is a reasoned request, with which *HaShem* needs Avraham's willing co-operation if the right outcome is to be obtained, for Avraham, Yitzchak and the Jewish people yet to come.

Rashi comments, "Why did He not reveal to him [that it was Yitzchak] from the start? In order to make the commandment more precious to him and to give him reward for each and every statement." It is as if *HaShem* wants to encourage Avraham to think through the request, to engage with it and to accept and surrender each step to His will. A number of commentators go as far as suggesting that the request should start, "It would be good for you if you could take your son".

The writer to the Hebrews offers a snapshot on Avraham's thought process: "By faith Avraham, when he was tested, offered up Yitzchak; and he who had received the promises was offering up his only begotten son; it was he to whom it was said, 'In Yitzchak your descendants shall be called.' He considered that God is able to raise men even from the dead; from which he also received him back as a type" (Hebrews 11:17-19, NASB). Avraham is here visualised as being prepared to completely surrender Yitzchak, because his faith assured him that God had promised that he would have descendants to realise the promise Avraham had been given. No matter what happened in the short term, even if it came to killing Yitzchak, Avraham knew that God would work it out some way, raising him back to life if necessary. By being obedient, then, Avraham's faith was challenged and strengthened, his character grew and he could be rewarded for his faithfulness. It was indeed good for him.

The three synoptic gospels all relate a strikingly similar event in Yeshua's ministry. They record how a certain young man who was both wealthy and a leader among the people came to him because he felt unsure about his relationship with God. "One of the leaders asked him, 'Good rabbi, what should I do to obtain eternal life?'" (Luke 18:18, CJB). Like many people today, the man was trying to make sure that he had done everything he needed to do and was canvassing Yeshua's opinion - as a rabbi who taught with authority - on the matter. Yeshua's response was startling: "Why are you calling Me good? No one is good but God! You know the mitzvot - 'Don't commit adultery, don't murder, don't steal, don't give false testimony, honour your father and mother ...'" (v. 19-20, CJB). Yeshua starts by making it clear that giving Him a title or compliment is wasted, because He doesn't set the rules: it is God alone who is the standard of righteousness and He must be recognised as such; then He points to the basic commandments - all to be found in the Ten Words in either Shemot 20 or D'varim 5 - how else is a Jew to be sure of God's favour other than by obeying His commandments? The man is taken aback by the simplicity of the reply: "I have kept all these since I was a boy" (v. 21, CJB); this I have already done - implying the secondary question: are You sure that is all I have to do, it seems so simple? "On hearing this Yeshua said to him, 'There is one thing you still lack. Sell whatever you have, distribute the proceeds to the poor, and you will have riches in heaven. Then come, follow Me!" (v. 22, CJB). Hear what Yeshua is saying here; He is not advocating poverty and subsistence living among all His followers - He is challenging the young man in exactly the same way as

Avraham was challenged: are you prepared to give up what is closest to you - your money, your wealth - in order to guarantee your relationship with God, putting Him first above all else? It is not that obeying the commandments is wrong, on the contrary, but that obedience to a covenant can only be meaningful when there is a covenant; in this case, the covenant is established by putting God first and having no other gods before Him.

Yeshua is inviting the young man to take a step of faith for his own benefit: it would be good for you to sell everything and give it to the poor. Who benefits the most from the transaction? We know from Yeshua's comments elsewhere that although the particular gift of money might bring immediate relief to some poor people, it would not solve the problem of poverty: "For the poor you always have with you, and whenever you wish, you can do them good" (Mark 14:7, NASB). Similarly, Yeshua was not seeking followers for His own sake, but in order to lead and disciple them in serving God; the "follow Me" was not an instruction to put Yeshua before Father God, but an invitation to join Yeshua's group of disciples learning how to put into practice Yeshua's own summary of the *Torah*: "'You shall love the Lord your God with all your heart, and with all your soul, and with all your mind.' This is the great and foremost commandment. The second is like it, 'You shall love your neighbor as yourself'" (Matthew 22:37-39, NASB).

We have been given great and powerful promises by God but no matter how great and powerful the promises are, God Himself and our relationship with Him must still come before any of the promises. We must be prepared to trust Him for the execution of those promises in His time and His way, all the while holding the promises lightly and making sure that we always surrender them to Him. Without Him the promises are worthless; without Him their fulfillment, however gratifying it might appear to be in the short term, would be but dust and ashes and of no lasting pleasure or benefit.

Further Study: Romans 4:19-21; Psalm 27:4-5

Application: Have you been able to keep God first in your life, or have His promises and blessings started to come between you? Why not search your heart today and ask Him the question: which is more important to me, You or Your promises? Like most of us, you might find that an attitude adjustment is required!

חַיֵּי שָׂרָה

Khayey Sarah - The life of Sarah

B'resheet / Genesis 23:1 - 25:18

רִאשׁוֹן	Aliyah One	B'resheet/Genesis 23:1 - 16
שֵׁנִי	Aliyah Two	B'resheet/Genesis 23:17 - 24:9
שְׁלִישִׁי	Aliyah Three	B'resheet/Genesis 24:10 - 26
רְבִיעִי	Aliyah Four	B'resheet/Genesis 24:27 - 52
חֲמִשִׁי	Aliyah Five	B'resheet/Genesis 24:53 - 67
שִׁשִׁי	Aliyah Six	B'resheet /Genesis 25:1 - 11
שְׁבִיעִי	Aliyah Seven	B'resheet/Genesis 25:12 - 18

חַיֵּי שָׂרָה 'א

Khayey Sarah - The life of Sarah - 1

B'resheet / Genesis 23:1 - 16

B'resheet/Genesis 23:1 Sarah's lifetime was one hundred years, and twenty years, and seven years; the years of Sarah's life.

וַיִּהְיוּ חַיֵּי שָׂרָה מֵאָה שָׁנָה וְעֶשְׂרִים שָׁנָה
shanah   v'esriym   shanah meyah   Sarah khayey vayih'yu
וְשֶׁבַע שָׁנִים שְׁנֵי חַיֵּי שָׂרָה:
Sarah khayey sh'ney shaniym v'sheva

The commentators spend a lot of time on the apparent redundancy of the *Torah's* words in this verse. Why does the *Torah*, usually sparing and terse in its use of words, repeat the word 'year' three times in the first phrase and then follow that with the repetitive second phrase?

Rashi attributes qualities of each age-group to Sarah's life, while the Sfat Emet suggests that Sarah's years are emphasised because they were good years - all fruitful and productive.

This leads us to the idea that each year was important; that Sarah lived each year as if it might have been the last - so that each year counted. There is a place in the Sifre comment to this passage (*Piska 41*) where the rabbis teach, "Whatever you do should be done out of love for God," suggesting that Sarah's life was good because she was always looking to serve God. A matter-of-fact reading of the Biblical text may lead us to think that that is a rather idealistic point of view, but we do know that Sarah showed remarkable loyalty to her husband during the course of a marriage probably lasting over a hundred years and going through some extremely trying circumstances, not the least of which was following Avram when he left their life in Haran for a nomadic existence who-knows-where just because "God said so".

Yeshua tells us, "Do not worry about tomorrow - tomorrow will worry about itself! Today has enough tsuris already" (Matthew 6:34, CJB), which clearly speaks to the importance of living each day at a time. Similarly, James, in his letter, warns us about presuming to say, "today or tomorrow we will go to such-and-such a city, stay there a year and make a profit!" when all we are is "a mist that appears for a little while and then disappears" (James 4:13, CJB). At the same time, Rav Sha'ul tells us that anyone who does not provide for the needs of his family "has denied the faith, and is worse than an unbeliever" (1 Timothy 5:8, NASB) - this is usually taken to imply financial planning and making regular commitments.

So how do we resolve these opposites: live only for today, but plan for tomorrow? By making responsible and prayerful plans before the Lord, but holding them lightly, recognising that all our days belong to Him and letting Him lead us each day.

Further Study: Hebrews 11:13-16, Proverbs 3:5-6

Application: Has your life become stuck in a round of routine, or are you living each day responsibly before the Lord as if it were your last?

חַיֵּי שָׂרָה ב'

Khayey Sarah - The life of Sarah - 2

B'resheet / Genesis 23:17 - 24:9

B'resheet/Genesis 23:17 So the field of Ephron in Machpelah, which was to the east of Mamre ... was made over

וַיָּקָם | שְׂדֵה עֶפְרוֹן אֲשֶׁר בַּמַּכְפֵּלָה אֲשֶׁר
asher ba'Machpeylah asher   Ef'ron   s'dey   vayakam

לִפְנֵי מַמְרֵא
Mamre   lifney

The verb that is used in this verse, וַיָּקָם from the root קוּם, means literally 'and he arose' or 'he rose up'. This verb is found in Isaiah 60:1 קוּמִי אוֹרִי, "Arise! Shine!" It will also be familiar from the words canted as the *Torah* is taken from the Ark and processed around the congregation on *Shabbat* morning: קוּמָה יהוה וְיָפֻצוּ אֹיְבֶיךָ, "Arise, O Lord, and let Your enemies be scattered" (B'Midbar 10:35, ESV). This is a sufficiently unusual use of the verb in this verse that it attracts the attention of the commentators. Rashi, for example, comments that although the simple meaning (*p'shat*) of the verse is that the field stood as Avraham's purchase, the field has an arising, an ascension in itself, because it "left the possession of a commoner for the possession of a king".

Consider what this means: the field, the first piece of *Eretz Yisra'el* to be legally owned by our people, was elevated - became more holy - when it was transferred into Avraham's ownership. But doesn't the *Torah* tell us that the whole land belongs to God and is His to give, so that it is all holy? Yes, it does, but although God is in possession of the freehold, peoples other than Avraham and his descendants either held a lease on the land or had declared squatters' rights to the areas where they lived, so that although Avraham walked the length and breadth of the land as God had commanded him, this was the only piece where God's authority was demonstrated "on the ground". So Ephron's field arose when it entered Avraham's ownership.

How much more then is there a change in status when we turn to God, confess our sins and enter fully into His kingdom, accepting the yoke of

Yeshua as Lord. Just as Avraham counted out four hundred shekels of silver to purchase Ephron's field, Rav Sha'ul tells us that "you were bought with a price" (1 Corinthians 6:20, CJB). We are owned by God; although we were already His, for He made us, He bought us back - redeemed us from the enemy who had claimed squatters' rights in our lives because of our sin. Yeshua says that "whoever hears what I am saying and trusts the One who sent Me has eternal life", he has "already crossed over from death to life!" (John 5:24, CJB). Peter speaks of those who have been "called out of darkness into His marvelous light" (1 Peter 2:9, NASB) and Rav Sha'ul quotes Yeshua's words to him when he (Sha'ul) was told to "open their eyes so that they may turn from darkness to light and from the dominion of Satan to God" (Acts 26:18, NASB). When we undergo that change, we also arise, we are elevated in holiness, for we are brought into God's kingdom and ownership.

Further Study: Judges 6:11-24; John 9:24-25

Application: How many times have you heard believers refer to themselves as sinners, even if "a sinner saved by grace"? This is simply not true - we are the children of The King, full members of His kingdom, even if we do still sometimes sin and need to ask forgiveness. Throw off the lie and stand tall in your real nature: you are a son or a daughter of The King!

חַיֵּי שָׂרָה 'ג

Khayey Sarah - The life of Sarah - 3

B'resheet / Genesis 24:10 - 26

B'resheet/Genesis 24:10 And he went and all the wealth of his master [was] in his hand

וַיֵּלֶךְ וְכָל־טוּב אֲדֹנָיו בְּיָדוֹ
b'yado adonayv tuv v'chol vay'eylech

Although indistinguishable in the consonantal text, טוֹב and טוּב have quite distinct though connected meanings. טוֹב is an adjective meaning 'good', whereas טוּב is a noun meaning 'goods' or 'wealth'. The Sages have a discussion as to whether this text means (B'resheet Rabbah 59:11): did Eli'ezer (cf. B'resheet 15:2) physically take all of Avraham's possessions with him - impossible, since he took only ten camels; had Avraham actually given his wealth to Eli'ezer in some transferable form to possess until he should pass them on - also impossible since Eli'ezer was a slave so had no right to property.

Rashi suggests that Avraham wrote a document describing his wealth and making it over to Yitz'khak so that a potential father-in-law would feel confident that his daughter would be properly provided for and that he would be allaying himself to a family of substance.

Mark tells us that, "the Pharisess came out and began to argue with Him, seeking from Him a sign from heaven to test Him" (Mark 8:11, NASB). As the religious leaders in a generation that was keenly anticipating Messiah - a messiah to free them from the Roman occupation and oppression - but had been plagued by a series of pretenders to the title who caused a lot of unrest and disturbance but failed to deliver on their claims, the *P'rushim* were trying to check Yeshua's credentials. "We've heard the words; now where's the beef!" Before endorsing Yeshua as Messiah - as a hundred or so years later, Rabbi Akiva endorsed Shimon ben Kosiba - the *P'rushim* wanted to be sure that Yeshua was the real thing. This is just like Rivkah's brother Lavan: "when he saw the nose-ring, and the bracelets on his sister's wrists besides, and when he heard his sister Rivkah's report of what the man had said to her, he ran out to the spring and found the man standing there by the camels.

'Come on in,' he said, 'you whom Adonai has blessed ...'" (B'resheet 24:29-31, CJB). It was the physical manifestation of wealth that brought credibility and assurance of status.

What is it that authenticates us today; what gives us credibility as witnesses and servants of the Most High God? What is it that makes people stop in their tracks and want to know and share in what we do and have to say? Simply (and only) one thing: the power of God being manifest in and through us. As the writer to the Hebrews says: "This deliverance, which was first declared by the Lord, was confirmed to us by those who heard Him; while God also bore witness to it with various signs, wonders and miracles, and with the gifts of the Ruach HaKodesh which He distributed as He chose" (Hebrews 2:3-4, CJB). Historically, the church advanced with the gospel, signs of power and healing. The church in the Southern Hemisphere is doing the same today - so should we!

Further Study: Acts 4:23-31; Mark 16:14-18

Application: Do you feel inadequate and frustrated at the lack of power and progress for the gospel and the coming of the kingdom in your life and congregation? Revisit the descriptions of the early followers of Yeshua, pray and expect the Lord to move in power and have boldness to proclaim the gospel of the kingdom!

חַיֵּי שָׂרָה 'ד

Khayey Sarah - The life of Sarah - 4

B'resheet / Genesis 24:27 - 52

B'resheet/Genesis 24:27 Adonai has led me in the way of the house of my master's brothers.

אָנֹכִי בַּדֶּרֶךְ נָחַנִי יהוה בֵּית אֲחֵי אֲדֹנִי׃

adoniy akhey beyt Adonai nakhaniy baderech anochiy

This is the concluding phrase of the prayer of thanks prayed by Avraham's servant, on the mission to find a wife for Yitz'khak, when he sees that *HaShem* has answered his earlier prayer for guidance: that he has indeed been led to the Avraham's family in Haran. Rashi comments: "**On the way**: the way which has been prepared, the straight way, on the way which I needed." This brings together three important aspects of God's guidance and sovereignty. First, God had already prepared the way for Avraham's servant to follow; *HaShem* already knew and planned that Yitz'khak was to marry Rivkah, and He knew perfectly well where she lived, what she would be doing that day and how best to introduce Rivkah and Avraham's servant; the way was prepared. Secondly, the way was straight; all the obstacles, twists and turns had been removed - this is not to say that the journey across the desert from Canaan was not dry, arduous, long, cold at night or did not have other difficulties that the servant had to overcome, but that the way was direct and straight. Thirdly, the way was the way that the servant needed to follow; no other way would have got him from there to there, it was the one way that he needed to fulfill his master's commission to find a wife for Yitz'khak.

When *HaShem* spoke to the northern of the two divided kingdoms, Israel, through the prophet Amos, Amos was challenged and rebuked by Amaziah the priest of Bethel. Amos responded by saying, "I am not a prophet, nor am I the son of a prophet; for I am a herdsman and a grower of sycamore figs. But the Lord took me from following the flock and the Lord said to me, 'Go prophesy to My people Israel'" (Amos 7:14-15, NASB). This was not Amos' natural role in life, neither had he been born or brought up to it, but God had prepared the way by calling him, removed the obstacles so that

Amos had access to the right people and places to deliver God's message, and this was the way that Amos himself needed to follow after God had shared some of His heart for His people (see Amos 7:1-9).

When King David wanted to build a house - the Temple - for the ark and God's presence to dwell in, Nathan the prophet was sent to give David a God's-eye view of his life: "I took you from the pasture, from following the sheep, that you should be ruler over My people Israel. And I have been with you wherever you have gone ... and I will make you a great name ... when your days are complete and you lie down with your fathers, I will raise up your descendant ... and your house and your kingdom shall endure before Me forever" (2 Samuel 7:8-9,12,16, NASB). All of a sudden, David could see jow God had prepared his way, what a straight way - in spite of the difficulties, the years running from King Saul, living rough - it had been and how much he needed to follow it in order to be what he was now.

It is no less true today - for God does not change - that God prepares a way for each of our lives, a way that has been carefully straightened so that we can walk along it. God does not want us to fall off or be unable to walk in His way - and it is the way that we need to follow, for there is no other way that leads where we need to go. God provides a custom-made way for each of us and He takes us from where we were and places us upon the way that leads to life and relationship with Him.

Further Study: Proverbs 3:5-6; 2 Samuel 7:18-29

Application: Which way are you going today? Are you walking in God's way - the straight way, the way you need - or have you gone off on a way of your own planning and devising, away from God and among the thorns and thistles of life? If so, then take heart that you are neither the first nor the last to do so but, know that God has a way for you, a better way, His way.

חַיֵּי שָׂרָה 'ה

Khayey Sarah - The life of Sarah - 5

B'resheet / Genesis 24:53 - 67

B'resheet/Genesis 24:53 items of silver and gold and garments he gave to Rivkah and precious things he gave to her brother

כְּלֵי־כֶסֶף וּכְלֵי זָהָב וּבְגָדִים וַיִּתֵּן לְרִבְקָה

l'Rivkah   vayiteyn oov'gadiym zahav oochley chesef k'ley

וּמִגְדָּנֹת נָתַן לְאָחִיהָ

l'akhiyha natan oomigdanot

  This text comes at the end of the negotiations between Avraham's servant (Eliezer) and Rivkah's family for Rivkah to come to the land of Canaan (as it was then) to be the wife of Yitz'khak. According to Davidson, - a feminine plural noun מִגְדָּנֹת - comes from a root מֶגֶד (that is not used in biblical Hebrew but means "to be honoured, noble or excellent" in Arabic), to mean choice or precious things. Rashi, who is probably trying to make a distinction between the gifts given to Rivkah and those given to her family, tells us that "this means 'delicacies', for he brought with him varieties of fruit from the Land of Israel", referring to the use of the word in Song of Songs 4:13. *Chazal* interpret the word as "parched ears of corn or nuts" (B'resheet Rabbah 60:11) quoting from Ezra 1:6. In either case, they make the point that the gifts given to Rivkah - the bride - are of a different calibre to those given to Rivkah's family.

  Nahum Sarna says that "the two types of gift ... most likely correspond to the 'bride price and gifts' mentioned in 34:12. The first was a fixed amount paid by the groom in compensation for the loss of the bride's services and her potential offspring, which will now belong to the groom's family; the second consisted of ceremonial marriage gifts to the bride's family." Notice that in Sarna's comment and in 34:12, the bride-price is paid not to the bride but to the bride's family, whereas our text is clear that the gifts of gold and silver were given to Rivkah herself. Hirsch, after confirming the difference in the gifts: "He gave precious gifts to the young bride; confectionery, polite attentions to the mother and brother; to the father - nothing!", comes down very firmly against reading more recent oriental customs and habits back into the text. He completely rejects the idea of a bride-price, citing Rachel and Leah's disgust at their father Laban allowing himself to be paid for them by Ya'akov: "Do we still have any portion or inheritance in our father's house? Are we not reckoned by him as foreigners? For he has sold us, and has also completely consumed our purchase price" (B'resheet 31:14-15, NASB).

We can use these ideas to help us see our relationship with God more clearly, both at an individual and corporate level. The Scriptures are clear that when Yeshua took the punishment for our sin by dying on the stake at Calvary, a ransom was paid - or a debt was settled. But to whom was the payment made? Not to the devil, the father or originator of sin; this was not a bride-price paid to someone who owned us, but a penalty paid to the court, a ransom or substitute so that we should not have to die - the appropriate punishment for our rebellion and sin. Although the forces of wickedness worked to bring about the crucifixion, thinking that they would thereby defeat God's plan ("Let us kill the heir, then the inheritance will be ours" (Mark 12:7)), not only did they not gain anything at all from the transaction - for nothing was due to them in any case - but they were themselves defeated in the process. Death, the price of sin, was both paid and vanquished at the same time, so that those who trust in Yeshua may be free of the "law of sin and of death" (Romans 8:2, NASB).

But look also at the gifts that have been given to the bride. We have redemption and forgiveness of sins (Ephesians 1:7), eternal life (John 3:16), the indwelling of the *Ruach* (John 14:16), the peace of God (Philippians 4:7) and peace with God (Romans 5:1), the gifts of the Spirit (1 Corinthians 12), and many other gifts, both individually and as the body/bride of Messiah, for "He who did not spare His own Son, but delivered Him up for us all, how will He not also with Him freely give us all things?" (Romans 8:32, NASB). As the bride, like Rivkah, we have received the choicest gifts both now and in the future. Why? Because God loves us and has chosen us; because God wants to show His love and generosity through us; because God delights in us; because God values us and wants to bless us.

Further Study: Deuteronomy 10:17-18; Matthew 6:33; 1 Corinthians 2:9

Application: Do you feel downtrodden and valueless? Do you struggle with self-worth or have a sneaky feeling that God only let you in by mistake? Lift up your head and know that you are a child of the King, chosen and precious to Him and He longs to bless you in more ways than you can ever imagine. Ask Him about it today!

חַיֵּי שָׂרָה ו׳

Khayey Sarah - The life of Sarah - 6

B'resheet / Genesis 25:1 - 11

B'resheet/Genesis 25:5 And Avraham gave all that was his to Isaac.

וַיִּתֵּן אברהם אֶת־כָּל־אֲשֶׁר־לוֹ לְיִצְחָק:

l'Yitz'khak   lo   asher   kol   et   Avraham vayiteyn

This verse, falling as it does among the verses leading to the account of Avraham's passing, appears to be addressing the issue of physical inheritance: Yitz'khak gets everything, Ishmael gets nothing. On the other hand, the context of the immediately surrounding verses is set before Avraham's death, at the time when Avraham's children from Keturah - whom he married only after Sarah had died - and his concubines were old enough to leave home and were sent off to the east with a gift to start their own lives and families. This statement - that "Avraham gave all that he had to Isaac" - is juxtaposed with the following verse: "but to the sons of his concubines, Avraham gave gifts while he was still living, and sent them away from his son Isaac eastward" (v. 6, NASB). There is a hint here that perhaps the text isn't talking about the physical estate after all. In the previous chapter, when Avraham's servant has gone back to Haran to find a wife for Yitz'khak, the servant tells Rivkah's family: "Now Sarah my master's wife bore a son to my master in her old age; and he has given him all that he has" (24:36, NASB). Similar words, but that verse is held to be the point at which Avraham had transferred title in all his possessions over to Yitz'khak, so that this later one must be talking about something else. Perhaps it is the transference of authority as head of the household, the responsibility of governing and caring for the rest of the family and the servants, the status among the other inhabitants of the land and a recognition that Yitz'khak is now "the man".

Rashi says, "Rabbi Nechemiah said: Avraham gave Yitz'khak his right to dispense blessing - for the Holy One, Blessed is He, said to Avraham 'And you shall be a blessing' (B'resheet 12:2, JPS), meaning that the blessings are given over to your hand, to bless whomever you wish. And Avraham gave them over to Isaac." The words of Rabbi Nechemiah come from B'resheet Rabbah 61:6 where the rabbis discuss what it was that Avraham gave Yitz'khak. "Rabbi Judah said: It means the birthright. R. Nechemiah said: The power of blessing. The Rabbis said: The family vault and a deed of gift." The first suggestion, the birthright, was covered above and the last suggestion means a place to be buried, and the legal document proving that he owned the land - the field of Ephron and the Machpelah Cave. By picking up on the middle proposal, Rashi points to an important idea. When Abram (as he was then) was first called to leave Haran, *HaShem* told him, "And I will make you a great nation, and I will bless you, and make your name great; and so you shall be a blessing" (B'resheet 12:2, NASB). From this, the rabbis concluded that *HaShem* was giving Avraham the power or ability to bless others; he had the ability to pass on or withhold the blessing to/from others. It was this power or ability, the delegated authority to direct blessing, that Rabbi Nechemiah suggested was being given to Yitz'khak so that in turn, he would be a blessing to the people around him and so fulfill *HaShem*'s promise that Avraham and his seed would be a blessing to the nations: "in you all the families of the earth shall be blessed" (12:3, NASB).

This inheritance, then, could be described as Avraham's essence, his character, his relationship with God - perhaps these were the qualities that Yitz'khak learned from and so inherited from his father; the means of being a blessing to others and to God. See also how Avraham gave of himself to Yitz'khak: not stintingly or in part, but whole-heartedly and without measure; everything - or, as the Hebrew text literally translates, "all that was to him" - was invested into Yitz'khak. Nothing was held back. The root of the Hebrew verb used here, נָתַן, has the most common meaning "to give", but can also mean "to grant, permit; to emit, yield or bear; to place, lay or put; to appoint; to make like" (Davidson) and could stretch to the idea of make an investment. Avraham poured himself into his son, so that he might be like him, he appointed him as his successor not only in physical and familial matters, but as the holder of the covenant with God, the means by which all the nations would eventually be blessed. Notice how much more powerful this investment is than the gifts which Avraham gave to his concubine's sons; this is to build character and purpose in the son to take the father's place, to represent him to the world and maintain the promise and the word of God, a deposit expecting a return or yield, while the gifts - well intentioned as they were - were simply material starting points to help each son find a wife, set up tents, purchase some livestock and establish their own family.

From here it is but a small step to perhaps the most well-known verse in the Bible, recited almost as many times as the *Sh'ma* (D'varim 6:4): "For God so loved the world that He gave His only Son that whoever believes in Him should not perish but have eternal life" (John 3:16, NASB). God the Father, who poured Himself totally into His Son - so that the Bible says that Yeshua was "the radiance of His glory and the exact representation of His nature" (Hebrews 1:3, NASB) and Yeshua Himself said, "I and the Father are one" (John 10:30, NASB) - and gave Himself, in the person of Yeshua, as a gift to the world as a deposit expecting a return and with a definite purpose: to save the world and raise up a family of believers who would follow and worship Him willingly because of His love for them. Yeshua shows the character and purpose of God, He represents God to the world and maintains the promise and the word of God, giving the gifts of His Spirit - the *Ruach HaKodesh* - that his brothers and sisters, the body of Messiah might grow in stature and become like Yeshua Himself.

What is the purpose of our lives? That we should give and invest of ourselves into the next generation, be that physical - for every man or woman's first field is their own family or children - or spiritual. We are called to be like Avraham, who himself modelled the character of God in this respect, and Yeshua, who gave His whole life to be a servant, investing our time, our money, our talents and skills, our very substance, into the job of raising up the next generation to follow us and labour in the harvest field of the Kingdom. Until the Lord returns there will always be a harvest to be gathered, there will always be disciples to train and teach in the ways of the Lord, so no shortage of investment opportunities for the resources of the Kingdom. May we all bring forth a harvest for Him who loved us: thirty-fold, sixty-fold or a hundred-fold!

Further Study: Zechariah 8:13; Colossians 1:18-19

Application: How many people do you invest in? Draw up an inventory and make sure that you know into whom God is calling you to invest your time and resources. Follow the model of Avraham and Yeshua and ask God how to make you a whole-hearted investor in people!

חַיֵּי שָׂרָה 'ז

Khayey Sarah - The life of Sarah - 7

B'resheet / Genesis 25:12 - 18

B'resheet/Genesis 25:16 ... and these are the names by their courtyards and by their strongholds, twelve chieftains ...

וְאֵלֶּה שְׁמֹתָם בְּחַצְרֵיהֶם וּבְטִירֹתָם
uvtiyrotam   b'khatz'reyhem sh'motam   v'eyleh
שְׁנֵים־עָשָׂר נְשִׂיאִם
n'siyim   asar sh'neym

    This summary follows a precise enumeration and naming of each of Yishmael's twelve sons, given in birth order, in verses 13-15. We know from other ancient Middle-East documents that these were real people, not just names put in a list. Adbeel, for example, is the tribe of Idiba'il who were subjugated by Tiglath-pileser III and assigned to guard duty on the Egyptian frontier. Nebaioth may be the progenitor of the Nabateans who built the rose-pink city of Petra in Jordan; but his descendants certainly occur in the accounts of Ashurbanipal's campaigns against the Arabs. All these peoples - tribes or clans - were known to be nomadic in lifestyle, herders of sheep and goats, roaming in sometimes quite dispersed areas of the Middle East, generally to the east and south of the Land of Israel; they were not city dwellers. This is hinted at by the word בְּחַצְרֵיהֶם - their courtyards - which comes from a root verb חָצֵר that is not used in the text of the Hebrew Bible. Davidson lists several derivative nouns with meanings such as "village, hamlet" or "enclosure, area, court". Rashi comments that these are "cities that have no walls, for they are open"; while *Targum Onkelos* translates the word as "open areas", which might suggest a camp consisting of tents pitched around a central area of open community space. Such a layout is typical of pastoral nomadic tribes.

    Given that Yitz'khak is the carrier of the promise, and that Yishmael effectively drops out of the story halfway through chapter 21, in *parasha Vayera*, to reappear briefly next to Yitz'khak at their father Avraham's burial in the cave of Machpela in Hevron, why does the biblical author pause at this point to devote a couple of paragraphs to a genealogy-style summary of Yishmael's descendants, life and death? Why also the use of the word נְשִׂיאָם - princes or chieftains? Is the number of the sons - twelve - important? The text this points back to is: "And as for Ishmael, I have heard you; behold, I will bless him, and will make him fruitful, and will multiply him exceedingly. He shall become the father of twelve princes, and I will make him a great nation" (B'resheet 17:20, NASB). Even though Yishmael was not the one with whom *HaShem* would establish His covenant, He is nevertheless faithful to keep His promise to Avraham with respect to Yishmael; he is indeed the father of twelve princes and does in time become the father of a great nation of peoples stretching far and wide throughout the Middle East. The writer therefore takes the time, before moving on with the main story, to show that *HaShem* has kept His promises to Yishmael in exact parallel to the promise that will be worked out through Ya'akov's twelve sons. The only difference between the sons of Ya'akov and the sons of Yishmael is that the former are the children of the covenant while the latter are not.

God made a covenant with Noach after the flood had ended and He had let Noach and his family out of the ark. He told him, "While the earth remains, seedtime and harvest, and cold and heat, and summer and winter, and day and night shall not cease" (B'resheet 8:22, NASB). Although the rains may be withheld for a season, as a sign of God's judgement for sin, that covenant still stands. One of Job's so-called comforters comments, "Dominion and awe belong to Him who establishes peace in His heights. Is there any number to His troops? And upon whom does His light not rise?" (Job 25:2-3, NASB), while the Psalmist several times proclaims that God provides for all of creation: "The Lord is good to all, and His mercy is over all that He has made ... The eyes of all look to You, and You give them their food in due season. You open Your hand; You satisfy the desire of every living thing" (Psalm 145:9,15-16, ESV). Yeshua teaches the people the same thing: "For He makes His sun shine on good and bad people alike, and He sends rain to the righteous and the unrighteous alike" (Matthew 5:45, CJB). God's common grace is upon the whole of creation to maintain it in its order and path.

In spite of God's goodness and faithfulness, mankind has failed to take notice of the evidence that is before them. Even when the southern kingdom of Judah is threatened with the same punishment as her northern neighbour Israel, whose refugees probably filled the countryside, God observes that "They do not say in their heart, 'Let us now fear the Lord our God, who gives rain in its season, both the autumn rain and the spring rain, who keeps for us the appointed weeks of the harvest'" (Jeremiah 5:24, NASB). Among the nations, the situation is even worse. Rav Sha'ul points out that, "What is revealed is God's anger from heaven against all the godlessness and wickedness of people who in their wickedness keep suppressing the truth; because what is known about God is plain to them, since God has made it plain to them. For ever since the creation of the universe His invisible qualities - both His eternal power and His divine nature - have been clearly seen, because they can be understood from what He has made. Therefore, they have no excuse; because, although they know who God is, they do not glorify Him as God or thank Him. On the contrary, they have become futile in their thinking; and their undiscerning hearts have become darkened" (Romans 1:18-21, CJB). Because of consistently ignoring the evidence that is all around us every day, the hearts and minds of those who choose to reject God become blinded to Him so that it is increasingly difficult for them to acknowledge Him.

Many people today deny God in their lives, either deliberately or deliberately. That is to say, some explicitly deny God, having looked at the evidence and rejected it; others ignore the evidence but without having considered it. Yeshua spoke about this in the well-known parable of the sower. The seed, or word of God, that fell on the rocky ground was eaten before it could germinate; the seed that fell on shallow ground couldn't grow roots to endure the heat and drought; the seed that fell among the weeds was choked by the thorns. Only the seed that fell on the good soil germinated, grew roots, had room to grow and brought forth a harvest. Our job is twofold: firstly to make sure that we are good soil, that we have weeded and prepared, that we receive the word gladly, make room for it, encourage it to grow and ensure that it stays watered. Secondly, we must encourage others who will also hear the word, to do the same. We must be prepared to scare away the crows, make sure that the seed is watered, risk pricking our hands by pulling a few thistles and even turn over some fallow ground to start the process. The question is: do you have what it takes and are you prepared to get your hands dirty? As God's sun and rain fall on you, will you share that with those who can't or won't recognise it falling on them?

Further Study: Psalm 19:2-4; Acts 14:17

Application: Why not start by recognising God's blessings in your life and thanking Him for them? Ask God who else needs to know about the blessing today and offer to help. Then keep your eyes open, because you'll find yourself being taken up on that offer to help someone else enter or grow in the kingdom.

תּוֹלְדֹת

Toldot - Histories

B'resheet / Genesis 25:19 - 28:9

רִאשׁוֹן	Aliyah One	B'resheet/Genesis 25:19 - 26:5
שֵׁנִי	Aliyah Two	B'resheet/Genesis 26:6 - 12
שְׁלִישִׁי	Aliyah Three	B'resheet/Genesis 26:13 - 22
רְבִיעִי	Aliyah Four	B'resheet/Genesis 26:23 - 29
חֲמִשִׁי	Aliyah Five	B'resheet/Genesis 26:30 - 27:27
שִׁשִׁי	Aliyah Six	B'resheet /Genesis 27:28 - 28:4
שְׁבִיעִי	Aliyah Seven	B'resheet/Genesis 28:5 - 9

א' תּוֹלְדֹת

Toldot - Histories - 1

B'resheet / Genesis 25:19 - 26:5

B'resheet/Genesis 25:19 Now these are the generations of Isaac, Abraham's son; Abraham became the father of Isaac.

וְאֵלֶּה תּוֹלְדֹת יִצְחָק בֶּן־אַבְרָהָם אַבְרָהָם
Avraham   Avraham   ben   Yitz'khak   tol'dot   v'eyleh

הוֹלִיד אֶת־יִצְחָק:
Yitz'khak   et   holiyd

This text bears a strong resemblance to the beginning of Mark's gospel: "The beginning of the gospel of Yeshua the Messiah, the Son of God" (Mark 1:1, NASB). Sforno takes the word תּוֹלְדֹת to mean "chronicles" or "the events of one's life", so using this verse to introduce the following chapters as the events of Yitz'khak's life. Rashi, on the other hand, understands the word to mean "offspring", so limiting them as an introduction to only the next ten verses describing the birth of Esav and Ya'akov.

It is interesting to see that the *Torah* takes the time to tell us not only that Yitz'khak was Avraham's son, but that Avraham begot (became the father of) Yitz'khak. In other words, it is emphasising that Avraham was the natural physical father of Yitz'khak and that he was not just his adopted son and legal heir. Rashi even suggests that *HaShem* created a strong physical resemblance between father and son, so that everyone would recognise the true relationship.

In Bible times, it was critical to know who your father was and the genealogy that you came from in order to claim inheritance rights, tribal descent and position in society. In today's Jewish world it is still very important to know if you are a '*cohen*' or 'Levi'; hundreds of the descendants of Aharon, the priestly line, gather at the *Kotel* to bless the people of Israel three times each year.

So the writer of Mark's gospel carries on the tradition in both senses. His text introduces the events of Yeshua's life: "This is the story of ...", but it also immediately declares who Yeshua is: He is the Son of God. That is who He is, the characteristics He inherits, whose resemblance He bears, so that everyone who sees Him can recognise the true relationship. And as the gospel travels through Yeshua's ministry years, we see Yeshua uniquely portrayed as both the Son of Man and the Son of God.

In John's gospel, chapter 8, Yeshua and the *P'rushim* had a sharp disagreement about parentage. "You know neither Me, nor My Father; if you knew Me, you would know My Father also" (v. 19, NASB), said Yeshua, "You are of your father the devil, and you want to do the desires of your father" (v. 44, NASB). You can often discern peoples' descent just by looking at them and their behaviour. We tell people who we are all the time without speaking a word, by our attitudes, our clothes and our body language - just the way we look.

Further Study: Romans 8:29; 12:2

Application: Who will you look like today? Are people going to be able to see the Father in you?

Toldot - Histories - 2

B'resheet / Genesis 26:6 - 12

B'resheet/Genesis 26:6 And Yitz'khak dwelt in Gerar

$$\text{וַיֵּשֶׁב יִצְחָק בִּגְרָר:}$$
big'rar Yitz'khak vayeyshev

The Hebrew verb יָשַׁב, here translated 'dwelt', 'settled' (ESV), 'lived' (NASB), has a range of meanings coming from the basic "to sit" or "to sit down"; these cover "remain, stay, abide", "dwell in or inhabit". All the meanings imply a degree of permanence or longevity, in sharp contrast to the verb גּוּר which is usually translated 'sojourn' or 'dwell' with an emphasis on this being only for a time or a season. Indeed, the latter verb gives rise to the noun גֵּר meaning 'a stranger' or 'a foreigner'.

So why is it significant that the *Torah* uses this word to describe Yitz'khak's residence at Gerar? In the preceding verses, God had told Yitz'khak to remain in the Land of Israel, in spite of the famine in the land; He had held up Avraham's obedience to God's commandments as an example and repeated His promise and intention to bless Yitz'khak and his descendants. Gerar, on the other hand, while still being in the Land, was in the territory then occupied by the P'lishtim - the Philistines - which was not necessarily the safest place for a follower of the One True God to live. Nevertheless, it was here that Yitz'khak not only lived, but put down settled roots; he remained there. Just a few verses further on (v. 12 ff.) the text tells us that Yitz'khak reaped a hundred-fold harvest and grew very wealthy as God blessed him. And Yitz'khak remained faithful to God's specific instructions to "stay in the land" (v2, NASB).

Rav Sha'ul had a similar experience: going into the face of danger in obedience to God's instructions. He told the elders of Ephesus gathered at Miletus, "And now, compelled by the Spirit, I am going to Jerusalem. I don't know what will happen to me there, other than that in every city the Ruach HaKodesh keeps warning me that imprisonment and persecution await me" (Acts 20:22-23, CJB). On the journey, Rav Sha'ul's party met *talmidim* at Tzor where "guided by the Spirit, they told Sha'ul not to go up to Jerusalem;

but when the week was over, we left to continue our journey" (21:4-5, CJB). Finally, "a prophet named Agav came down from Y'hudah to visit us. He took Sha'ul's belt, tied up his own hands and feet and said, 'Here is what the Ruach HaKodesh says: "The man who owns this belt - the Judeans in Jerusalem will tie him up and hand him over to the Goyim"'" (vv.10-11, CJB). Yet, persistently, Rav Sha'ul pushed on, walking out the vision and the call that God had placed on him.

Yeshua rebuked Simon Peter when he tried to stop Him going ahead with God's plan: "'God forbid it, Lord! This shall never happen to you.' But He turned round and said to Peter, 'Get behind Me, Satan! You are a stumbling block to Me; for you are not setting your mind on God's interests, but man's'" (Matthew 16:22-23, NASB).

Further Study: Hosea 1:1-3; Isaiah 20:1-6; Luke 21:10-19; John 16:33

Application: Many times we are called by God to resolutely sit in an uncomfortable place, for reasons that we don't understand, so that God can work out His purposes both in our lives and those around us. If you are there and finding it difficult, stop struggling and seek God for His grace to "dwell" and see your assignment through to the end.

תּוֹלְדֹת ג׳

Toldot - Histories - 3

B'resheet / Genesis 26:13 - 22

B'resheet/Genesis 26:13 And the man grew great and he walked to walk and he grew until very great.

וַיִּגְדַּל הָאִישׁ וַיֵּלֶךְ הָלוֹךְ וְגָדֵל עַד כִּי־גָדַל
gadal kiy   ad   v'gadeyl haloch vayeylech ha'iysh vayig'dal

מְאֹד:
m'od

The word גָּדַל is used three times in this verse, twice as a verb and once as a noun. The root meaning is 'to be or become great' or 'to grow'. We find the word used of children growing up and also as part of the title of the High Priest, הַכֹּהֵן גָּדֹל. But in between, the *Torah* uses two instances of the root הָלַךְ, to walk or go - this time as both an active and an infinitive verb. Although this attracts translations such as "he kept becoming greater" (Artscroll), "he continued to grow richer" (NASB), "prospered more and more" (CJB), which are supported by the dictionaries, it is interesting to take the alternative, more literal, translation and notice that the *Torah* is telling us that in the midst of growing wealth, Yitz'khak "walked the walk". In other words, in spite of his increasing substance, wealth, responsibility - the next verse tells us, "flocks and herds and much industry" - he continued to be upright and righteous; the Sages tell us that he was meticulous about tithing (B'resheet Rabbah 64:6) and Sforno cites Malachi 3:10 as the reason for *HaShem*'s blessing in these verses.

Many of the kings of Israel turned away from following the Lord because of their riches, wives and positions. "King Shlomo loved many foreign women ... He had 700 wives, all princesses, and 300 concubines; and his wives turned his head away. For when Shlomo became old, his wives turned his heart away toward other gods, so that he was not whole-hearted with Adonai his God, as David his father had been" (1 Kings 11:1-4, CJB). Many stories within the Jewish heritage, from biblical times until today, tell of people who once rich have neglected the poor, failed to tithe and give *tz'daka*, and become arrogant and proud; yet there were also those who gave deeply from their riches to the poor, the community and those in need. History teaches us that while wealth and blessing can distract us from our service to God (and His people), it is not certain that they will because each person has a choice, like Yitz'khak, to "walk the walk" and not just "talk the talk".

In the parable of the Sower, Yeshua explains to His *talmidim* about the seed that fell among thorns: "they hear the message; but the worries of the world, the deceitful glamour of wealth and all the other kinds of desires push in and choke the message; so that it produces nothing" (Mark 4:18-19, CJB). Anyone who owns a big house will tell you about the time and money it takes to maintain that property: painting, gardening, repairs - which, while necessary and certainly not bad of themselves, can sap our energy and resources so that we have to draw back from kingdom work and activities. At the same time, larger houses provide venues and opportunities for hospitality, meetings and other ministry functions if they are used for the Kingdom of God. The question is: how do we handle them - do we walk the walk?

Further Study: Luke 12:22-34; Psalm 112:1-3; Philippians 3:12-16

Application: Have you allowed yourself to be distracted by God's blessings so that you have lost focus on God in the midst of the blessings? Are you still walking the walk in the midst of growing great, so that you can grow greater in service and honour to God?

תּוֹלְדֹת 'ד

Toldot - Histories - 4

B'resheet / Genesis 26:23 - 29

B'resheet/Genesis 26:24 You shall not fear, for I am with you and I will bless you.

אַל־תִּירָא כִּי־אִתְּךָ אָנֹכִי וּבֵרַכְתִּיךָ
ooveyrach'tiycha anochi   itcha   kiy   tiyra   al

These words are spoken to Yitz'khak during a rather turbulent period in his life. Earlier in the *parasha*, we have read that *HaShem* had blessed him with a hundredfold yield on his crops (v. 12) and Yitz'khak became so rich that the Philistines envied him (v. 14). Then followed a period of dispute when Yitz'khak and the Philistines argue over the ownership of several wells as - in effect - the Philistines force Yitz'khak to move out of their area. Finally, just before the resolution that is about to come (v. 26) Yitz'khak goes up to Be'er Sheva and the Lord appears to him at night with these words. "I am the God of your father Avraham", God says earlier in the verse, to remind Yitz'khak of the past, of *HaShem*'s covenant and relationship with Avraham, and to stress both continuity and constancy. "Fear not, for I am with you" God continues, moving from the past to the present: I am here, now, so you do not need to fear. This is emphasised by the verb form אַל־תִּירָא: not imperative, do not fear, but prefix form indicating present or future incomplete action - you shall not, you will not. Then God moves to the future: "I will bless you and I will increase your seed" - despite the currently prevailing difficulties, I will bless you, I will be keeping My promise anyway.

The theme of God being with His people in the midst of trials and suffering, rather than taking them out of trouble - which does happen sometimes but not, apparently, often - is picked up by David. He writes: "Even though I walk through the dark valley of death, because You are with me, I fear no harm. Your rod and Your staff give me courage. You prepare a banquet for me while my enemies watch" (Psalm 23:4-5, GWT). Even in the darkest times, God is with us and blesses us. The prophets echo the same: "When you go through the sea, I am with you. When you go through rivers, they will not sweep you away. When you walk through fire, you will not be burned, and the flames will not harm you" (Isaiah 43:2, GWT). No mention here of an easy life or a trouble-free existence for Israel - rather the contrary: a life full of constant physical and spiritual challenge. See how the challenges are a part of life and a result of moving forward; not "If the sea washes over you, I will be with you" but "When you go through the sea, I am with you". As we follow the Lord, we will go through times of challenge and opposition, but He is already there with us.

Rav Sha'ul reported exactly the same thing: "The first time I had to present my defence, no-one stood by me ... but the Lord stood by me and gave me power to proclaim the full message for all the Goyim to hear, and I was rescued from the lion's mouth. The Lord will rescue me from every evil attack and bring me safely into His heavenly kingdom" (2 Timothy 4:16-18, CJB). Yeshua too, told the disciples that He would be with them always (Matthew 28:20), that He would not leave them as orphans (John 14:18), and: "I will ask the Father, and He will give you another comforting Counsellor like Me, the Spirit of Truth, to be with you forever" (John 14:16, CJB).

Further Study: John 16:32-33; 2 Corinthians 12:7-10

Application: Do you find yourself almost swamped by the pressures and challenges of life? Although seemingly without end or purpose, God is there with you, in the midst of those trials and He is - even now, though you may have difficulty seeing it - blessing you and others through you. And there is yet more blessing to come!

תּוֹלְדֹת ה׳

Toldot - Histories 5

B'resheet / Genesis 26:30 - 27:27

B'resheet/Genesis 26:30 And he made for them a feast and they ate and they drank

וַיַּעַשׂ לָהֶם מִשְׁתֶּה וַיֹּאכְלוּ וַיִּשְׁתּוּ:
vayishtu   vayochlu   mish'teh   lahem   vaya'as

The word מִשְׁתֶּה, here translated 'feast', comes from the root שָׁתָה, which usually means "to drink" (e.g. Job 15:16) but many translations (KJV, RSV, NRSV, NIV, ESV) also suggest "to banquet, feast, dine" from contexts such as Esther 7:1. The noun is constructed from the verb root by adding a מ prefix, which is commonly taken as the location where the verb activity takes place; another example is the noun מִזְבֵּחַ, an altar, from the root זָבַח, to slaughter or kill animals, especially for sacrifice. Here, eating and drinking take place at a feast or banquet that Yitz'khak has made for Abimelech the king of the Philistines, Ahuzzath the king's advisor and Phicol the commander of his army.

Sarna comments that "In the ancient world, treaty-making often was accompanied by a ceremonial meal, the purpose of which was to create an atmosphere of harmony and fellowship for the pact to go into effect." The Scriptures provide us with a number of examples of high hospitality - for this is not just the sharing of a meal together - being used as a diplomatic tool. "Then Ya'akov offered a sacrifice on the mountain and called his kinsmen to the meal; and they ate the meal and spent the night on the mountain. And early in the morning Laban arose, and kissed his sons and his daughters and blessed them. Then Laban departed and returned to his place" (B'resheet 31:54-55, NASB). Here after Ya'akov, his wives and children have fled from Haran and been chased by the indignant Laban before *HaShem* intervenes to protect Ya'akov by warning Laban in a dream, Ya'akov - on the one side - and Laban - on the other - make a covenant before God not to harm each other in the future. They share a formal meal, prepared by Ya'akov and his household, before each leave in the respective directions.

Another example, somewhat enigmatic in its images that are reminiscent of the visions seen many centuries later by Ezekiel and Daniel, comes at the end of the formal giving of the *Torah* to Israel at Mt. Sinai: "Then Moshe went up with Aharon, Nadab and Abihu, and seventy of the elders ... and they beheld God, and they ate and drank" (Shemot 24:9,11, NASB). God provided the feast, either by a miracle or from the sacrifices that had just been made; and in the context of a ceremonial meal to celebrate the offer and acceptance of covenant, "they saw the God of Israel; and under His feet there appeared to be a pavement of sapphire, as clear as the sky itself" (v. 10, NASB).

Years later, when David was king of Judah, Abner - who was serving Saul's son Ishbosheth - came to David at Hebron to deliver the other eleven tribes into his kingdom, "and David made a feast for Abner and the men who were with him. And Abner said to David, 'Let me arise and go, and gather all Israel to my lord the king that they make a covenant with you, and that you may be king over all that your soul desires.' So David sent Abner away, and he went in peace" (2 Samuel 3:20-21, NASB). Abner was switching sides, from the house of Saul to the house of David, who was effectively at war with Saul's son Ishbosheth, and offered to bring the other tribes to accept David as king over them. David laid on a ceremonial meal for Abner and his men and they departed in peace.

Taking another big step forward in time, we find another meal that was arranged in order to effect covenant. A group of fishermen had been out all night on the Kinneret, but had failed to catch anything. At daybreak, Yeshua met them and after repeating the miracle that He had first used to catch their attention when calling those same fishermen to be His first disciples (see Luke 5:1-11), He invited them to a fish breakfast that He had already prepared for them. But this was no ordinary men's breakfast meeting, this was a meal to confirm and establish covenant. "After breakfast, Yeshua said to Shim'on Kefa, 'Shim'on Bar-Yohanan, do you love Me more than these?'" (John 21:15, CJB). After repeating the question twice more, each time with Peter's reply that he loved Him, "Yeshua said to him" - again echoing His original call in Mark 1:17 - "'Follow Me!'" (v. 19, CJB).

No less certain is that God is still providing meals for people and uses the context of a meal in order to call people to know Him - the Alpha courses, all of which centre around a meal, run by churches all over the UK are testimony to that - to deeper commitment to Him and to send them out or commission them to serve Him in their immediate location or around the world. Mellowed by the hospitality and food, sitting down and talking afterwards over a cup of coffee, people are much more open to hear what God has to say to them and respond to His voice.

Further Study: Matthew 25:35; Hebrews 13:2

Application: When did you last set up a meal for people so that you and they could hear from the Lord? Why not think of who you could invite round to share some food and what God has been speaking to you about. Go on, right now - pick up the 'phone and your address book - and see what God can do!

תּוֹלְדֹת ו׳

Toldot - Histories - 6

B'resheet / Genesis 27:28 - 28:4

B'resheet/Genesis 27:28 And may God give you from the dew of the heavens and from the fatness of the earth ...

וְיִתֶּן־לְךָ הָאֱלֹהִים מִטַּל הַשָּׁמַיִם וּמִשְׁמַנֵּי

oomish'maney hashamayim   mital   ha'Elohiym l'cha v'yiten

הָאָרֶץ

ha'aretz

The word וּמִשְׁמַנֵּי, with a preceding conjunction 'and' and preposition 'from', is the construct form of שְׁמָנִים, which according to Davidson is to be translated "fatness" or "rich production". In turn, it is the plural of שֶׁמֶן, a noun with the meanings "fatness, oil, ointment" and, when used specifically of the land, "fertility"; it is often used for olive oil. All these words are based on the root verb שָׁמַן, which means to be or become fat. Although the phrase "the fatness of the earth" may sound a little strange to a modern ear, it nevertheless conveys a picture of fullness, bounty, plentiful harvest, productive crops, a heavy yield. *Targum Onkelos* paraphrases the word 'fatness' to 'goodness' as another word that would speak more literally to its hearers, and many commentators have picked up on the scale of Yitz'khak's blessing to Ya'akov. The Ba'al HaTurim, for example, notices that there are ten words in this verse (although seven are quoted in our text above) and ten components to the whole blessing:

1. the dew of the heavens
2. the fatness of the earth
3. abundant grain
4. and wine
5. peoples will serve you
6. regimes will bow to you
7. to be a lord to your kinsmen
8. your mother's sons will bow to you

9. those who curse you are
cursed

10. those who bless you are
blessed

Radak points out that Yitz'khak does not include rain in his blessing, for excessive rain can cause damage, while dew is always a blessing. Chizkuni comments that while rain is seasonal in Israel, dew falls all year long; and the Sforno adds that everyone likes dew and it never impedes a person's going and coming. The Sforno goes on to comment that God will give His blessing, as the Creator of the world, when Ya'akov appreciates God's goodness; he seems to be saying that the giving of the blessing is in some way conditional upon the recipient being aware of and relating to the giver; when Ya'akov acknowledges God, then he will be in a position to receive the blessing and to enable God to give it.

Noticing that this blessing follows Yitz'khak's observation that Ya'akov - dressed in Esav's clothes - smells "like a field the Lord has blessed" (v. 27), the Sages commented, "May He give again and again; may He give you blessings and give you the means for holding them; may He give you yours and your father's; may He give you yours and your brother's" (B'resheet Rabbah 66:3). Rashi explains that since God had already given the fragrance of the field, these additional blessings were just that: additional, and were to be repeated again and again.

Rashi and Sforno both make a further point, however, that goes beyond the specific meaning of the words, to ask why the blessing is given. Rashi compares the blessing given to Ya'akov with that later given to Esav and suggests that while Esav's blessing is unconditional: "of the fatness of the earth shall be your dwelling" (v. 39), the blessing for Ya'akov is constrained by whether he deserves it. Rashi derives this from the use of הָאֱלֹהִים rather than יהוה as the name for the Almighty at the start of the blessing. הָאֱלֹהִים, translated "God" rather than "the Lord" is considered to be the name of God's attribute of justice, so that the blessing would only be given to Ya'akov according to his entitlement by law, on the basis of the way he was using it. Sforno provides the purpose for the blessings: "to be able to support others as we find, 'And you will lend to many nations, but you will not borrow' (D'varim 28:12)"; the blessing, the wealth, the provision, was to enable Israel to support its own poor and needy and to be a blessing to the surrounding nations and peoples of the world. To the extent that the descendants of Ya'akov fulfill that purpose, Rashi claims, and prove themselves worthy of the blessing, will it be given to them. This is echoed in the words of Solomon's prayer concerning the people of Israel when the Temple was dedicated: "Render to each according all his ways, whose heart You know ... that they may fear You all the days that they live in the Land which You have given to our fathers" (1 Kings 8:39-40, NASB).

The same principles of purpose apply to us as believers; the purpose of our blessing is to support the family and household of faith and to overflow that blessing to the nations. Yeshua told the *talmidim*, "Give, and it will be given to you; good measure, pressed down, shaken together, running over, they will pour into your lap. For by your standard of measure it will be measured to you in return" (Luke 6:38, NASB). As we share the blessing with others, so it will be returned to us in proportion. Believers are included in this expression of God's economy as Rav Sha'ul explains: "So then, you are no longer foreigners and strangers. On the contrary, you are fellow-citizens with God's people and members of God's family" (Ephesians 2:19, CJB). Jew and Gentile alike share in the blessing and the distribution of the blessing. Sha'ul has the immediate physical family in view when he writes, "Anyone who does not provide for his own people, especially for his family, has disowned the faith and is worse than an unbeliever" (1 Timothy 5:8, CJB), but the focus is more general when he says, "So then, while we have opportunity, let us do good to all men, and especially to those who are of the household of faith" (Galatians 6:10, NASB). While needy believers take precedence, the blessing is also to be made available to those who are not believers. As we have received - one blessing after another - so may we give so that God's heart of compassion should be seen in the world.

Further Study: D'varim 33:13-16; Zechariah 8:12-13; James 2:13

Application: Have you considered the many blessings that you have received from God? How could you respond and pass on that blessing to others this week? Remember that blessings need not always be financial, but ask God how you can play your part in His kingdom economy.

תּוֹלְדֹת 'ז

Toldot - Histories - 7

B'resheet / Genesis 28:5 - 9

B'resheet/Genesis 28:5 And Yitz'khak sent Ya'akov and he went to Padan Aram.

וַיִּשְׁלַח יִצְחָק אֶת־יַעֲקֹב וַיֵּלֶךְ פַּדֶּנָה אֲרָם
Aram Padenah vayeylech Ya'akov et Yitz'khak vayishlakh

Taken in isolation, the first verse of the seventh *aliyah* of this *parasha* does not seem particularly significant. In context, however, it is part of a sequence that points to what should be an important characteristic of our behaviour both as Jews and as believers in Messiah Yeshua.

The backdrop to this event is that following Ya'akov's successful ruse to gain the blessing of the firstborn by impersonating his brother Esav, Rivkah - Ya'akov's mother, who engineered the misappropriation of the inheritance - fears for Ya'akov's safety and has been urging Yitz'khak - the blind father who was duped by the goat-skins - to send Ya'akov "back home" to find himself a wife from among her family in Haran. Yitz'khak may have been reluctant; he was born in Canaan and never left the country. Ya'akov nevertheless saw the wisdom in putting a little space between himself and his brother and probably welcomed the opportunity to travel and see the world. Between his wife and his son, Yitz'khak therefore decided to send Ya'akov to Padan Aram, to the house of his brother-in-law (Ya'akov's uncle) Laban, to cool his heels and see what matrimony and a little responsibility could do to improve his interpersonal skills. Ya'akov's obedience and prompt exit from the bosom of his family is both the key event and the trigger to what follows.

How does Esav take Ya'akov's departure? Only a few verses before, he says to himself, "The days of mourning for my father will soon draw near; then I will kill Ya'akov my brother" (27:41). This, after all, is why Rivkah wants Ya'akov away from there! We also know that just before this story starts, "[Esav] took as a wife Judith the daughter of Beeri the Hittite and Basemath the daughter of Elon the Hittite" (26:34) and that this was an irritation to both his parents (26:35 and 27:46). What does Esav now think -

is he disappointed at Ya'akov's relocation so that he will no longer have the opportunity to carry out his plans? Rashi comments that "Esav saw that Yitz'khak had blessed Ya'akov and that he sent him off to Padan Aram and that Ya'akov obeyed his father and went to Padan Aram." Simply seeing that in spite of the deception over of the firstborn blessing, his father still blessed Ya'akov and sent him off to take a wife from the family back home, and that Ya'akov obediently went, caused Esav to look hard at what he was doing. In spite of Yitz'khak's liking for him, was he honouring his parents and being the son they wanted him to be? He reaches the conclusion that "the daughters of Canaan displeased his father Yitz'khak" (28:8, NASB), so he went and took another wife from the family of Ishmael. Because of Ya'akov's obedience, Esav tried to rectify the relationship with his parents and obey their wish for him to marry "in" rather than "out". Even though Esav hated Ya'akov, he learned from and wanted to emulate his brother's behaviour in order to please his parents.

On one occasion when He was questioned about His authority by the Pharisees, Yeshua told a story. "'But give me your opinion: a man had two sons. He went to the first and said, "Son, go and work today in the vineyard." He answered, "I don't want to"; but later he changed his mind and went. The father went to his other son and said the same thing. This one answered, "I will, sir"; but he didn't go. Which of the two did what his father wanted?' 'The first,' they replied. 'That's right!' Yeshua said to them" (Matthew 21:28-31, CJB). The Pharisees recognised that the eventual obedience of the first son, even though his initial words were contrary, was the right thing to do; they could also see that the words of the second son, although favourable in themselves, were not matched by action and so proved to be worthless. The behaviour of the two sons in the story was a powerful example that Yeshua used to teach the Pharisees about their behaviour: "I tell you that the tax-collectors and prostitutes are going into the Kingdom of God ahead of you! For Yochanan came to you showing the path to righteousness, and you wouldn't trust him. The tax-collectors and prostitutes trusted him; but you, even after you saw this, didn't change your minds later and trust him" (vv. 31-32, CJB).

As might be expected, the letters of the *shluchim* - the Apostles - to the young community of believers also pick up on this theme: behaviour and obedience and its effect upon those who see. It is not certain which of Rav Sha'ul or Peter wrote their letters first, but we do have their words recorded for us. Peter not only encourages good behaviour but gives a key reason or motivation: "Dear friends, I urge you as aliens and temporary residents ... to live such good lives among the pagans that even though they now speak against you as evil-doers, they will, as a result of seeing your good actions, give glory to God on the Day of His coming" (1 Peter 2:11-12, CJB). By their behaviour, the believers will give such a strong witness of good conduct that although their contemporaries may dismiss them and describe them as evil at the time, they will eventually have to agree that the believers were doing the right thing and give God the glory for that. In other words, the witness of the believers was accurate and adequate and even though those who saw them were not prepared to accept it and become obedient themselves to the Gospel, they won't be able to claim that they hadn't seen or heard.

Rav Sha'ul, picking up on an image first used by the prophet Daniel: "those who can discern will shine like the brightness of heaven's dome, and those who turn many to righteousness like the stars forever and ever" (Daniel 12:3, CJB), addresses not just behaviour but attitude. "Do everything without kvetching or arguing, so that you may be blameless and pure children of God, without defect in the midst of a twisted and perverted generation, among whom you shine like stars in the sky, as you hold on to the Word of Life" (Philippians 2:14-16, CJB). It is not enough simply to be obedient and do the right thing; the attitude that accompanies the action must also be wholesome and willing. Good actions accompanied by a bad attitude will be swamped, so that all that will be seen is the negative expression; there will be no good witness - on the contrary, the overall effect will be bad and discourage others from wanting to be involved with the Kingdom of God. In order to shine, to stand out from the actions and attitudes of the world in which we live, we must not only do the right thing but do it willingly and enthusiastically. Then both behaviour and delivery will combine to provide a powerful positive witness for the Kingdom.

In spite of his previous offences, Ya'akov quietly submitted to his father's instructions to head back east and take a wife from his mother's relatives. This had a sufficient effect on even a resentful and aggressive Esav that he recognised that his choice of wives had offended his parents so he took steps to ameliorate the situation. Yeshua's story demonstrates that actions rather than words signify real obedience and convey our true commitment. Sha'ul's and Peter's letters call us both to good actions and good attitudes so that our witness for God may be consistent and an attractive invitation to join the Kingdom of God. How is your witness? Are you careful always to obey God without complaining and protesting about it? Do you proclaim your membership of the Kingdom by your cheerful attitude and graceful compliance to God's instructions and regulations? We all probably need to do some work in this area! We must not let our current situation control our future behaviour or who we are called to be.

Further Study: 1 Corinthians 15:58; Ephesians 4:17-18

Application: Start with something small: keeping the speed limit when driving is an amazing witness in a culture that generally doesn't and is always noticed by passengers in your car, particularly if they are themselves able to drive. A cheerful and willing submission to this simple regulation opens the door to talk about larger issues in the Kingdom. Try it and see!

וַיֵּצֵא

Vayetze - And he went out

B'resheet / Genesis 28:10 - 32:3

רִאשׁוֹן	Aliyah One	B'resheet/Genesis 28:10 - 22
שֵׁנִי	Aliyah Two	B'resheet/Genesis 29:1 - 17
שְׁלִישִׁי	Aliyah Three	B'resheet/Genesis 29:18 - 30:13
רְבִיעִי	Aliyah Four	B'resheet/Genesis 30:14 - 27
חֲמִשִׁי	Aliyah Five	B'resheet/Genesis 30:28 - 31:16
שִׁשִׁי	Aliyah Six	B'resheet /Genesis 31:17 - 42
שְׁבִיעִי	Aliyah Seven	B'resheet/Genesis 31:43 - 32:3

וַיֵּצֵא א׳

Vayetze - And he went out - 1

B'resheet / Genesis 28:10 - 22

B'resheet/Genesis 28:10 Ya'akov went out from Be'er-Sheva and travelled toward Haran

וַיֵּצֵא יַעֲקֹב מִבְּאֵר שָׁבַע וַיֵּלֶךְ חָרָנָה׃

kharanah vayeylech shava   mib'eyr   Ya'akov vayeytzey

Why does the *Torah* tell us both that Ya'akov left Be'er Sheva and that he went to Haran? Rashi suggests that the first clause is to reconnect the narrative with 28:5, because it was interrupted by the story of Esav taking a wife from the house of Ishmael. The Dubna Maggid, on the other hand, points out that a person makes a journey for one of two reasons: either he is obliged to leave one place, or he wishes to go to another. In Ya'akov's case, his mother Rivkah told him that Esav was looking to kill him (27:42), while his father Yitz'khak told him to go and take a wife from the family at Padan Aram (28:2). So Ya'akov both 'went out' and 'went to'.

When Peter wrote to our people in the *Diaspora* he said that God has "called you out of darkness into His wonderful light" (1 Peter 2:9, CJB). See the two directions at work again: out of darkness, into the light. Remember also the words of the man blind from birth whose sight had been restored by Yeshua when he was being questioned by the *P'rushim*; he said, "One thing I do know: I was blind, now I see" (John 9:25, CJB). Again, we can clearly see the two states of before and after, with the blind man having been taken from one world (that of blindness) to another (the world of sight).

Rav Sha'ul also speaks to this in his first letter to the believers in Corinth. After listing some of the lifestyles that mark those who will not share in the Kingdom of God he writes, "Some of you used to do these things. But you have cleansed yourselves, you have been set apart for God, you have come to be counted righteous through the power of the Lord Yeshua the Messiah and the Spirit of our God" (1 Corinthians 6:11, CJB). Here, Sha'ul is extending the principle to the spiritual realm: believers have been called out of lives of sin - which we were all in, to greater or lesser extent (Romans 3:23) - into a life of "righteousness, shalom and joy in the Ruach

HaKodesh" (Romans 14:17, CJB).

Yeshua said that, "whoever hears what I am saying and trusts the One who sent Me has eternal life ... he has already crossed over from death to life" (John 5:24, CJB). The only question to ask is - have we done this, and do we live in the good of it, or have we failed to leave our old lives behind?

Further Study: Isaiah 42:14-17; Acts 26:16-18

Application: Are you living the new life, the true life, the real life of freedom and righteousness in Messiah Yeshua, or are you still half-living in the old life of the past? Ask God to show you where you stand today.

וַיֵּצֵא ב׳

Vayetze - And he went out - 2

B'resheet / Genesis 29:1 - 17

B'resheet/Genesis 29:1 And Ya'akov lifted his feet and went to the land of the sons of the East

וַיִּשָּׂא יַעֲקֹב רַגְלָיו וַיֵּלֶךְ אַרְצָה בְנֵי־קֶדֶם:

kedem v'ney   ar'tzah vayeylech rag'layv Ya'akov   vayisa

So Ya'akov, our intrepid hero, actually goes down from the Land to visit his family in Haran. He has had his dream, struck his bargain and anointed a stone with oil; there is nothing left to do but walk: hundreds of miles! Our text tells us two interesting things about the way that Ya'akov looked at this next stage of his journey. There are many places in the Tanakh where the Scriptures tell us that somebody went somewhere, or walked in a particular direction, and they nearly all use the verb הָלַךְ, to walk or go, and this is no exception. It is the preceding clause that is different: Ya'akov lifted his feet.

The first thing we learn is that Ya'akov realised that he had to do the walking. He wasn't able to hitch a lift in a passing lorry, he couldn't catch a train; neither could he fly - there were no scheduled flights between Bethel and Haran in those days. If he was going to get there, then he had no option but to get on with it and walk. He had to put one foot in front of the other and keep on doing that for days until he got there - it was the only way to do it. Secondly, the verse shows something of his attitude: Ya'akov didn't trudge along or drag his feet, he lifted his feet and walked. The verb נָשָׂא means to lift, raise or support; in its *Pi'el* voice it is often translated 'strengthen' or 'establish'. Ya'akov had a journey to make and he set off with enthusiasm and determination.

In that well-known passage from the book of Isaiah: "And your ears will hear a word behind you, 'This is the way, walk in it,' whenever you turn to the right or the left" (Isaiah 30:21, NASB), the same dynamic is at work. One cannot be turning to the right or the left unless engaged in motion, and the voice of the *Ruach HaKodesh* will encourage us to walk in the footsteps of our Teacher. Rav Sha'ul uses the image of the games: "Don't you know that in a race all the runners compete, but only one wins the prize? So, then, run to win!" (1 Corinthians 9:24, CJB). Just as Ya'akov lifted his feet, so we are to exert ourselves as we journey through life.

Yeshua spoke to His disciples in the same way: "Therefore, go and make people from all nations into talmidim" (Matthew 28:19, CJB). Many commentators have written about whether this passage is calling everyone to go to a mission field overseas, or simply to be aware of the call to share the gospel with those around us. In Hebrew, Yeshua would have used the same verb הָלַךְ, to walk or go, showing that this is a matter of lifestyle rather than location. What matters is to be on the journey and lifting our feet as we go.

Further Study: Isaiah 40:28-31; 1 Corinthians 9:25-27

Application: Has your walk slowed down and your feet started to drag recently? Do you feel discouraged or forsaken? Why not ask God for a fresh renewing of vision and try lifting your feet as you go.

וַיֵּצֵא ג׳

Vayetze - And he went out - 3

B'resheet / Genesis 29:18 - 30:13

B'resheet/Genesis 29:18 I will serve you seven years for Rachel, your younger daughter.

אֶעֱבָדְךָ שֶׁבַע שָׁנִים בְּרָחֵל בִּתְּךָ הַקְּטַנָּה:

hak'tanah bit'cha b'Rakheyl shaniym sheva e'evad'cha

"Love will find a way," the saying, several books, many songs and CDs, say. Here is Ya'akov making a way to marry Rachel, the girls he loves despite the odds against him. Rashi points out how specific Ya'akov is being here: not just 'Rachel', for Lavan might buy another girl called Rachel from the marketplace; not just 'your daughter' for Lavan might (and, as it happened, did) marry Ya'akov to another daughter; but also 'your younger' so that there should be no doubt about the contract they were agreeing. All this, of course, was to no avail since Lavan does marry Leah to Ya'akov first and then extracts another seven years' work from his nephew for Rachel. And because of his love for Rachel, Ya'akov submits.

Sforno, on the other hand, suggests that the seven years of labour that Ya'akov did before marrying was both a means of demonstrating his ability to properly provide for a wife and family, as well as a dowry for Lavan. When Ya'akov arrived in Haran, he later confessed, he had only the clothes he stood up in: "For with my staff I crossed the Yarden" (B'resheet 32:11), and the Sages said, "A man may marry many wives provided he possesses the means to support them" (*b*. Yevamot 68*a*).

That aside, the text goes on to tell us that "Ya'akov worked seven years for Rachel and they seemed to him a few days because of his love for her" (29:20). Was this just infatuation or did Ya'akov see some essential quality in Rachel that he knew marked her out as a woman of worth? Seven years is a long time by anyone's counting, yet Ya'akov not only ended up working seven but fourteen years for Rachel. He knew that he had to marry her, so he gritted his teeth and worked in spite of his uncle's duplicity.

The writer to the Hebrews tells us that Yeshua "for the joy set before Him endured the cross, despising the shame and has sat down at the right hand of the throne of God" (Hebrews 12:2, NASB). Yeshua went ahead and pushed on through the physical and spiritual agony of the cross, His humiliation at the hands of both the Romans and the Jewish leaders of His day and the separation from His Father, in order to reach the prize set before Him: the victory over sin and death, the resurrection, the outpouring of the Spirit and the bringing of many sons to glory. This is why the gospel writer tells us that, "As the time approached for Him to be taken into heaven, He made His decision to set out for Jerusalem" (Luke 9:51, CJB); He knew what had to be done; He knew that only He could do it; He knew that the time had come and "He humbled Himself becoming obedient to the point of death, even death on a cross" (Philippians 2:8, NASB). In the older and more literal translations of the Bible, Luke's words present an even more graphic picture of Yeshua's determination: "When the time was come ... He steadfastly set His face to go to Jerusalem" (KJV).

Further Study: Isaiah 50:4-7; Ezekiel 3:4-9

Application: What is our level of commitment to obedience to God's word, particularly when it becomes inconvenient or unpleasant? Should we not, as Rav Sha'ul says, "have the same mind in you as was in Messiah Yeshua" (Philippians 2:5) and serve God both obediently and willingly?

וַיֵּצֵא ד׳

Vayetze - And he went out - 4

B'resheet / Genesis 30:14 - 27

B'resheet/Genesis 30:25 And Ya'akov said to Lavan, "Send me out and I will go to my place, my land."

וַיֹּאמֶר יַעֲקֹב אֶל־לָבָן שַׁלְּחֵנִי וְאֵלְכָה

v'eylchah shal'kheyniy Lavan el Ya'akov vayomer

אֶל־מְקוֹמִי וּלְאַרְצִי׃

ool'artziy m'komiy el

There are two issues in this text: one of substance and one of interest. The interest is the Hebrew grammar at the end of Ya'akov's sentence. He uses the preposition אֶל, "to, towards, into", with "my place" but the shorter ל, "to, for" with "my land", where it might have been more natural to finish וְאֶל־אַרְצִי, repeating the same preposition. Hirsch comments on this to point out that while Ya'akov had a place, a home, perhaps where his father was still living, "to or towards" which he can go, the land - to be the property of his descendants - is not yet his, so that "to, for" is a better usage. Indeed, it almost conveys the idea that although he will be in his place, he will be no nearer his land than in Haran, except that he will be living more for the land of his future and bringing up his family in the land that is one day to be theirs.

The substance, on the other hand, concerns the verb שַׁלְּחֵנִי and Ya'akov's attitude in making his request. The verb is a *Pi'el* imperative from the root שָׁלַח, which in its *Qal* form is most often translated as 'send'. In the *Pi'el* stem, it carries a permissive quality: send away, let go, dismiss; let loose, set free, set at liberty. So even though in imperative (or command) form, Ya'akov is essentially asking for permission to leave Lavan's household and employ in order to return to the land of Canaan. Here is a grown man, with two wives and a dozen children plus, no doubt, his own - still small at this stage - household of maids and other servants. Moreover, he had the call of God on him; he has a future, a land, a place and a life to live that doesn't consist of making his devious uncle any richer than he already is. Why is he asking permission and not just telling Lavan that they are going? The answer to that question is an excellent example of how things are supposed to work in the Kingdom of God.

Firstly, as we will find out in a later *parasha*, God has not yet told Ya'akov to leave. He may have been speaking to him about making changes in their life and reminding him of His promises and some of the things that are to come, but He hasn't taken the starting pistol out of its holster, let alone pulled the trigger. Oftentimes, God speaks to us about something that He is going to do, at some point in the future; He prepares us for what is yet to come: "'For I know the plans I have for you', declares the Lord, 'plans for welfare and not calamity to give you a future and a hope'" (Jeremiah 29:11, NASB). But it is not yet and we have to wait for God's specific timing and instructions before actually moving out and walking into that vision.

Secondly, there is the question of oversight. Ya'akov may only have been Lavan's son-in-law and Lavan may have been taking shocking advantage of him, but he was nevertheless living in Haran as a part of Lavan's household and enjoying his protection, patronage and position. Lavan is providing the roof over his head, the food on his table and even - in a sense, as the next verse goes on to say - his family. Ya'akov had come with nothing but his wits and to some extent, even though he had earned them, all that he had belonged to Lavan. He was under Lavan's authority, so it was only right and proper that Ya'akov should ask for Lavan's permission before just walking out, breaking all the family relationships and leaving hurt feelings and loose ends.

The writer to the Hebrews says: "Obey your leaders and submit to them, for they keep watch over your lives, as people who will have to render an account" (Hebrews 13:17, CJB). Obviously there are situations, such as leadership abuse or sin, when God calls people to move on a more unilateral basis, although even then there is an expectation that we should attempt to communicate and be orderly, but the normal assumption is that when it is time for people to move on, not only will the people concerned know, but their current leaders also will be aware that it is right; God will have spoken to both leaders and people. Then there can be a blessing and a sending out, proper maintenance of relationships and a smooth transition.

Further Study: Proverbs 12:14-15; 1 Corinthians 14:33

Application: Do you feel that God has been telling you to do something, that it is time to be moving on into new areas of work, ministry or life? If so, make sure that you have talked with your leaders, pastors or the people to whom you are accountable - you might be surprised how receptive they are to the idea and can confirm your calling.

וַיֵּצֵא 'ה

Vayetze - And he went out - 5

B'resheet / Genesis 30:28 - 31:16

B'resheet/Genesis 30:28 And he said, "Specify your wage to me and I will pay it."

וַיֹּאמַר נָקְבָה שְׂכָרְךָ עָלַי וְאֶתֵּנָה:
v'eteynah alay   s'char'cha nak'vah vayomar

After Ya'akov's beloved wife Rachel has finally given birth to a son, Ya'akov's thoughts turn to home and he asks Laban, his uncle and father-in-law, to release him "so that I can return to my own place, to my own country" (B'resheet 30:25, CJB). Laban, reluctant to let a good thing go, pretends to think that this is the opening shot in a salary negotiation and responds first with a little flattery and then this invitation for Ya'akov to put his initial bid on the table. The word נָקְבָה only occurs once in the Hebrew Scriptures and at first glance looks like a *Qal* affix 3fs form of the verb נָקַב, which includes the meanings "to bore or pierce; to mark out, determine, specify or name", but since שָׂכָר is a masculine noun, that cannot be the subject and translation becomes difficult. Rashi, pointing to *Targum Onkelos* - פָּרֵשׁ אַגְרָךְ, spell out your wage - explains instead that נָקְבָה is a *Qal* imperative ms form with a paragogic *hay*: a command or instruction - let's have it then, what are you after!

The *Torah* is insistent that wages should be paid promptly: "The wages of a hired man are not to remain with you all night until morning" (Vayikra 19:13, NASB), and "You shall give [a hired servant] his wages on his day before the sun sets, for he is poor and sets his heart on it; so that he not cry out against you to the Lord and it become sin in you" (D'varim 24:15, NASB). James picks up the theme in his letter: "Behold, the pay of the labourers who mowed your fields, and which has been withheld by you, cries out against you; and the outcry of those who did the harvesting has reached the ears of the Lord of Hosts" (James 5:4, NASB). Rich farmers and landowners would hire workers for their fields and then not pay them until it was convenient for themselves, putting the workers in dire financial

133

circumstances and starving their families.

The negotiation between Ya'akov and Laban shows that it is important to set and pay appropriate wages. God rebuked the rich people who returned from the exile in Babylon because they "oppress the wage earner in his wages" (Malachi 3:5, NASB), while Yeshua told the disciples on a mission trip to "stay in the house, eating and drinking what they give you; for the worker is worthy of his wages" (Luke 10:7, NASB). Rav Sha'ul quotes these words in his first letter to Timothy, applying the same principle to elders and "those who work hard at preaching and teaching" (1 Timothy 5:17, NASB). Even Judas Iscariot received the preset wages for betraying Yeshua into the hands of the Chief Priests (Matthew 26:14-15, Zechariah 11:12).

From all this we can see that God attaches great importance to people receiving the appropriate wages, and receiving them on time. How blessed is mankind that God does not operate the same timeliness with us in regard to our dealings with Him. Rav Sha'ul tells us clearly that "the wages of sin is death" (Romans 6:23); perhaps one of the most well-known and frequently quoted verses from the Bible, although the verse which gives the other side of the coin - "The wages of the righteous is life" (Proverbs 10:16, NASB) - is rather less well-known. We have all sinned in our lives, a fact that becomes painfully aware to many people just before they pass out of this life, and there are consequences which will be faced, no matter who we are. Are we not blessed that God doesn't immediately bring the just and appropriate wages for our sin down on our heads the minute we commit it, but instead gives us an opportunity to repent and set things right with Him? "The Lord is not slow in keeping His promises, as some people think of slowness; on the contrary, He is patient with you; for it is not His purpose that anyone should be destroyed, but that everyone should turn from his sins" (2 Peter 3:9, CJB).

God's judgement is certain and we must not take Him for granted as Peter's letter continues, "However, the day of the Lord will come 'like a thief'" (v. 10, CJB). Our lives will catch up with us on that day when we stand before Him. Peter urges his readers, "You should lead holy and godly lives, as you wait for the Day of God and work to hasten its coming ... do everything you can to be found by Him without spot or defect and at peace - think of our Lord's patience as deliverance" (vv. 11 - 15, CJB). It is as if we are Ya'akov, hearing God say through Laban, "Specify your wage and I will pay it."

Further Study: Malachi 3:5; Matthew 20:1-16

Application: Where do you stand before God today? Are your accounts with Him all resolved, or are you delaying coming to terms with Him, hoping either that you won't have to do this or that a miracle will happen to make everything come right? Don't delude yourself either way: you will and it has - Yeshua the Messiah has come!

וַיֵּצֵא י׳

Vayetze - And he went out - 6

B'resheet / Genesis 31:17 - 42

B'resheet/Genesis 31:18 And he led away all his livestock and all his possessions that he had acquired; the purchase of his livestock that he had acquired

וַיִּנְהַג אֶת־כָּל־מִקְנֵהוּ וְאֶת־כָּל־רְכֻשׁוֹ אֲשֶׁר

asher   r'chusho kol   v'et   mikneyhu kol   et vayinhag

רָכָשׁ מִקְנֵה קִנְיָנוֹ אֲשֶׁר רָכַשׁ

rachash asher kinyano   mikney rachash

The Hebrew text here is full of repeated words, so bears some analysis to find out what is being said. The verse starts with the verb וַיִּנְהַג, an ordinary enough *Qal* prefix 3ms form in the *vav*-conversive structure; this is normally translated in the past tense. The root נָהַג is used for driving cattle, to lead or conduct or, most interestingly here, to lead or carry away as spoil. Given that 'he' is Ya'akov, that this text comes in the narrative of Ya'akov leaving his uncle Laban after twenty years of what was at best frustrating and at worst acrimonious service to return to his father Yitz'khak in Canaan, and in Laban's later somewhat bitter comment that, "The daughters are mine, the children are mine, the flocks are mine, and everything you see is mine!" (31:43, CJB), it is significant that the verb has at least one meaning that is suggestive of taking spoil or plunder. Might the text be hinting that Ya'akov - helped, of course, by *HaShem* - has triumphed over Laban's dishonesty and double-dealing, that Ya'akov's work-ethic and integrity during those years have, metaphorically, tied up the strong man so that the house may be plundered (Matthew 12:29)?

The root קָנָה generates the noun מִקְנֶה, present here in two forms, and the verb קִנְיָנוֹ - from the basic meaning of "to get, acquire; to buy, purchase". So מִקְנֶה means a possession, riches or wealth, but chiefly consisting of cattle or flocks. רָכָשׁ, here as two verbs and a noun, has a similar meaning: "to get, gain, acquire", but with more of an emphasis on

135

non-livestock possessions. Together the words suggest a wealth that is substantially in livestock, but that also includes other material possessions that had been purchased by the sale of livestock. Hirsch suggests that both words are present to emphasise that all Ya'akov's possessions did belong to him, because even though the previous narrative only records Ya'akov being paid in livestock, he had traded some of his animals in order to purchase other non-stock possessions. Indeed, Rashi, quoting the Sages, "that which he acquired with his possessions" (B'resheet Rabbah 74:5), goes as far as to specify "slaves, slave-women, camels and donkeys". The whole cluster of words leads Nahum Sarna to comment that this "underscores Ya'akov's claim to absolute and rightful ownership of all his possessions, thus refuting in advance Laban's assertion in verse 43."

Comparing Ya'akov's departure from Padan Aram with his grandfather Avraham's departure, we see a similar pattern. Avraham had been told to leave his country, his family and his father's house, yet the text records that "Abram took Sarai his wife and Lot his nephew, and all their possessions which they had accumulated, and the persons which they had acquired in Haran" (B'rehseet 12:5, NASB); that sounds like a fairly comprehensive description of "everything". So too, Ya'akov, sensing that the Lord was now calling him back to the Land of Canaan after twenty years building a family and a financial base, after consulting with both Leah and Rachel, took absolutely everything that was indisputably his and set off for home. In a nomadic society, you own everything that you have and can drive or carry; you don't own the land or facilities on the land - such as wells - even if you dug or built them yourself. Wherever a nomadic people travel, therefore, they take everything with them as a matter of course; they leave nothing behind. Ya'akov and his family were going home, that was where their hearts were calling; they felt that they had no ties to where they were currently living, so everything that could be moved was! Even the kitchen sink!

During the Sermon on the Mount, Yeshua taught his disciples and the crowd who had flocked from all over the Galil to hear him, a different view of material possessions. In the centuries since Ya'akov's time, although nomads were still a part of the Israelite society - as indeed the Bedouin still are today - many people had settled down and lived in houses or permanent structures, the houses were clustered in villages and towns and the majority of the population was much less mobile than before. Matthew records: "Do not store up for yourselves wealth here on earth, where moths and rust destroy, and burglars break in and steal. Instead, store up for yourselves wealth in heaven, where neither moth nor rust destroys, and burglars do not break in or steal. For where your wealth is, there your heart will be also" (Matthew 6:19-21, CJB). Yeshua is saying that wealth that is secure against the routine depredations of this life is not physical possessions accumulated here in our houses or barns, but investments of time, money and possessions that are made in the . He is not saying that we shouldn't have material wealth or possessions that we need and use in our daily lives, but that they should not be regarded as real wealth. Just as Ya'akov traded some of his livestock, which would inevitably grow old or get diseases and die, for other possessions that might last longer or perform a different task, so we are to trade our money and possessions as investments in people, ministries and Kingdom opportunities in order to gain eternal holdings that will never perish or be destroyed. Our riches in heaven, held by Messiah Himself, are proof against the worst stock-market crashes or downturns.

In a story that Yeshua told, according to Luke's account also during the Sermon on the Mount, He said, "There was a man whose land was very productive. He debated with himself, 'What should I do? I haven't enough room for all my crops.' Then he said, 'This is what I will do: I'll tear down my barns and build bigger ones, and I'll store all my wheat and other goods there. Then I'll say to myself, "You're a lucky man! You have a big supply of goods laid up that will last many years. Start taking it easy! Eat! Drink! Enjoy yourself!"' But God said to him, 'You fool! This very night you will die! And the things you prepared - whose will they be?' That's how it is with anyone who stores up wealth for himself without being rich toward God" (Luke 12:16-21, CJB). Once again, see what Yeshua is saying - it isn't the possessions themselves that are the problem, it is the attitude towards them and the fastness with which we hold them. Ya'akov had to take all his stuff with him because there was nowhere else to put it. Middle Eastern culture in those days held possessions lightly; hospitality and provision for family, strangers and the poor were acts of charity or righteousness that were a part of the fundamental fabric of society. The West is now an almost exclusively resident society; although we may move for a job or family reasons, and travel on a daily basis to work, many people own houses and have lived in them for many years - in some cases, generations. Our basic society now owns land, even if in tiny parcels, or rents ownership rights; unless invited in, even government officials require a court warrant to enter private property or seize material goods. This has created walls and barriers between people and broken down the patterns of sharing and hospitality; instead of taking all our stuff with us and being an open people, we have become a closed people, locking our stuff up in our individual fortresses.

Today God is challenging people to come back to a more open and flexible attitude. Yeshua promised, "Truly I say to you, there is no one who has left house or wife or brothers or parents or children, for the sake of the Kingdom of God, who shall not receive many times as much at this time and in the age to come, eternal life" (Luke 18:29-30, NASB). God does not steal from us; He wants to give us much more than we could ever gain for ourselves; He even provides the security guard and a receipt for the deposit as we cash in our valueless (from the point of view of eternity) earthly possessions to buy "gold refined by fire, that you may become rich, and white garments, that you may clothe yourself" (Revelation 3:18, NASB). Open homes, hands and hearts are the way of the !

Further Study: Ezekiel 18:4-9; 1 Timothy 6:17-19

Application: Are you going through stress to maintain or keep your finances or material possessions at the moment? Are you uncertain of their real value and unclear how to handle their investment? Why not ask the only truly independent financial adviser what He would recommend?

וַיֵּצֵא ז׳

Vayetze - And he went out - 7

B'resheet / Genesis 31:43 - 32:3

B'resheet/Genesis 31:43 the daughters are my daughters and the children and my children and the flock is my flock ...

הַבָּנוֹת בְּנֹתַי וְהַבָּנִים בָּנַי וְהַצֹּאן צֹאנִי

tzo'niy v'hatzo'n banay v'habaniym b'notay habanot

Following Ya'akov's outburst against Laban, his somewhat unscrupulous and devious uncle, these words are Laban's response to the charges of dishonesty and deception that flowed from Ya'akov's mouth as he unburdens himself from twenty years hard work and constant struggle to build a life for his wives and children. Accused rightly of consistently attempting to defraud his nephew of a just wage for his work, Laban tartly responds that everything Ya'akov claims to own actually belongs to him. The Sforno helps Laban express his feelings: "Even if I changed your wage, or sent you away empty handed, I would not have been taking away anything from you since everything belongs to me; and whatever you possess is through fraud, not by right." But is this correct? Do Ya'akov's wives and children, his flocks and herds, tents and household belong to Laban after all? We know from contemporary history that it was unusual for the son-in-law to join his father-in-law's household; normally the new bride and groom would join the groom's family since that was the place of their inheritance. Although the bride would have a dowry provided by her father, that was a gift over which he would not be expected to retain control or ownership. So much so that Nahum Sarna dryly observes that "Now publicly exposed as a scoundrel, Laban lamely tries to cover his loss of face with empty rhetoric, that has no legal force behind it, only emotion."

In our times, wages once earned are very clearly the property of the employee and strict legislation governs the way in which it must be paid (and taxed, of course). Not paying wages on time is a criminal offence. The suggestion that the employee's house, family and savings were still in some way the property of the employer would be considered ridiculous. There are certain exceptions - such as tied houses, where accommodation belonging to the employer is provided either free of charge or at a subsidised rent, or share/stock purchase schemes - but these are clearly demarcated in the contract of employment, protected by law and often administered by independent trustees. Whatever has been paid to the employee belongs to him and that is that!

Doing an Internet search on Google for the words "It's mine! It's all mine" - what Laban meant and the words put into the mouth of the wimpish Prince John as he cuddles the bags of gold tax money in the cartoon version of "Robin Hood" - produces a staggering count of more than 52 million references. These range from song lyrics, to advice on divorce settlements, scientific reports on the behaviour of cats marking their territory and a few word-plays from the mining industry. Even a few seem to be from disgruntled employees, complaining about or trying to expose their former employers' activities! To one extent or another, however, they are all about claiming disputed ownership and usually in a fairly strident and forthright way. Human beings seem to have little difficulty staking their claims, with or without the help of the Internet.

Yeshua paints a very different picture of the way that life is meant to be lived in the Kingdom. In the Sermon on the Mount, He says, "If someone wants to sue you for your shirt, let him have your coat as well! ... When someone asks you for something, give it to him; when someone wants to borrow something from you, lend it to him" (Matthew 5:40,42, CJB). This sounds like a very loose way to hold your possessions. In fact, Yeshua goes on to explain just how "expensive" discipleship is: "If anyone wants to come after Me, let him say 'No' to himself, take up his execution-stake, and keep following Me. For whoever wants to save his own life will destroy it, but whoever destroys his life for My sake will find it. What good will it do someone if he gains the whole world but forfeits his life? Or, what can a person give in exchange for his life?" (Matthew 16:24-26, CJB); challenging words indeed. Certainly avaricious wealth-gathering for its own sake is not acceptable Kingdom behaviour, but what about normal people? After all, we are not all Russian oil magnates, buying up football clubs and businesses with the small change from our back pockets - how should we apply Yeshua's words in our lives?

Perhaps the key is in understanding that true ownership is not and never has been ours. The cry "It's all mine" is exactly the opposite of the truth: none of it is ours. We are stewards of all that God has made in this world; mightily blessed stewards, that is true, but stewards none the less. When our people were nomads without a home-land of their own in the desert on the way to Israel, while describing the sabbatical year and redemption of property, *HaShem* makes this clear: "The land, moreover, shall not be sold permanently, for the land is Mine; for you are but aliens and sojourners with Me" (Vayikra 25:23, NASB). Israel may hold the head lease on the Land, but they are still only lease-holders; *HaShem* retains the freehold. The Preacher in Jerusalem somewhat bitterly observed that we start this life with nothing and we leave it in the same way: "As he had come naked from his mother's womb, so will he return as he came. He will take nothing from the fruit of his labor that he can carry in his hand" (Ecclesiastes 5:15, NASB). Job expressed the same thought but was able to makes sense of it because he correctly recognised the hand of God: "Naked I came from my mother's womb, and naked I shall return there. The Lord gave and the Lord has taken away. Blessed be the name of the Lord" (Job 1:21, NASB).

The early church was apparently not immune to those who accumulated wealth at the expense of others. James writes them a stinging rebuke: "Next, a word for the rich: weep and wail over the hardships coming upon you! Your riches have rotted, and your clothes have become moth-eaten; your gold and silver have corroded, and their corrosion will be evidence against you and will eat up your flesh like fire! This is the acharit hayamim, and you have been storing up wealth!" (James 5:1-3, CJB). These are the last days, he tells them: they are abusing their power to collect wealth for themselves that is not only of no real eternal value but is already destroying both itself and them. He goes on: "Listen! The wages you have fraudulently withheld from the workers who mowed your fields are calling out against you, and the outcries of those who harvested have reached the ears of Adonai-Tzva'ot. You have led a life of luxury and self-indulgence here on earth - in a time of slaughter, you have gone on eating to your heart's content. You have condemned, you have murdered the innocent; they have not withstood you" (vv. 4-6, CJB). It is not the possessions themselves, nor the possession of them that is the problem, but the attitude towards them and the way in which they are amassed and used.

The Kingdom of God has within it great financiers and philanthropists who generate large amounts of wealth from ethical but efficient businesses and channel much of these monies into supporting the works of the churches, big and small. Many individuals who simply have normal jobs and incomes set aside a proportion of their income to give to the work of the Kingdom, be that in organised forms or often in spontaneous charity to other individuals and groups. The essence is that all these people see themselves as part of the Kingdom, as stewards or channels through which the Lord is moving His finances to bless others. Finance, of itself, is a necessary medium for making things happen; you cannot run even a simple soup kitchen without money - someone has to buy the raw materials to make the soup and the mugs or flasks in which to give it away. We must all learn to hold the Kingdom resources that have been entrusted to our care less tightly, not to wrap our arms around them amidst cries of "It's all mine!" but to recognise that it is the Lord who owns "the cattle on a thousand hills" (Psalm 50:10) who provides and wants to direct all things that pass through our hands.

Further Study: 1 Chronicles 29:14-15; Hebrew 11:8-10

Application: Are you holding something too tightly, so that God is not able to use it? If He can't use it, you'll find that you can't use it either - you need to let go in order to release its use. Why not ask God today what you need to release to Him and then let Him show you how to use it.

וַיִּשְׁלַח

Vayishlakh - And he sent

B'resheet / Genesis 32:4 - 36:43

רִאשׁוֹן	Aliyah One	B'resheet/Genesis 32:4 - 13
שֵׁנִי	Aliyah Two	B'resheet/Genesis 32:14 - 30
שְׁלִישִׁי	Aliyah Three	B'resheet/Genesis 32:31 - 33:5
רְבִיעִי	Aliyah Four	B'resheet/Genesis 33:6 - 20
חֲמִשִׁי	Aliyah Five	B'resheet/Genesis 34:1 - 35:11
שִׁשִׁי	Aliyah Six	B'resheet /Genesis 35:12 - 36:19
שְׁבִיעִי	Aliyah Seven	B'resheet/Genesis 36:20 - 42

וַיִּשְׁלַח א'

Vayishlakh - And he sent - 1

B'resheet / Genesis 32:4 - 13

B'resheet/Genesis 32:4 And Ya'akov sent messengers ahead of him to Esav his brother

וַיִּשְׁלַח יַעֲקֹב מַלְאָכִים לְפָנָיו אֶל-עֵשָׂו אָחִיו
akhiyv   Esav   el   l'fanayv   malachiym   Ya'akov vayishlakh

There are some things that can only be done face-to-face. Not by email, nor by telephone or letter; simply face-to-face, in person. One such was the resolution of the conflict between Ya'akov and his brother Esav. Reading both last and this week's *parashiyot*, we find Ya'akov seeing the face of God as he struggles with the Messenger of the Lord, and seeing the face of God in Esav's face. It is mentioned here in this first phrase from the reading, "ahead of him". The Hebrew word לְפָנָיו literally means 'to his faces' and is used in many places in the Hebrew Scriptures to mean 'before' or 'in the presence of' as well as the meaning here.

Sometimes, you have to look someone square in the face before you know exactly who they are or whether they mean what they say. Only when you look them straight in the eye do you feel a level of confidence. Perhaps this was one of the purposes for the event known as the Transfiguration related in the first few verses of Matthew 17. Yeshua took just three *talmidim* up into a high mountain and there His glory was revealed as He spoke with Moshe and Elijah. Matthew tells us, "He began to change form - His face shone like the sun, and His clothing became as white as light" (Matthew 17:2, CJB). The *talmidim* saw Yeshua revealed as they saw His face.

Rav Sha'ul points out that this same glory has been placed in each of us, "for God, who said, 'Light shall shine out of darkness,' is the One who has shone in our hearts to give the light of the knowledge of the glory of God in the face of Messiah" (2 Corinthians 4:6, NASB), and he goes on in the next verse to talk of us as "jars of clay"(v7, ESV) so that God's glory may be seen and recognised for what it is. Not only do we have the light and knowledge in our hearts, but others are to see the face of Messiah in us; when they search our eyes, they are to find Yeshua looking out at them. Yeshua Himself said,

"You are the light of the world" (Matthew 5:14, CJB) - how is this to be? When other people look intently at us, when they want to know who we really are, whether they can trust what we say, they want to catch our eye, to look us square in the face, to see whether we will engage them without flinching or turning away.

Just as Ya'akov sent messengers ahead of him to Esav, we are the messengers sent ahead by Yeshua to prepare for His coming. What do people see when they look into our eyes?

Further Study: 1 Corinthians 13:12; Matthew 5:14-16

Application: Before we can share the face of God with others, we need to know His face for ourselves. Ask God today for a fresh revelation of the face of Yeshua in your life and spend those extra few minutes relaxing in His presence and soaking Him into your heart.

וַיִּשְׁלַח 'ב

Vayishlakh - And he sent - 2

B'resheet / Genesis 32:14 - 30

B'resheet/Genesis 32:14 And he took from what came into his hand, a present for his brother Esav

וַיִּקַּח מִן־הַבָּא בְיָדוֹ מִנְחָה לְעֵשָׂו אָחִיו:

akhiyv   l'Esav   min'kha   v'yado   ha'ba   min   vayikakh

The Ramban points out that Scripture is here saying that Ya'akov prepared a gift for Esav from what he had around him. The following verses describe this in detail: sheep, goats, camels, cows and donkeys; all of definite and significant worth, but not items such as silver and gold. Where, Ramban asks, in the desert, was Ya'akov to get such material from? All his wealth, considerable though it was, was represented by his livestock, his household, his herdsmen and his drovers. Moreover, Ya'akov presented his gift to his brother in terms that his brother would relate to and understand easily. Esav too had flocks and herds and he understood the value of milking ewes and their young, of correctly matched cows and bulls; this was a carefully thought-out strategy to play to Esav's character. Esav was a man of the fields, a hunter and herdsman by nature, rather than Ya'akov who had had to learn the skills as a matter of survival while working for his uncle, Lavan.

What do we bring as gifts to God? Everything that we have is already His and comes from Him. Micah the prophet struggled with the same question: "With what shall I come to the Lord and bow myself before the God on high? Shall I come to Him with burnt offerings, with yearling calves? Does the Lord take delight in thousands of rams, in ten thousand rivers of oil?" (Micah 6:6-7, NASB) Is great expense and arrangement of huge, costly offerings what God desires of us? No, essentially like Ya'akov, we are to offer what we already have, what is immediately to hand; the word of prophecy continues: "Human being, you have already been told what is good, what Adonai demands of you - no more than to act justly, love grace and walk in purity with your God" (v8, CJB). Our lives and conduct are to be our offering to God, that which pleases Him.

The synoptic gospels bring us a picture of Yeshua being confronted with the same question by a group of scribes and *P'rushim* who were out to catch Him saying something for which they might have Him arrested by the Romans (Matthew 22:15-22; Mark 12:13-17; Luke 20:19-26). "Is it lawful for us to pay taxes to Caesar or not?" (Luke 20:22, NASB). Yeshua responded by asking to see a coin and asking whose face or inscription it bore, before saying, "Render to Caesar the things that are Caesar's, and to God the things that are God's" (Luke 20:25, NASB). Yeshua was relating to Caesar (and his officials) in the way that he would relate to and understand: paying taxes with physical signs of earthly wealth, even bearing the emperor's own insignia. While Yeshua is not saying that tithes and offerings in the Kingdom of God should not be given in the legal currency of one or another country, or be given exclusively in some other form, He is saying that the quality of the gift should be appropriate to the recipient and, like Ya'akov's gift to Esav, from what we have around us: ourselves and our lives.

Further Study: Luke 21:1-4; Psalm 51:15-17

Application: Are you so involved in the mechanical computation of your income and tithe, sending money here and there to match the level of giving that you think God requires of you, that you have lost sight of the gift that God really desires - yourself?

וַיִּשְׁלַח ג׳

Vayishlakh - And he sent - 3

B'resheet / Genesis 32:31 - 33:5

B'resheet/Genesis 32:31 "For I have seen God face-to-face and my soul has escaped."

כִּי־רָאִיתִי אֱלֹהִים פָּנִים אֶל־פָּנִים וַתִּנָּצֵל

vatinatzeyl paniym el paniym Elohiym ra'iytiy kiy

נַפְשִׁי:

naf'shiy

While the English word for 'face' twice in this verse is singular, the Hebrew word פָּנִים is plural - literally, "faces" - and hardly ever appears in the singular in biblical Hebrew. A face may be viewed from the front, in profile, in silhouette or something in between; similarly, a face may show joy, pain, elation, sorrow, surprise and many other emotions. The Hebrew idiom recognises this and reflects the many faces that human beings can show by using the word in the plural. Judaism traditionally talks of the attributes of God: the attribute of mercy, the attribute of justice, and so on; this leads to the idea of God also having many faces, depending on which attribute you focus on or see.

The Hebrew scriptures present a mixed report as to whether we can see the face of God. Moshe, for example, is told very clearly, "But My face ... you cannot see, because a human being cannot look at Me and remain alive" (Shemot 33:20, CJB). Isaiah, on the other hand, saw *HaShem* "sitting on a high lofty throne! The hem of His robe filled the temple" (Isaiah 6:1, CJB), recognised that he was "doomed! Because I, a man with unclean lips ... have seen with my own eyes the King, Adonai-Tzva'ot!" (v5, CJB), yet survives to tell the tale. Another example of God being seen is when Gideon is commissioned: the text clearly has *Adonai* speaking to Gideon, but only the Angel of the Lord is seen - "[Gid'on] said, 'Oh no! My Lord! Adonai! Because I've seen the angel of Adonai face-to-face!' But Adonai reassured him, 'Shalom to you, don't be afraid, you won't die!'" (Judges 6:22-23, CJB). There is much debate in scholarly circles as to who the *Malach Adonai*, the Angel of the

149

Lord, is - who can be seen without causing death, but speaks in the first person singular as God to Avraham and others.

The New Covenant scriptures are more definite: "No man has ever seen God" (John 1:18a, CJB). Then who have they seen? John goes on, "the only and unique Son, who is identical with God and is at the Father's side - He has made Him known" (v18b, CJB). Did John know what he was saying? "The Word became flesh and dwelt among us, and we beheld His glory, glory as of the only begotten from the Father, full of grace and truth" (v14, NASB). This was a real, tangible, physical, visible person, as John later says on his first letter: "What was from the beginning, what we have heard, what we have seen with our eyes, what we beheld and our hands handled, concerning the Word of Life" (1 John 1:1, NASB); Yeshua in the flesh, God made man.

Rav Sha'ul picks up the word-play when he writes, "For now we see in a mirror dimly, but then face to face" (1 Corinthians 13:12, NASB), looking forward to the day when we shall be with God for ever. J. Sidlow Baxter[4] comments: "then the One who we now know heart-to-heart, we shall see face-to-face".

Further Study: Judges 13:2-3; Ezekiel 1:22-28; Daniel 17:9-14

Application: Do you know God well enough heart-to-heart that when you see Him face-to-face it won't be a shock? Make good use of the time you have now to work on your relationship with Yeshua so that although He still awes you, He becomes like an old familiar friend.

---

4. J. Sidlow Baxter, 1903-1999: Pastor and theologian; born in Australia, brought up in Lancashire, attended Spugeon's college in London

וַיִּשְׁלַח 'ד

Vayishlakh - And he sent - 4

B'resheet / Genesis 33:6 - 20

B'resheet/Genesis 33:9 And Esav said, "I have much, my brother; let what is yours be yours."

וַיֹּאמֶר עֵשָׂו יֶשׁ־לִי רָב אָחִי יְהִי לְךָ
l'cha y'hiy akhiy rav liy yeysh Eysav vayomer

אֲשֶׁר־לָךְ:
lach asher

What could Esav mean by this response to Ya'akov? Was he rejecting Ya'akov's attempts at reconciliation as well as his gifts? The Sforno translates the first phrase of the reply as "I have plenty" and adds as comment "... and need naught." This is saying that Esav already had many flocks and herds of his own, so is in no need of the gift that Ya'akov is trying to give him. To the second phrase, Sforno adds, "Since you are my brother, you need not honour me with this gift," as if Esav is saying that the relationship between them should make such a gift unnecessary. Ya'akov, on the other hand (see verses 10 and 11) presses him to accept it, for Esav's acceptance of the gift is the sign of accepting Ya'akov - at least in some measure - and reconciliation. It would be much more difficult for Esav to attack Ya'akov later after accepting such an extravagant gift.

Rashi, by contrast, sees a different idea behind Esav's words. Rather than seeing a negotiation over the current gifts, Rashi suggests that Esav continues with his spurning of the birthright: "Here Esav conceded to Ya'akov with regard to the blessings." Esav is content with the material blessings that he has and does not want to take up the family responsibilities, so he accedes to Ya'akov's request to accept the gift before him and once again symbolically gives up the right of the first-born. By this action, Esav accepts that he is being "bought out" by Ya'akov - a compensation payment, "in full and final settlement", reflecting the reality that Ya'akov is the head of the family and will take God's promise on to the next generation.

The question of rightful authority over material things was used by Yeshua's enemies to try and trick Him into making a public statement that could be used against Him. Knowing that the people opposed paying taxes to the Roman authorities at least partly on the basis that it was improper to give any of the (holy) produce or money of the Land to the (pagan, unholy) Roman emperor, they asked Him whether *Torah* permitted them to pay taxes to Rome. Neatly detecting their subterfuge, Yeshua replies, "Give the Emperor what belongs to the Emperor. And give to God what belongs to God!" (Luke 20:25, CJB). That is, Yeshua acknowledges that although all things belong to God at an absolute level, it is necessary - and appropriate before God - to submit to the authorities that God Himself has placed around us, in the areas for which they have responsibility.

Like Ya'akov, we often have a choice what we do with out stuff. We can attempt to brazen it out and protect what we see as our rights, or we can choose to "buy" peace and an undisputed claim to what remains by acknowledging the rightful authority of others. This is clearly the case in the matter of taxation: there are very few countries that allow believers not to pay tax on the grounds that they and the money they earn belong to God and so are not subject to income tax! But it is also true in other areas such as family relationships, where we acknowledge the rightful claims of spouses, parents and children to a proportion of our time and financial resources.

Further Study: Romans 13:6-8; 1 Timothy 5:8

Application: Do you find it difficult allocating your time and resources, perhaps even resenting the way that others seem to press for more of a limited supply? Perhaps an attitude adjustment is called for, to seek balance and recognition of the needs and position of others around us.

וַיִּשְׁלַח ה׳

Vayishlakh - And he sent - 5

B'resheet / Genesis 34:1 - 35:11

B'resheet/Genesis 34:1 And Dinah, the daughter of Leah, went out ... to see the daughters of the land.

וַתֵּצֵא דִינָה בַּת־לֵאָה ... לִרְאוֹת בִּבְנוֹת
biv'not   lir'ot   ...   Le'ah   bat   Diynah vateytzey

הָאָרֶץ:
ha'aretz

The verb לִרְאוֹת, here a *Qal* infinitive from the root רָאָה, is most often translated either as "to see" or "to look (at)". Here, followed by the בְּ prefix, "in", it takes on an overtone of "inspect" or "look over" (Artscroll), so telling us that Dinah had not necessarily gone simply to socialise, but to assess, to evaluate, to weigh up, the local girls. Given the narrative that follows, of Dinah being taken and raped by the son of a local prince or leader, she must have been without male escort, spending time with the Hivvite girls and women, probably on a repeated basis, so that her behaviour and conduct could be noticed by Shechem and her habits of coming and going mapped in order to make the assault possible.

Rashi asks why the verse refers to Dinah as the daughter of Leah and not the daughter of Ya'akov. He answers his own question: "because of her 'going out' she is called 'the daughter of Leah', for Leah too was one who would go out, as it says: 'Leah went out to meet him' (B'resheet 30:16). Of her they coined the aphorism: 'Like mother, like daughter'." The saying is a quote from Ezekiel 16:44 and it is used in an extensive discussion of this episode in B'resheet Rabbah 80:1ff. The rabbis disapproved of Leah going out to meet Ya'akov on his way home from the field and telling him that he was to sleep with her that night, deeming it forward and inappropriate conduct, although Leah - being a matriarch - is elsewhere generally praised and held up as perfect in almost every way. However, Dinah's behaviour is taken as inheriting this lamentable trait and the rabbis portray it as a family failing that leads directly to Dinah's undoing, which could not have occurred if she had not learnt this flawed behaviour from her mother.

Another notable example of the inheritance of bad characteristics is found in John 8 where we observe Yeshua in a heated exchange with some of the Jewish leaders. Calling on the well-known fact that many sons resemble their fathers - if not in appearance, then in manner, speech and behaviour - Yeshua told them, "I say what My Father has shown Me; you do what your father has told you" (John 8:38, CJB). The leaders retort that their father is Avraham, but Yeshua says, Not so - "You belong to your father, Satan, and you want to carry out your father's desires" (v. 44, CJB). What can have provoked this level of acrimony? Yeshua knew that those Jewish leaders hated the things that He was saying and were seeking an opportunity to kill Him (or have Him killed); this, of course, is contrary to the *Torah* - they are not obeying God, so must be obeying Satan. By following the behaviour patterns of the enemy - Yeshua tells them, "from the start he was a murderer ... a liar - indeed, the inventor of the lie!" (v. 44, CJB) - as a son models the behaviour of his father, they are demonstrating their spiritual inheritance.

Like those Jewish leaders in Yeshua's time, we too inherit learned behaviour and attitudes from our physical parents, from our society and environment, from father figures or mentors in our lives and even from our peer group around us every day. Some of the influences can be very good and positive: being brought up in a strong believing home; godly teachers at school, church or synagogue; a caring and challenging mentor or older people who encourage us. For other people, sadly, those same figures can be a source of discouragement, bad attitudes and habits, leading us into trouble. All too frequently we can be swayed by our peer-group - those around us at work, college, camp or leisure - and we find ourselves rejecting our real values in order to identify with our peers and be considered part of the crowd. And bad habits, once learned, can be almost impossible to break.

How can we break the power and control of the past, those inherited and learned behaviours that sometimes seem to dog our path? The key is to recognise the truth that God speaks to us; Rav Sha'ul writes: "If anyone is united with the Messiah, he is a new creation - the old has passed; look, what has come is fresh and new!" (2 Corinthians 5:17, CJB). Once we know Yeshua and have truly given our lives to Him, we are new; the old has ceased to exist and have any legitimate hold over us; we are new, fresh and clean. Certainly old habits may take time to stop but they have no right to hold us, there is no legal ownership that allows them tenure - they have to go. As we walk in and declare the truth that the enemy has no claim over us, unless we choose to invite him back, we can and will experience freedom from "the sin which doth so easily beset us" (Hebrews 12:1, KJV). Let it no more be said of us, "Like mother, like daughter", but that we are the children of the King!

Further Study: 1 Kings 21:25-26; Romans 6:4-7

Application: Do you struggle with inherited behaviour or expectations that drag you down? Stand firm today in the knowledge that you are a new creation. Talking with someone who understands these issues may be a good thing, but start today to experience the freedom that God has for you!

וַיִּשְׁלַח

Vayishlakh - And he sent - 6

B'resheet / Genesis 35:12 - 36:19

B'resheet/Genesis 35:12 And the land I gave to Avraham and to Yitzkhak, I will give to you; and to your descendants after you

וְאֶת־הָאָרֶץ אֲשֶׁר נָתַתִּי לְאַבְרָהָם וּלְיִצְחָק
ool'Yitzkhak   l'Avraham   natatiy   asher   ha'aretz   v'et

לְךָ אֶתְּנֶנָּה וּלְזַרְעֲךָ אַחֲרֶיךָ
akhareycha ool'zaracha et'nenah l'cha

Nahum Sarna suggests comparing this text with B'resheet 17:8, where the promise of the Land was given to Avraham. There the text reads: "And I will give to you and to your descendants after you, the land of your sojournings, all the land of Canaan, for an everlasting possession" (NASB). Avraham repeats the promise to his servant whom he is sending to find a wife for Yitz'khak, "The Lord ... who spoke to me, and who swore to me, saying, 'To your descendants I will give this land'" (B'resheet 24:7, NASB) and *HaShem* repeats it to Yitz'khak: "to you and your descendants I will give all these lands, and I will establish the oath which I swore to your father Avraham" (B'resheet 26:3, NASB). Now that Ya'akov has returned to the Land with his family, ready to take up residence there and by that residence to actualise his inheritance of the promise, *HaShem* confirms both the promise and His readiness to fulfill it. For Ya'akov, who has been on a long journey - in many ways - to arrive at this point in time and space, this is a pivotal moment. He has just returned from Padan Aram; he has gone - at *HaShem*'s instruction - to the place of his momentous vision before he left the Land twenty years ago; he has built there an altar to *HaShem*; he has tied himself and his household to the Land by burying his mother's nurse under a nearby oak tree; he has arrived! Then, once he is committed - lock, stock and barrel - *HaShem* appears to him and confirms the promise of the Land for him and for his descendants after him, just as He had done for Avraham and Yitz'khak. The rightness of Ya'akov's actions in returning and coming home to Canaan is sealed by the word of *HaShem*.

Sforno comments, "**And to your offspring after you I will give the land**: In the end of days I will give your offspring the entire earth, not only *Eretz Yisrael*, as it says, 'You will spread powerfully westward, eastward, northward and southward' (B'resheet 28:14); and as it is said, 'and break down all the sons of Seth' (B'Midbar 24:17, ESV)". Here Sforno is picking up on the repetition of the word הָאָרֶץ at the end of the verse; it is not redundant, he suggests, but the first instance in the verse applies to the Land, while the second should be taken to mean the whole earth. The quote from 28:14 are the words that *HaShem* speaks to Ya'akov concerning his descendants (of which at the time he had none, nor wives) at Bethel when he was leaving the Land to go to Padan Aram. Sforno is perhaps thinking of the way in which the book of D'varim speaks of Israel being the chief among the nations, or Zechariah's prophetic visions of the time when all the nations will come up to celebrate the Feast of Tabernacles in Jerusalem. This is not a vision of military conquest, but as Hirsch points out, the natural result of the whole world coming to recognise the God of Israel as the One True God and coming into the one united Kingdom of God. Hirsch quotes from Psalm 37 (vv. 11, 22, 29) the phrases:

וַעֲנָוִים יִירְשׁוּ־אָרֶץ - the humble will inherit the earth,

מְבֹרָכָיו יִירְשׁוּ אָרֶץ - those blessed by Him [*Adonai*] will inherit the earth,

צַדִּיקִם יִירְשׁוּ־אָרֶץ - the righteous shall inherit the earth

to source his comment that "to those that truly follow in your footsteps, the whole world will fall as their spiritual heritage".

The Ramban is interested in the way the promises have been repeated. He says, "This alludes to an oath, for the Land was given to them with an oath so that sin should not cause annulment of the gift." He points out that later on the *Torah* says, "the land of which I swore to Avraham, to Yitz'khak and to Ya'akov" (Shemot 33:1, CJB) and suggests while there is no explicit giving of an oath recorded, "that the repetition of the prophecy constitutes an oath". His concern is to stress that the giving of the Land is not conditional upon Israel's behaviour because God has sworn to do it. That does not, of course, mean that every generation will live securely in the land regardless of their behaviour, for we know that Israel has spent significant periods of time either in the Land under oppression from their neighbours - in the time of the Judges and to some extent today - or exiled from the Land altogether - Babylon and the dispersion after the destruction of the 2nd Temple. No, it is simply that the promise that the descendants of Ya'akov will inherit the Land is a promise that God has given and God will fulfill, for individuals, for groups of Israelites and - ultimately - for the whole nation, in His time. Israel's good or bad behaviour cannot void that promise or release God from His own obligation.

At the start of the Sermon on the Mount, Yeshua echoes some of the phrases from Psalm 37: "Blessed are the meek, for they shall inherit the earth" (Matthew 5:5, ESV). The word 'meek' can also be translated 'humble' to align exactly with Psalm 37:11, but it clearly also aligns with verse 22. He also mentions possession of the Kingdom of Heaven in two of the other beatitudes (vv. 3 and 10). Here too, the promise is given on an unconditional basis - it is a statement of God's fixed purposes and intent: the meek will inherit the earth, whether anyone else minds or not; God has said so! Those who truly follow the ways of God will exhibit those character traits and will qualify to inherit those blessings that naturally follow from our relationship with God. It depends only on God.

The writer to the Hebrews picks up this issue when he writes, "Therefore, when God wanted to demonstrate still more convincingly the unchangeable character of His intentions to those who were to receive what He had promised, He added an oath to the promise; so that through two unchangeable things, in neither of which God could lie, we, who have fled to take a firm hold on the hope set before us, would be strongly encouraged" (Hebrews 6:17-18, CJB). The writer is referring to the promise that God gave to Avraham: that He would bless him and give him many descendants; this has happened - indeed, the very existence of the Jewish people has been cited as a proof for the existence of God! More than that, the spiritual descendants of Avraham are found in every corner of the globe, even some places where the Jewish people are not to be found.

When God says that He is going to do something, we can and must be sure that He is going to do it. When He does it is more open, since God's timing and ours do not always align in the way that we would like. Sometimes He doesn't follow the line of action that we expected either and He surprises us while remaining consistent with Himself and His words. Be that as it may, whether the timing or the event is not what we thought, with hindsight we can always see that God's way was the best and the outcome is better than we could have planned or imagined. As Rav Sha'ul, who by the sound of it had some experience in this area, wrote: "Now to Him who by His power working in us is able to do far beyond anything we can ask or imagine, to Him be glory in the Messianic Community and in the Messiah Yeshua from generation to generation forever. Amen" (Ephesians 3:20-21, CJB).

Further Study: Micah 7:20; Revelation 21:6-7

Application: Now is the time to remember that whatever happens, and stuff certainly does happen, God's promises are absolutely certain and can be trusted in the face of any challenge. If you are finding it tough holding on against the tide, take a moment to thank God for His faithfulness and then push on regardless because His word is for ever!

וַיִּשְׁלַח ז׳

Vayishlakh - And he sent - 7

B'resheet / Genesis 36:20 - 42

B'resheet/Genesis 36:20 These are the children of Se'ir, the Horite, the ones who dwelt in the land ...

אֵלֶּה בְנֵי־שֵׂעִיר הַחֹרִי יֹשְׁבֵי הָאָרֶץ

ha'aretz yosh'vey hakhoriy   Seyiyr   v'ney   eyleh

While the word הָאָרֶץ is most frequently used without a name to mean the Land of Israel, here its context - in the middle of genealogies for the descendants of Esav and the other tribes who lived in the area known as Se'ir or Edom - makes it clear that "the land" is the land that *HaShem* had designated for Esav and his sons to occupy. Rashi, quoting from *Targum Jonathan*, tells us: "For they were its inhabitants before Esav came there"; the clans of Se'ir the Horite had inhabited that land before Esav moved to the area.

The Sages held that the Horites were expert agriculturalists who instinctively knew which kind of crops could be supported by a particular tract of land: "Rabbi Samuel ben Nahmani said in Rabbi Johanan's name - they were thoroughly versed in the cultivation of the earth. For they used to say, This measure for olives, this measure for vines, this measure for figs. The word 'Horite' implies that they smelled the earth" (*b. Shabbat 85a*) to determine how many crops and of what type the land would best suit. This is based upon a word play: the name 'Horite' is drawn from the unused root חוּר meaning to dig or bore, while reversing the letters gives the root רוּחַ meaning to smell.

We might, nevertheless, wonder why the *Torah* is taking the time and trouble to record the names and genealogy of a people who seem only tangentially related to the main narrative of Avraham's descendants. The Sforno suggests that "The *Torah* records the names of these mighty men of repute to tell us that even so, the children of Esav were able to destroy them, for this was the will of the Almighty, as it says, 'As He did for the children of Esav who dwell in Se'ir' (D'varim 2:22)". Esav and his descendants had been given the land of Se'ir as their inheritance, so even though the men who

161

previously lived there were worthy of note, "we see that the land belongs to God who gives it to whomever He wishes" (Radak). After Moshe's death, when Joshua - although well schooled - is about to lead the people into the Land, God says to him: "Moses My servant is dead; now therefore arise, cross this Jordan, you and all this people, to the land which I am giving to them, to the sons of Israel. Every place on which the sole of your foot treads, I have given it to you, just as I spoke to Moses" (Joshua 1:2-3, NASB). Just because the local or human leadership has changed, there is no change in God's plans; the people are still going to enter the Land and God is still going to clear away the obstacles in their path.

In our day, we see eloquent and persuasive leaders of the nations who seem to exercise power and influence far beyond the borders of their own countries on the world stage. Individual nation states are grouping themselves together in federations and communities in order to increase their voice when they speak and are submerging their individual identities into that of their group. Vast commercial enterprises, employing thousands of people in many countries, pursue their own revenue-earning agendas regardless of national boundaries and without concern for the opinions or benefit of the countries within which they work. Financial empires, with revenues far exceeding those of many individual countries, control the ways in which even the nations of the world relate to each other, enabling or preventing international trade at the whim of a senior manager. Communication giants, linking all the parts of the world with cables, fibres and satellites, route the transfer of voice, documents and even people via their privately owned and operated networks, while remaining totally unaccountable to the countries and peoples that they serve. Gradually, the barriers of language and culture are being broken down to enable people the world over to work with each other and be governed as one.

Taken together, this picture looks and sounds amazingly like the ancient world: "Now the whole earth used the same language and the same words" (B'resheet 11:1, NASB). We have heard the language of that era from kings and politicians for centuries, "And they said to one another, 'Come, let us make bricks and burn them thoroughly.' And they used brick for stone, and they used tar for mortar. And they said, 'Come, let us build for ourselves a city, and a tower whose top will reach into heaven, and let us make for ourselves a name; lest we be scattered abroad over the face of the whole earth'" (B'resheet 11:3-4, NASB). Despite the rise of many world empires - Roman, Mongol, Indian, British, Russian - they have been unable to find enough cohesion to hold them together; each in turn has fallen and crumbled, the individual components making up the empire struggling to re-assert their independence. Now, perhaps, we may sense shadowy figures in the background who may just be able to exert enough control to make a world empire a possibility, manipulating politicians and commercial interests alike to bring a single international authority into being, despite the wishes of the people or nations themselves. Such an authority would either be entirely non-elected or only pseudo-democratic, enabling those in power to remain so and suppress disagreement. To many, who think they see the writing on the wall, this is a frightening prospect and conspiracy theories abound, linking largely unknown people through obscure "private" meetings and places in a web of interconnected intrigue.

More worrying is the way that many of the nations and corporations that wield such disproportionately high influence over all of our lives are implacably hostile to the Kingdom of God. Although "human rights" is a universal cry and banner used by parts of the world to throw off the shackles of tradition and religion, these "rights" somehow don't seem to be relevant to those who follow Yeshua and are blatantly ignored by some countries with the active connivance of others. The action that God took at the Tower of Babel - "And the Lord said, 'Behold, they are one people, and they all have the same language. And this is what they began to do, and now nothing which they purpose to do will be impossible for them. Come, let Us go down and there confuse their language, that they may not understand one another's speech.' So the Lord scattered them abroad from there over the face of the whole earth; and they stopped building the city" (B'resheet 11:6-8, NASB) - is no longer relevant, since mankind is already scattered over the face of the earth but has managed to get joined up again regardless of distance and time.

The text above points the way to the correct perspective. The Horites were nameworthy in their time with a reputation for agricultural skill, yet they gave way to the household of Esav. God had given the land to Esav and so, despite the qualities and strengths of the Horites, they were conquered and subdued by what may have been an inferior force. Archeology confirms that such a conquest did take place and that it was a fairly violent affair. The new owners of the land took possession according to God's mandate. The Psalmist asks the question: "Why are the nations in an uproar, and the peoples devising a vain thing?" (Psalm 2:1, NASB). The nations of the world, driven by the forces of wickedness that seek to destroy the Kingdom of God, are flexing their muscles and formenting revolt: "The kings of the earth take their stand, and the rulers take counsel together against the Lord and against His Anointed: 'Let us tear their fetters apart, and cast away their cords from us!'" (vv. 2-3, NASB). But God's response remains constant: "He who sits in the heavens laughs, the Lord scoffs at them. Then He will speak to them in His anger and terrify them in His fury" (vv. 4-5, NASB).

Just as in days past, God has an agenda and a plan; His plans are unshakeable and will be fulfilled perfectly, on time and within budget. Men with mighty names, eloquent voices, powerful influences, significant connections and more, may stand against the Kingdom of God but they will rail in vain and shall not succeed. God has given all the world to His Son,

Messiah Yeshua, saying, "I will surely give the nations as Your inheritance, and the very ends of the earth as Your possession. You shall break them with a rod of iron, You shalt shatter them like earthenware" (Psalm 21:8-9, NASB). The word has gone out and God waiting for the nations to bow before Him: "Do homage to the Son, lest He become angry, and you perish in the way, for His wrath may soon be kindled. How blessed are all who take refuge in Him!" (v. 12, NASB).

Further Study: Psalm 5:11; Revelation 19:11-16

Application: If you are nervous about the political and economic events that are happening in your life and the larger world around you, take comfort that God has it all in hand. Now is the time to depend fully on Him and put His plan into action. Ask Him today what you should be doing to speed the day of Messiah's return.

וַיֵּשֶׁב

Vayeshev - And he dwelt

B'resheet / Genesis 37:1 - 40:23

רִאשׁוֹן	Aliyah One	B'resheet/Genesis 37:1 - 11
שֵׁנִי	Aliyah Two	B'resheet/Genesis 37:12 - 22
שְׁלִישִׁי	Aliyah Three	B'resheet/Genesis 37:23 - 36
רְבִיעִי	Aliyah Four	B'resheet/Genesis 38:1 - 30
חֲמִשִׁי	Aliyah Five	B'resheet/Genesis 39:1 - 6
שִׁשִּׁי	Aliyah Six	B'resheet /Genesis 39:7 - 23
שְׁבִיעִי	Aliyah Seven	B'resheet/Genesis 40:1 - 23

וַיֵּשֶׁב 'א

Vayeshev - And he dwelt - 1

B'resheet / Genesis 37:1 - 11

B'resheet/Genesis 37:1 Ya'akov settled in the land of his father's sojournings

וַיֵּשֶׁב יַעֲקֹב בְּאֶרֶץ מְגוּרֵי אָבִיו
aviyv   m'gurey   b'eretz   Ya'akov vayeyshev

Today we stand in a rich tradition; a tradition of study, prayer and worship; a tradition that has not only preserved the customs and faith of our people over the generations, but has endured for thousands of years. There is great value in tradition, provided that it does not become our master. When Ya'akov returned from over twenty years in Padan Aram at the house of his Uncle Lavan, he returns to the land of his birth, *Eretz Yisrael*. He returns in a different state to that in which he left: then he had only the clothes he stood up in, used a rock for a pillow and was something of a fugitive from his older brother; now he is a man of substance, with flocks and herds, twelve sons and a whole household. Older and wiser, he settles down in the land where his father sojourned, where the Lord told him to stay (B'resheet 26:2-3).

Speaking through the prophet Jeremiah, the Lord said, "Stand by the ways and see and ask for the ancient paths, where the good way is, and walk in it; and you shall find rest for your souls" (Jeremiah 6:16, NASB). Some chapters later, He adds, "My people ... have stumbled from their ways, from the ancient paths, to walk in bypaths, not on a highway" (Jeremiah 18:15, NASB). Our relationship with God is founded on certain principles that do not change: He is God and there is no other; He created the world and all that is in it; He has made covenant with us ever since the days of Noach and Avraham, supremely in the body and blood of Yeshua, His Son; the cross/stake is the way of atonement, reconciliation and peace with God. These are the givens and the unshakeable foundations of our faith, that we come back to time after time.

In all three synoptic gospels, the writers record that Yeshua taught about the effects of trying to put new wine into old wineskins - that the acid would destroy the old skins, thus wasting both them and the wine. Only in Luke's gospel is the concluding phrase found: "No-one, after drinking old [wine] wishes for new; for he says, 'The old is good enough'" (Luke 5:39, NASB). In our search for the new things that God is always doing (Is 48:6), we must be careful not to throw the baby out with the bath-water, but to remain rooted and grounded in the unalterable precepts of the faith that we have inherited, the faith once delivered to the saints (Jude 3), the faith of our fathers Avraham, Yitz'khak and Ya'akov.

Further Study: Luke 5:37-39; Isaiah 48:6-7; Jude 3

Application: A question we all need to ask ourselves is: are we standing firm on the traditional faith and values described in the pages of Scripture or have we been drawn off course by something new.

וַיֵּשֶׁב ב׳

Vayeshev - And he dwelt - 2

B'resheet / Genesis 37:12 - 22

B'resheet/Genesis 37:12 And his brothers went to pasture the flock of their father in Shechem

וַיֵּלְכוּ אֶחָיו לִרְעוֹת אֶת־צֹאן אֲבִיהֶם

aviy'hem   tzon   et   lir'ot   ekhayv vayeyl'chu

בִּשְׁכֶם
bish'chem

In the *Torah* scrolls, the word אֶת in this verse has a dot written above each letter. According to the manuscript tradition, this is a way of marking scribal mistakes in a non-erasable medium - by putting dots over letters or words, the proof-reader would indicate that they should not be present in the text. Nevertheless, both this word and its annotation are preserved in the Masoretic Text. The function of the word אֶת is to denote that what follows is the direct object of the (usually) preceding verb, and in this verse its purpose is to link "the flock of their father" to "pasture". But what if it were absent? What then would the brothers be going to pasture?

Rashi suggests that the brothers went to Shechem to pasture themselves! We read earlier in the *parasha* (37:2) that Yosef had already cast doubts upon the brothers' dedication as shepherds and here they were, setting off out of father's sight and control, ostensibly to pasture the sheep, but quite possibly to pasture themselves - take it easy, have a lazy time and a few laughs - while paying a little cursory attention to the sheep. Even their father Ya'akov is suspicious, sending Yosef after them to see what they are really up to, and asking for a report on their activities.

Early in the book of Isaiah, the prophet draws a picture of a vineyard and workers, representing the house of Y'hudah and Yisra'el. *HaShem* had built and planted the vineyard with the expectation of a harvest. "What more was there to do for My vineyard that I have not done in it? Why, when I expected it to produce good grapes did it produce worthless ones?" (Isaiah 5:4, NASB). Over the rest of the chapter, the prophet highlights ways in which the men of Y'hudah and Yisra'el in those days had pastured themselves rather than pasturing God's people. Building on the same passage, Yeshua also spoke of a man who "planted a vineyard, and put a wall around it" (Mark 12:1, NASB). Once the vineyard was let out to tenants, the owner set off for a journey, expecting a return in his investment. But here again, once out of sight and effective control of the owner, the workers are seeking their own profit and comfort, even to the extent of killing the owner's son: "This is the heir; come, let us kill him and the inheritance will be ours!" (Mark 12:7, NASB)

Does this idea also speak to us? God doesn't always seem to be paying attention to what we are doing and, as the Psalmist notes on many occasions, the wicked seem to be getting away with everything they do. We should be both challenged and comforted by the assurance that God does see everything and nothing escapes His notice. As Rav Sha'ul writes: "Do not be deceived, God is not mocked; for whatever a man sows, this he will also reap" (Galatians 6:7, NASB). God sees and is interested in the smallest things we do and is always ready to share our confidences with us and encourage us.

Further Study: Matthew 7:21-23; Job 13:7-9

Application: If the prospect of Yeshua turning up in your home or work place today and watching what you do and say is disturbing, perhaps it would be a good idea to talk this through with Him sooner rather than later.

וַיֵּשֶׁב ג'

Vayeshev - And he dwelt - 3

B'resheet / Genesis 37:23 - 36

B'resheet/Genesis 37:23 and they stripped off Yosef his undergarment, his garment of long sleeves

וַיַּפְשִׁיטוּ אֶת־יוֹסֵף אֶת־כֻּתָּנְתּוֹ אֶת־כְּתֹנֶת

k'tonet   et   kootan'to   et   Yosef   et   vayaf'shiytiy

הַפַּסִּים

ha'pasiym

Since the next verse tells us that the brothers "took him", Hirsch deduces that Yosef offered no resistance to being stripped of his coat, but only begged not to be treated in this way. In fact, we don't learn until much later that the brothers would say, "we are all guilty concerning our brother in that we saw the anguish of his soul when he entreated us and we would not hear" (B'resheet 42:21, Hirsch). To a significant extent, then, Yosef submitted to his brothers in the humiliation of having his clothing removed from him and being thrown into the pit and, apparently, in the subsequent sale to the merchants bound for Egypt. Perhaps even at this point, Yosef had some inkling of God's hand on him; he was later to say after Ya'akov's death, "You meant to do me harm, but God meant it for good - so that it would come about as it is today, with many people's lives being saved" (B'resheet 50:20, CJB).

The prophets speak of another who would submit to unjust treatment, this time in silence without even complaining: "He was oppressed and He was afflicted, yet He did not open His mouth; like a lamb that is led to slaughter, and like a sheep that is silent before its shearers, so He did not open His mouth" (Isaiah 53:7, NASB). Knowing this, Yeshua taught His own disciples, "We are now going up to Jerusalem, where the Son of Man will be handed over to the head cohanim and the Torah-teachers. They will sentence Him to death and turn Him over to the Goyim who will jeer at Him, spit on Him, beat Him and kill Him; but after three days, He will rise" (Mark 10:33-34, CJB). Later in the text we find the fulfillment: "He remained silent and made no reply" (Mark 14:61,

CJB) to the *Cohen HaGadol*; "But Yeshua made no further response, to Pilate's amazement" (Mark 15:5, CJB); Herod "questioned Him at great length, but Yeshua made no reply" (Luke 23:9, CJB). His only expression of anguish was in the Garden: "My Father, if possible, let this cup pass from Me! Yet - not what I want, but what You want!" (Matthew 26:39, CJB).

Three times each day, immediately following the individual reading of the *Shemoneh Esrei*, in the concluding prayer of Rabbi Mar, son of Rabina (*b*. Berachot 17*a*), Israel prays, "To those who curse me, let my soul be silent; and let my soul be like dust to everyone" (Artscroll); or "Help me ignore those who would slander me. Let me be humble before all" (Sim Shalom). We pray for the grace to ignore insults and attacks, not to respond in an unsuitable way to those who may be mocking or ridiculing us, and to keep a low and humble profile. Little wonder that Rav Sha'ul writes, "As much as it is possible, live in peace with everyone" (Romans 12:18, GWT), urging us to pursue things that lead to peace and to build each other up at all times (Romans 14:19), as He echoes the Master: "Have salt in yourselves, and be at peace with one another" (Mark 9:50, NASB).

Further Study: Matthew 5:38-41; Matthew 10:16-22

Application: Have you witnessed or been the subject of unfair attention or treatment recently? Did you try to defend or justify yourself, or were you able to "endure the slings and arrows of outrageous fortune" and overcome them by your peace? Pray for God's grace today.

וַיֵּשֶׁב 'ד

Vayeshev - And he dwelt - 4

B'resheet / Genesis 38:1 - 30

B'resheet/Genesis 38:1 And it was at this time that Y'hudah went down from his brothers.

וַיְהִי בָּעֵת הַהִוא וַיֵּרֶד יְהוּדָה מֵאֵת אֶחָיו

ekhayv mey'eyt Y'hudah vayeyred hahiv   ba'eyt vay'hiy

This text starts the story fragment - just this one chapter - that deals with Y'hudah's marriage, the birth of his sons and grandsons, including his relationship with Tamar, his daughter-in-law and the mother - with him - of his grandsons/sons. The whole chapter is only thirty verses, yet must span some fifteen to twenty years, inserted into the main narrative of the Yosef story which immediately picks up again in the following chapter. Naturally, the insertion of this important piece of story - for from the union of Y'hudah and Tamar would eventually come King David and, of course, Messiah - at this point has attracted the attention of the commentators.

Rashi asks, "Why is this passage juxtaposed at this point - interrupting the story of Yosef?" He answers that the key word is וַיֵּרֶד, "and he went down", from the root יָרַד, which means to go down or descend - the opposite of the root עָלָה, to go up or ascend. While these verbs are often used in a very physical way: going down to Egypt, going up to Bethel, they always have a spiritual under-thread running through them. Jerusalem, in the mountains of Judea, while not the highest point of altitude in the whole land of Israel, is certainly among the highest points physically in Judea; it is also seen as the highest spiritual place in the Land, so that pilgrims would come up to see the House of the Lord, go up to Jerusalem, from all over both the Land and the world, to seek the God of Israel. As they ascended physically they also ascended to a holier place and a higher level of holiness. Returning home reversed the process as they went down. This sense is preserved in the modern words *"aliyah"*, to immigrate to Israel and *"yeridah"*, to emigrate from Israel.

But why did Y'hudah go down from his brothers? Rashi continues, "To teach that his brothers took him down from his position of leadership in the family when they saw the distress of their father." The brothers held Y'hudah responsible for his idea of selling Yosef to the Ishmaelite/Midianite traders and then telling Ya'akov that his favourite son had been attacked and killed by wild animals. Because of his obviously (with hindsight) bad judgement, his brothers now looked down on him and probably spurned him. The text goes on: "he turned away to an Adullamite man named Hiram" and the following verses relate that he married out - a local merchant's daughter - and lived apart from his father and brothers for enough time to have two grown-up sons and arrange a local marriage for them also.

This teaches us two things. Firstly, that sin causes a separation and a barrier, not only between men and God, but also between men and within families. Secondly, one sin inevitably leads to another unless God intervenes to stop the process. As Rav Sha'ul wrote: "For sin, seizing the opportunity afforded by the commandment, deceived me; and through the commandment killed me" (Romans 7:11, CJB). So from Y'hudah's one sin came a distancing, a cooling of relationship, followed by a turning away, a breaking of fellowship and regular contact, leading to the other events of the chapter: the sin of his sons, not honouring his commitment to his daughter-in-law, consorting with a prostitute, being unable to redeem his pledge to pay the prostitute, condemning his daughter-in-law to death for becoming pregnant without a husband, until finally he stood up to his failures and admitted his part.

Further Study: Proverbs 9:13-18; Hebrews 3:12-14

Application: Are you on the edge of a slippery slope of sin away from God, your family and those close to you? Even if you have already started "going down" it is never too late to acknowledge what is going on and call out to God to help you. "Everyone who calls on the name of the Lord will be saved" (Romans 10:13, ESV).

וַיֵּשֶׁב 'ה

Vayeshev - And he dwelt - 5

B'resheet / Genesis 39:1 - 6

B'resheet/Genesis 39:1 And Yosef was brought down to Egypt and Potiphar bought him

וְיוֹסֵף הוּרַד מִצְרָיְמָה וַיִּקְנֵהוּ פּוֹטִיפַר
Po'tiphar vayik'neyhu Mitzraymah hoorad v'Yoseyf

The Sforno opens this passage by commenting on the placement of the וְ - "and" - at the beginning of this section of the narrative. The last chapter dealt with the affairs of Yosef's brother Judah, back in the land of Canaan, and Sforno says that the וְ is placed at the beginning of this narrative block, with the proper name Yosef rather than with the verb that follows, in order to emphasise that these events (i.e. chapter 38 and chapter 39 ff.) took place at the same time. The verb הוּרַד is a *Hof'al* Affix 3ms from the root יָרַד, to go down or descend, the *Hof'al* stem is both causitive and passive: Yosef did not of his own volition go down to Egypt, but he was caused to go down - as the modern JPS translation says: "When Yosef was taken down to Egypt". The same verb is used of Judah in the previous chapter, וַיֵּרֶד יְהוּדָה, "and Judah went down", although there it is in the *Qal* stem, denoting active action; this invites a comparison of the two events.

Rashi accepts the invitation and comments that the *Torah* deliberately positioned the narrative sequences - interrupting the Yosef story with the seemingly out-of-place story of Judah's life - "in order to juxtapose the descent of Judah with the sale of Yosef." Rashi has previously commented that Judah was to some extent removed from his position of authority among the brothers because with hindsight they disapproved of his advice to sell Yosef to the Midianites, so that Judah could have been said to have "gone down" or been taken down a peg or two, but here our attention is focused on the difference between the two events: Judah - feeling the disapprobation of his family - turns aside and goes down into the land of Canaan by marrying a local merchant's daughter and having children; he chose to do that. Yosef, on the other hand, went down to Egypt against his will, with no choice in the matter, because he had been sold to the Midianite slave traders. Perhaps he initially entertained some thoughts that this was at least better than being killed or left in the pit to die, and besides he'd easily be able to slip away and make for home, but his hopes in that direction would soon have been disillusioned. He had to face not only being taken many miles to a foreign country away from his home, but the emotional descent in status from the favourite son of a rich father to the indignity of being sold in a slave market and becoming the personal slave to a man of stature and reputation as the chief executioner in Pharaoh's court!

In the Yosef story - as we shall see in the coming weeks as we read on through the text - *HaShem* brings Yosef down so that He may bring him up again in a different and better place to accomplish His plans. Like a duck or a grebe that dives below the water and only re-appears some time later and often yards away from the point of disappearance, Yosef bobs out of sight on the Canaan stage, only to re-appear - eventually - as the Grand Vizier of Egypt; second in command only to Pharaoh himself, in order to save his family from the famine across the whole region, and effect their transfer to Egypt thus fulfilling God's promise to Avraham. Although Yosef never loses touch with God during the process, it is only with hindsight that he can say to his brothers, "God sent me ahead of you to ensure that you will have descendants on earth and to save your lives in a great deliverance" (B'resheet 45:7, CJB). He later added, "God meant it for good - so that it would come about as it is today, with many people's lives being saved" (50:20, CJB).

Yosef's life was a pointer, a worked example, of Messiah who was to come. Our rabbis recognise this when they write about Messiah ben Yosef - Messiah, son of Yosef. We can see here a model of the life and ministry of Yeshua: "though He was in the form of God, He did not regard equality with God something to be possessed by force. On the contrary, He emptied Himself, in that He took the form of a slave by becoming like human beings are. And when He appeared as a human being, He humbled Himself still more by becoming obedient even to death - death on a stake as a criminal! Therefore God raised Him to the highest place and gave Him the name above every name; that in honour of the name given Yeshua, every knee will bow - in heaven, on earth and under the earth - and every tongue will acknowledge that Yeshua the Messiah is Adonai - to the glory of God the Father" (Philippians 2:6-11, CJB).

Further Study: Isaiah 50:4-7; Isaiah 45:23-25

Application: Do you feel cast down and despondent, thinking that God has forgotten about you and that you are languishing away in a corner out of His sight? Never fear, for God has a purpose for your life; if He has cast down or put on one side it is for the purpose that He may yet bring you out and use you to bless and encourage others in the unfolding of His kingdom plans.

וַיֵּשֶׁב י׳

Vayeshev - And he dwelt - 6

B'resheet / Genesis 39:7 - 23

B'resheet/Genesis 39:9 And how should I do this great evil; should I sin against God?

וְאֵיךְ אֶעֱשֶׂה הָרָעָה הַגְּדֹלָה הַזֹּאת וְחָטָאתִי
v'khatatiy   *hazot*   *hagdolah*   *ha'ra'ah*   *e'eseh*   *v'eych*

לֵאלֹהִים:
lEylohiym

The wife of Potiphar, whom Rashi likens to a bear because she had no shame in her demands, has been pestering Yosef that he should have sexual relations with her. In an ancient slave-owning culture, this was not necessarily an unusual event, slaves were often treated as sexual objects; the text might be hinting at this when it describes the behaviour of Potiphar's wife: "And it came about after these events that his master's wife looked with desire at Joseph, and she said, 'Lie with me'" (39:7, NASB) - just a command, without any pretence at relationship. Nahum Sarna points out that Yosef responds with a three-tier argument: firstly, that it would be a breach of the trust between Potiphar - his master - and himself; secondly, that it would be a violation of the husband's proprietory rights over his wife; and, thirdly, that it would be a religious offence against God - a great evil in His sight. As we know from the story, Potiphar's wife is not impressed by Yosef's arguments and continues to importune him, finally taking revenge by accusing him of attempting to instigate the sexual activity!

Targum Onkelos, in its relentless campaign to remove anthropomorphisms, translates the verb "sin against" as "be guilty before" lest it should appear that any human action can actually directly impact or offend God. *Onkelos* also changes the name of God at the end of the verse from Elohim to the tetragrammaton; this serves to remove any possibility that a reader might suppose that there was a plural deity; this happens 31 times in B'resheet alone, including the first creation narrative 1:1-2:4. Oddly, in this verse, that change serves to hide an important part of Yosef's speech - Yosef uses the name Elohim for God rather than the tetragrammaton because he is talking to an Egyptian who would not have known whom he was talking about had he used the personal covenant name of *Adonai*. The general Egyptian attitude to the God of the Hebrews can be seen from Pharoah's response to Moshe when the latter first comes before Pharoah to present *Adonai's* demand that he let the Israelites go: "Pharoah said, 'Who is the Lord that I should obey His voice to let Israel go? I do not know the Lord, and besides, I will not let Israel go'" (Shemot 5:2, NASB).

The Sforno is interested in the words הָרָעָה הַגְּדֹלָה הַזֹּאת - this great evil or wickedness; he paraphrases this as "repaying good with evil". Yosef is conscious that Potiphar has been very good to him, trusting him with all the affairs of his household, so that he is able to enjoy position and status within that establishment; as a slave he is entitled to nothing, but with God's hand upon him, he has been granted his master's favour and trust. For Yosef to now have sexual relations - even at her instigation - with Potiphar's wife, the one thing in the household that had not been given into his care, would be repaying his master's goodness with evil; to quote a modern aphorism: biting the hand that feeds him.

Rashi is bothered that this incident occurs before the *Torah* has been given to the Israelites and that nowhere in the book of B'resheet so far has an explicit command been given that would make the act of Yosef having sexual relations with Potiphar's wife, at her command, however unwise in human terms, a great sin before God. God appears to assume that men know that this is so in the story of Avraham and Sarah in Gerar when "God came to Abimelech in a dream of the night, and said to him, 'Behold, you are a dead man because of the woman whom you have taken, for she is married'" (B'resheet 20:3, NASB). To explain this, Rashi references the Talmud (*b.* Sanhedrin 56*a*), where the Sages list the seven Noachide commandments; the commandment against sexual immorality and unfaithfulness, either married or unmarried (adultery or fornication) is derived from the instructions for marriage given to Adam and Eve: "For this cause a man shall leave his father and his mother, and shall cleave to his wife; and they shall become one flesh" (B'resheet 2:24, NASB). Certainly the instructions given to Noach to "Be fruitful and multiply, and fill the earth" (B'resheet 9:1, NASB) are going to be difficult in the face of human jealousy and hurt that naturally spring from improper sexual conduct and infidelity. The rabbis consider the Noachide commandments to be binding upon all humanity, as descendants of Noach.

The detailed prohibition against and definition of sexual sins are outlined in Vayikra chapter 18 and repeated later in the *Torah*; they are binding upon Jews. The New Covenant Scriptures also carry that command forward explicitly for Gentile believers; the account of the Jerusalem Council records in both versions - the original minutes of the meeting and the letter written to the Gentiles afterwards - that sexual immorality was forbidden for Gentiles as one of the essential basics for fellowship between Jews and Gentiles: "For it seemed good to the Holy Spirit and to us to lay upon you no greater burden than these essentials: that you abstain from things sacrificed to idols and from blood and from things strangled and from fornication; if you keep yourselves free from such things, you will do well" (Acts 15:28-29, NASB) and see also the original minute in verse 20. Yeshua similarly linked adultery with other sins when he told the story about the Pharisee and the tax-collector: "The Pharisee stood and was praying thus to himself, 'God, I thank Thee that I am not like other people: swindlers, unjust, adulterers, or even like this tax-gatherer'" (Luke 18:11, NASB). Indeed, according to Rav Sha'ul, sexual sin prohibits entry to the Kingdom of Heaven: "Or do you not know that the unrighteous shall not inherit the Kingdom of God? Do not be deceived; neither fornicators, nor idolaters, nor adulterers, nor effeminate, nor homosexuals ..." (1 Corinthians 6:9, NASB).

Physical adultery is also an important spiritual type for spiritual adultery and the same rules apply to us as believers if we are unfaithful in our relationship with the Lord. Worshipping other gods, be that a formal religious experience, dabbling with fortune telling or the horoscope in a newspaper, an obsession with sport - playing or watching - or becoming a work-aholic, inevitably leads to relationship breakdown between us and God. Just as fornication - sexual activity before marriage - damages the people involved, so that they then enter marriage with memories, fantasies and expectations that do not involve their marriage partner, so people who mess about with the occult, horoscopes and the false religions will have to spend some time straightening out their relationship with God once they get to know Him. Yeshua's words, "You have heard that our fathers were told, 'Do not commit adultery.' But I tell you that a man who even looks at a woman with the purpose of lusting after her has already committed adultery with her in his heart" (Matthew 5:27-28, CJB), certainly apply to human sexual relationships but also apply to sins such as covetousness, envy and jealousy; they take our eyes off Yeshua and cause us to put something else - our neighbour's car, a football game, a certain salary - before Him and we become a slave to that lust, dishonouring Him. Perhaps this is the link that Rav Shaul sees: "Saying, 'Thou shalt not commit adultery,' do you commit adultery? Detesting idols, do you commit idolatrous acts?" (Romans 2:22, CJB).

Just as Yosef recoiled from the sin of committing adultery with his master's wife, even in a culture and society where this was often the norm, and despite her bidding, so we too need to flee from both physical and spiritual adultery. We must remain faithful to our God and be scrupulous to avoid falling into idolatry, allowing something or someone else to come between us and God. We must not repay His goodness with evil.

Further Study: Hebrews 13:4; James 2:11

Application: If you have become aware that you are involved in an improper relationship, with a member of the opposite sex, or with an object or desire that has become an obsession in your life, now would be an excellent time to flee from it and return wholeheartedly to God. You may find it useful to discuss this with your partner or a trusted spiritual friend or leader who can help you to restore your relationship with God and to hold you accountable for maintaining your distance and staying clear of such temptations in future.

וַיֵּשֶׁב ז׳

Vayeshev - And he dwelt - 7

B'resheet / Genesis 40:1 - 23

B'resheet/Genesis 40:1 And it was after these things ...

וַיְהִי אַחַר הַדְּבָרִים הָאֵלֶּה

ha'eyleh   hadvariym   akhar vay'hiy

This set of words form a common Hebrew phrase, used to mark an indefinite period of time - see also, for example, 15:1. Although the word הַדְּבָרִים comes from the root דָּבַר - to speak - and is often translated "the words", it is also frequently used to mean "things" or "matters". Nahum Sarna points out that although we can guess that Joseph was 28 years old at this point - he is thirty when entering Pharaoh's service (41:46), which was at least two years after this event (41:1) and has been away from his family since the age of 17 (37:2) - "we have no way of determining how many of those years he spent in the service of Potiphar and how many in prison." The time is not insubstantial and just as Avraham had to wait a quarter of century from the giving of God's promise of progeny to its fulfillment at the birth of Yitzchak, Joseph has to serve his time in God's economy before his promises, given in his dreams in chapter 37, become reality.

Commenting on the start of this narrative unit, when Pharaoh's chief cup-bearer and baker are placed for a while in the same prison as Joseph, Rashi suggests (based a little loosely on B'resheet Rabbah 88:1) that *HaShem* arranged their imprisonment as a distraction among the Egyptian court so that they should squabble among themselves rather than becoming aware of Joseph in prison before his time had come: "so that relief should come to the righteous one through them." Be'er Yitzchak aligns the text with the word "therefore"; in the light of Joseph's confinement in prison, while at the same time finding favour with the prison governor, *HaShem* sends two high-ranking personal servants of Pharaoh on a temporary sojourn to the same prison in a way that will comfort Joseph in the short term and, at the same time, set up the connection that will lead to his eventual freedom from imprisonment.

Similar phrases appear many times in the gospels: "And it came about that when Yeshua had finished these words" (Matthew 19:1, NASB), "About a week after Yeshua said these things" (Luke 9:28, CJB); linking phrases that move us on from one narrative or teaching unit to the next without being specific about either time or place. They indicate that one event or set of sayings has ended and that another is about to begin. Just as the curtain closes briefly, or the lighting on stage changes, we know that the play has moved on to the next scene. Much of the Bible is written from a historical point of view - that is, with hindsight, recording events that happened in the past of the writers - and so the individual milestones can be clearly seen and the major events lined up in sequence to show the overall design that lies behind the day-to-day happenings. As *Qohelet* wrote: "For everything there is a season, and a time for every matter under heaven" (Ecclesiastes 3:1, ESV).

Yeshua is keenly aware of God's timing and sequence during His earthly ministry; the gospel accounts, particularly John, have Yeshua making this point on many occasions: the wedding at Cana at the start of His ministry, "Yeshua replied, 'Mother, why should that concern me? - or you? My time hasn't come'" (John 2:4, CJB); teaching in the Temple in Jerusalem, "At this, they tried to arrest Him; but no one laid a hand on Him; because His time had not yet come" (John 7:30, CJB); after the event of the woman caught in adultery, "He said these things when He was teaching in the Temple treasury room; yet no one arrested Him, because His time had not yet come" (John 8:20, CJB). Yeshua knows that there is a script to follow, so that everything happens in its time and place. Finally, in the days leading up to the Last Supper, John observes, "It was just before the festival of Pesach, and Yeshua knew that the time had come for Him to pass from this world to the Father. Having loved His own people in the world, He loved them to the end" (John 13:1, CJB).

Living our lives, coping with the events of each day: piano lessons, doctor's appointments, house-group, work - mustn't forget work! - and our families, we tend to lose sight of God's plans in our normal busy round of activity. When something dramatic or tragic happens - the marriage of a son or daughter, death of a parent, a road accident - we go into panic mode, dealing with the extra pressure on an emergency basis, often exhausting ourselves and the patience of those around us. The urgent overrides the important and survival becomes the name of the game. Our eyes get so close to what we are immediately dealing with that our perspective becomes totally compromised. We forget that God still has a plan for everything to happen in its proper place and time. Even the pressures that we endure are part of God's process to shape us and touch other people through us.

Ancient Israel went through times of distress and anguish; bad decisions and sinful behaviour impaired their relationship with God, so that He allowed the surrounding nations to prevail against our people as a means of discipline or a wake-up call. In those times of stress, however, God continued to speak to the prophets and those who would hear Him, to offer encouragement and assurance that however bad things looked, everything was still under His control. The Psalmist cries out to God with confidence, "You will arise and have pity on Zion; it is the time to favor her; the appointed time has come" (Psalm 102:13, ESV), and the prophets announce God's future plans for the people: "This third I will bring into the fire; I will refine them like silver and test them like gold. They will call on My name and I will answer them; I will say, 'They are My people,' and they will say, 'The Lord is our God'" (Zechariah 13:9, NIV). All the time, God is working to purify and cleanse His people so that they may be wholehearted and righteous before Him.

Exactly the same process is happening to both Jew and Gentile believers in Messiah Yeshua today. So that Rav Sha'ul's prophetic words may be realised - "Messiah loved the Messianic Community, indeed, gave Himself up on its behalf, in order to set it apart for God, making it clean through immersion in the mikveh, so to speak, in order to present the Messianic Community to Himself as a bride to be proud of, without a spot, wrinkle or any such thing, but holy and without defect" (Ephesians 5:25-27, CJB) - we are being lovingly and individually moulded to bring us to perfection. Those encouraging words that Sha'ul wrote to the community in Rome really do apply to us as well: "Furthermore, we know that God causes everything to work together for the good of those who love God and are called in accordance with His purpose; because those whom He knew in advance, He also determined in advance would be conformed to the pattern of His Son, so that He might be the firstborn among many brothers; and those whom He thus determined in advance, He also called; and those whom He called, He also caused to be considered righteous; and those whom He caused to be considered righteous He also glorified!" (Romans 8:28-30, CJB).

Wouldn't it be nice if we had some foreknowledge of the events that are scheduled in our lives so that we can be ready for them? Not according to Yeshua! Although He spoke these words in reply to the disciples' question about the restoration of the kingdom to Israel, the words are still appropriate for us: "You don't need to know the dates or the times; the Father has kept these under His own authority" (Acts 1:7, CJB). We would be swamped by knowing what was ahead and would try to avoid or circumnavigate those times of trial that we didn't think that we could survive, let alone enjoy. We must go through the times of trial and testing in the order that He knows best, "for you know that the testing of your trust produces perseverance. But let perseverance do its complete work; so that you may be complete and whole, lacking in nothing" (James 1:3-4, CJB).

It is only when we look back through our lives that we can recognise the hand of God at work. We persevere now so that we too may say, "After those days" and know that although difficult, they have been worth living with God. "Even gold is tested for genuineness by fire. The purpose of these trials is so that your trust's genuineness, which is far more valuable than perishable gold, will be judged worthy of praise, glory and honor at the revealing of Yeshua the Messiah. Without having seen Him, you love Him. Without seeing Him now, but trusting in Him, you continue to be full of joy that is glorious beyond words" (1 Peter 1:7-8, CJB).

Further Study: 2 Corinthians 4:15-16; 2 Thessalonians 1:5-7

Application: If you are now at a place of testing, where your faith and endurance are being stretched, perhaps beyond what you think you can bear, take comfort that all these times are in God's hand and He knows exactly what we can withstand and the fruit that He will produce in our lives if we co-operate with Him. In time to come, you too will be able to recognise, "After those days ..."

מִקֵּץ

Mikketz - At the end

B'resheet / Genesis 41:1 - 44:17

רִאשׁוֹן	Aliyah One	B'resheet/Genesis 41:1 - 14
שֵׁנִי	Aliyah Two	B'resheet/Genesis 41:15 - 38
שְׁלִישִׁי	Aliyah Three	B'resheet/Genesis 41:39 - 52
רְבִיעִי	Aliyah Four	B'resheet/Genesis 41:53 - 42:18
חֲמִשִׁי	Aliyah Five	B'resheet/Genesis 42:19 - 43:15
שִׁשִׁי	Aliyah Six	B'resheet /Genesis 43:16 - 29
שְׁבִיעִי	Aliyah Seven	B'resheet/Genesis 43:30 - 44:17

מִקֵץ א׳

Mikketz - At the end - 1

B'resheet / Genesis 41:1 - 14

B'resheet/Genesis 41:1   And it was at the end of two years

וַיְהִי מִקֵץ שְׁנָתַיִם יָמִים
yamiym   sh'natiym   mikeytz vay'hiy

Literally meaning 'from the cutting off', the word מִקֵץ is translated in *Targum Onkelos* as מִסוֹף, related to the word we use for the final forms of some letters when they appear at the end of a word, 'at the end'. It had been two years, two long years for Yosef, languishing in jail while Pharaoh's chief cup-bearer was restored to his position of honour and trust at Pharaoh's court. How often had Yosef wondered what on earth was going on, how much longer he would have to endure before the promises of the famous (or infamous) dreams he had had started to come right.

The issue of timing comes up again and again in the Hebrew Scriptures. We hear Eliyahu HaNavi (Elijah the Prophet) chiding the people of Israel on Mt. Carmel: "How long are you going to jump back and forth between two positions?" (1 Kings 18:21, CJB). King David cries out to God, "How long, Adonai? Will you forget me for ever? How long will You hide Your face from me?" (Psalm 13:2, CJB). Daniel hears two heavenly beings discussing the vision he has just been shown, "How long will the events of the vision last?" (Daniel 8:13, CJB), while the prophet Jeremiah's heart weeps for his people and land, "How long must the land mourn and the grass in all the fields wither?" (Jeremiah 12:4, CJB).

Even Yeshua Himself is concerned about timing. In all three synoptic gospels are recorded, "O faithless and perverse generation, how long shall I be with you? How long shall I bear with you?" (Jeremiah 12:4; Mark 9:19; Luke 9:41, NKJV). The *P'rushim* challenge Yeshua with the same question, "How long do You keep us in doubt?" (John 10:24, NKJV).

A number of contemporary writers have come up with memorable phrases to capture the way in which this question is answered, in essence saying: the moment when God's power is revealed is when His timing and His promises intersect. That is to say, God has a time for each of His

187

promises to be fulfilled and He will bring every circumstance (and, if necessary, all of heaven and earth) to bear to keep His promise and to be shown faithful. Nothing can stand in the way of God's promise when the timing is right for it to happen. We can see this matter-of-fact approach taken in the gospel narratives of Yeshua's birth: "Here is how the birth of Yeshua the Messiah took place. When His mother Miryam was engaged ..." (Matthew 1:18, CJB), "Around this time, Emperor Augustus issued an order for a census to be taken ... In the country nearby were some shepherds spending the night in the fields ..." (Luke 2:1,8, CJB).

Further Study: Romans 5:1-5; Hebrews 12:1-3

Application: Are you aware of the sense of God's timing in your life? Have you felt let down when something didn't happen when you thought it ought to? Pray about seeking God's timing for today.

מִקֵּץ ב׳

Mikketz - At the end - 2

B'resheet / Genesis 41:15 - 38

B'resheet/Genesis 41:15 I dreamed a dream, and to interpret there is not one ...

חֲלוֹם חָלַמְתִּי וּפֹתֵר אֵין אֹתוֹ

oto   eyn   oofoteyr khalam'tiy khalom

In the previous verses we have read that one night Pharaoh, the absolute monarch of Egypt, held by his subjects to be at least semi-divine, had a dream. Not only was he unable to understand it, but after asking all his advisors and court magicians, "there was no-one who could interpret the dream for Pharaoh" (41:8). Pharaoh is troubled: here is an important message from heaven, specially for Pharaoh, delivered personally and very vividly, but Pharaoh cannot understand it and he cannot find anyone in his regular circle who can tell him what it means. So, Yosef is sent for, after the Chief Cupbearer's (belated) testimony and, after a quick shave and change of clothes, is ushered into the royal presence. The text gives us an insight into how desperate Pharaoh is: in front of his whole court, he admits to a Hebrew slave, just dragged in from his own prison, that he dreamed a dream and cannot find anyone to interpret it. The whole spiritual force of Egypt is bankrupt.

Later, at a low point in the spiritual life of our own people, we find Isaiah saying, "So the word of the Lord to them will be, 'Order on order, order on order, line on line, line on line, a little here, a little there'" (Isaiah 28:13, NASB). Amos paints an ever starker picture: "The days are going to come, declares the Almighty Lord, when I will send a famine throughout the land. It won't be an ordinary famine or drought. Instead, there will be a famine of hearing the word of the Lord. People will wander from sea to sea and roam from the north to the east, searching for the word of the Lord. But they won't find it" (Amos 8:11-12, GWT). In Rav Sha'ul's day, the situation was still the same: "For Jews demand signs and Greeks seek wisdom, but we preach Messiah crucified, a stumbling block to Jews and folly to Gentiles" (1 Corinthians 1:22-23, ESV). In all ages and times, people are seeking God but not understanding what they are hearing; they try to interpret what God says to them using the standards and methods of the world but it makes no sense to them.

This need that man has to hear from God is why Peter the *Shaliach* writes, "Always being ready to make a defence to everyone who asks you to give an account for the hope that is in you" (1 Peter 3:15, NASB). We must be ready to share and explain what God has done for us because "a natural man does not accept the things of God; for they are foolishness to him, and he cannot understand them, because they are spiritually appraised" (1 Corinthians 2:14, NASB). Our part is to show patience and concern, to explain without criticising and not making people feel embarrassed when they have to confess - like Pharaoh - that their spiritual state is bankrupt.

Further Study: Romans 10:14-15; 2 Corinthians 5:19-20

Application: How can you be ready today to share with those around you and help to explain their confusion? God can use the simplest words to touch people's lives but you have to be prepared to say them.

מִקֵּץ ג׳

Mikketz - At the end - 3

B'resheet / Genesis 41:39 - 52

B'resheet/Genesis 41:39 After God has caused you to know all this ...

אַחֲרֵי הוֹדִיעַ אֱלֹהִים אוֹתְךָ אֶת־כָּל־זֹאת
zot   kol   et   ot'cha   Elohiym   hodiy'a akharey

Variously translated as "informed" (Artscroll, NASB), "made known" (NIV) and "shown" (ESV, CJB), the verb הוֹדִיעַ is the *Hif'il* - or causative - stem of the root יָדַע which means "to know". The use of this term tells us something important about the process that is happening here: God didn't just tell Yosef what was going to happen, He didn't play the DVD or read the script, God caused Yosef to know. When God causes something to happen it is because this is a part of His plans being moved forward - almost despite the people involved, although in this case Yosef was a willing partner in the proceedings - as He moves people around on the world stage to make things happen. As Pharaoh's words go on to say: "After God has caused you to know all this, there is no-one so discerning or wise as you". The result of Yosef being able to interpret the dream is that Pharaoh is so impressed with Yosef's abilities that he knows that he must have him as his number two; never mind all the other people who had been standing in line for promotion or recognition - none had anything to touch what Yosef had just done.

Throughout Israel's history God continued to arrange external forces to judge and correct our people. "And it will come about in that day, that the Lord will whistle for the fly that is in the remotest part of the rivers of Egypt, and for the bee that is in the land of Assyria. And they will all come ..." (Isaiah 7:18-19, NASB). Not only to rebuke, however, but also to comfort and encourage: "It is I who says of Cyrus, 'He is My shepherd! And he will perform all My desire.' And he declares of Jerusalem, 'She will be built,' and of the temple, 'Your foundation will be laid'" (Isaiah 44:28, NASB). Here it is Cyrus, the king of the Medes and Persians who is used by God to start the rebuilding in the Land and the restoration of the temple after the exile in Babylon. Neither is it only where Israel is concerned that God causes action: "Thus says the Lord

God, 'I will also make the multitude of Egypt cease by the hand of Nebuchabnezzar king of Babylon. He and his people, the most ruthless of the nations, will be brought in to destroy the land; and they will draw their swords against Egypt'" (Ezekiel 30:10-11, NASB).

The Psalmist writes, "Why are the nations in an uproar, the peoples grumbling in vain? The earth's kings are taking positions, leaders conspiring together, against Adonai and His anointed" (Psalm 2:1-2, CJB). The Lord is seen laughing and scoffing at the nations (v4) and terrifying them by speaking to them (v5) before He sets the Son over them to "break them with a rod of iron ... shatter them like earthenware" (v9, NASB). Finally, the Psalmist warns, "Now therefore, O kings, show discernment; take warning, O judges of the earth. Worship the Lord with reverence, and rejoice with trembling. Do homage to the Son, lest He become angry and you perish" (v10-12a, NASB). God is both the director and producer of the largest show on earth, starring none other than His Son!

Further Study: Isaiah 45:1-7; Revelation 19:11-16

Application: In the hurly-burly of every day life, it is very easy to lose sight of just who God is. When we hear on the radio of leaders being raised up or cast down, or revolutions springing up, we should bless our God who holds the whole world in His hand and is certainly still working His purposes out in the affairs of men.

מָקֵּץ 'ד

Mikketz - At the end - 4

B'resheet / Genesis 41:53 - 42:18

B'resheet/Genesis 41:53 And the seven years of abundance were completed

וַתִּכְלֶינָה שֶׁבַע שְׁנֵי הַשָּׂבָע

hasava sh'ney sheva vatich'leynah

Amazingly, none of the major commentators make any reference to this text at all. It is perhaps seen only as the half-way point in the playing out of the prophetic dream that God gave to Pharaoh and Yosef interpreted for him: seven years of plenty followed by seven years of famine. Nahum Sarna merely comments on the prevalence of seven year famines in ancient Egyptian and other Middle Eastern texts, including a reference in the Mesopotamian Gilgamesh Epic.

This obscures the significance that the text relates. The noun הַשָּׂבָע, literally "the abundance", is derived from the root שָׂבַע, which means "to be or become satiated, satisfied, filled" and so has the sense of full satisfaction. These were not just seven years of enough; they were seven years of plenty, of abundance; they were seven years when God poured out His blessing, both in the rainfall producing the annual Nile flooding into the fields and the irrigation reservoirs, and in the fertility and productiveness of the fields themselves. At the same time, the verb וַתִּכְלֶינָה, most often translated simply "ended" comes from the root כָּלָה, which means "to be completed, finished, ended". It was not just that the time period of seven years had elapsed since God has spoken through Yosef and the dream; seven full years of God's blessing had been completed - there was neither day nor bushel of grain missing from what God had said would happen; the years and the harvests were brought to their full completion.

God's consistency with His word and His faithfulness in fulfilling His promises is reinforced time and again in the biblical narratives. At the end of Joshua's life, he gathers the people of Israel, their elders, judges and officers and reminds them of the way in which God has fulfilled the promises to bring them into the Land and clear it before them. "Now behold, today I am going the way of all the earth, and you know in all your hearts and in all your souls that not one word of all the good words which the Lord your God spoke concerning you has failed; all have been fulfilled for you, not one of them has failed" (Joshua 23:14, NASB). In all the years that Joshua had been leading Israel, and in the years before that when he had been Moshe's assistant, God always kept His word. Several hundred years later, as King Solomon is dedicating the Temple, we find him using very similar words: "Blessed be the Lord, who has given rest to His people, according to all that He promised; not one word has failed of all His good promise, which He promised through Moshe His servant" (1 Kings 8:56, NASB). During those intervening years, although there had been many ups and downs through the time of the judges until the kingdom was united under David, God's promises - of both blessing and discipline - had been faithfully kept by Him, and His people were the living witness of that as they stood with Solomon before the Temple.

In the years that followed, some of them dark years with much trouble and strife, God spoke again lest any should think either that the promises were all fulfilled so that there was nothing left to do, or that God had somehow changed His mind about the whole thing: "For as the rain and the snow come down from heaven, and do not return there without watering the earth, and making it bear and sprout, and furnishing seed to the sower and bread to the eater; so shall My word be which goes forth from My mouth; it shall not return to Me empty, without accomplishing what I desire, and without succeeding in the matter for which I sent it" (Isaiah 55:10-11, NASB). God promises continuity in His word being fulfilled: as the cycle of nature continues year by year, so God's word and promises will continue to be fulfilled.

Further Study: Psalm 34:8-14; 1 Thessalonians 5:23-24

Application: If you find yourself questioning whether God can still be trusted, whether He has forgotten you, or whether He can still reach into your life and circumstances, take heart from the seven fully completed years. Just as God did exactly what He said in the days of Yosef and Pharaoh, He has demonstrated over and over again what He can and will do today!

מִקֵּץ ה'

Mikketz - At the end - 5

B'resheet / Genesis 42:19 - 43:15

B'resheet/Genesis 42:19-20 If you are honest ... and your words will be true and you will not die

אִם-כֵּנִים אַתֶּם ... וְיֵאָמְנוּ דִבְרֵכֶם וְלֹא
v'lo   div'reychem v'yey'am'nu ...   atem   keynim   im

תָּמוּתוּ
tamutu

These are Yosef's words to his brothers; Yosef, who might be pardoned a little wariness and skepticism with the men who had so hated him that they had sold him to a band of passing slave traders! כֵּנִים is a plural adjective from the root כּוּן, which has a variety of meanings around being fixed, established, confirmed; כֵּן is used as an adverb to mean "thus, so, rightly", and the adjective form is usually translated as "upright, true, honest". The context here is the brothers' first trip to Egypt, at the behest of their father, to buy grain because of the famine in Canaan; Yosef knows who they are, but they will not know his identity until the show-down at the end of their second visit. Yosef has accused them of being spies, and after keeping them in prison for three days is now giving them an opportunity to bring Benjamin down to Egypt to "verify" their story about their family origins and their intentions in Egypt.

The root אָמַן, here in the form of וְיֵאָמְנוּ, includes the meanings "to be firm, true, faithful" and is the source of the word אֱמוּנָה, steadiness, truth, faithfulness which is the word most frequently used in the Hebrew Scriptures for "faith". It is fascinating that the *Torah* - in Yosef's mouth - links the truth of the brother's vows with them staying alive. Sforno comments - as Yosef is about to send the brothers back home - that Yosef is implying, "for even in Canaan I can have you put to death if you do not return to verify your story"; the power of Yosef's Egyptian arm can reach that far!

195

Rashi amplifies the phrase, "your words will be verified" by connecting it to two other verses. The first is the response that the woman accused of adultery has to say before the Priest when she accepts the imprecations of the curse of the water of bitterness upon herself: "And the woman shall say, 'Amen, Amen'" (B'Midbar 5:22, NASB) - may it be so; she is accepting the trial by ordeal, trusting in the Lord to vindicate her against her husband's suspicions: may the water of bitterness show that I have not been unfaithful. Rashi's second illustration comes from Solomon's prayer of dedication when the temple has been built and the Ark of the Covenant has been brought in; Solomon stands before the altar in the presence of all the people and prays, "Now therefore, O God of Israel, let Your word, I pray you, be confirmed which You have spoken to Your servant, my father David" (1 Kings 8:26, NASB). This echoes David's own words: "Now therefore, O Lord God, the word that You have spoken concerning Your servant and his house, confirm it forever, and do as You have spoken" (2 Samuel 7:25, NASB). Both David and Solomon are saying in essence: let Your word come true, let Your word be proved true by Your fulfillment of it.

Yeshua addresses the issues of our words and our actions being consistent in the Sermon on the Mount in Matthew's gospel. After reminding His audience that God requires people to keep their vows, and pointing out what nonsense it is to suggest that a vow must be kept if sworn on some holy object, but may be broken if sworn on some other - perhaps not so holy - object, He tell us that a simple 'Yes' or 'No' should be enough. When we have made a commitment - given our word - we need to make sure that we always follow through and do what we have said we will (Matthew 5:33-37).

But there is another side to this that Yosef's original words to the brothers reveal: "If you are men of truth, your words will be true and you won't die." True words validate that a person is true. We have focussed so far on validating our words by our actions, but anyone can do that on occasion. Yosef is challenging his brothers about whether they are true people: established, firm, reliable, men of integrity. The answer to his question will come later when, at the crux of the story, Judah steps forward and offers to take Benjamin's punishment for stealing Yosef's cup, so that their father will not loose another son. It is at this point that Yosef can see that the brothers - well, some at least - have become men of truth and honour. To use a modern example, parents (rightly) urge their children not to watch 18/R-rated movies, citing Rav Shaul: "In conclusion, brothers, focus your thoughts on what is true, noble, righteous, pure, lovable or admirable, on some virtue or on something praiseworthy" (Philippians 4:8, CJB), but then have a few 18/R-rated DVDs sitting on their own shelves that they don't watch in front of the children - thus completely undermining their admonitions because the words are not coming from the parents' own practice. The words themselves are true, but they do not come from a place of truth. God calls us not only to speak the truth, but to speak it from a heart and mind of truth; a life of truth committed to Him.

Further Study: Psalm 119:57-60; Jeremiah 11:4b-5

Application: How consistent is your life with what you say? Can God use you to speak to people because you will speak from truth? Now is the time to "break up your fallow ground" (Jeremiah 4:3) and allow the Lord to move in your life.

מִקֵּץ 'ו

Mikketz - At the end - 6

B'resheet / Genesis 43:16 - 29

B'resheet/Genesis 43:16 ... for the men shall eat with me at noon.

כִּי אִתִּי יֹאכְלוּ הָאֲנָשִׁים בַּצָּהֳרָיִם:

batza'harayim ha'anashiym   yochlu   itiy   kiy

While some commentators are interested in why this dinner appointment is being arranged - Sforno, for example, suggests that Yosef wanted to test his brothers by watching to see if they exhibited signs of jealousy when Benjamin was given larger portions of food than the others - most of the interest in this verse seems to be drawn to the last word, בַּצָּהֳרָיִם. Usually translated "at noon" (NASB, ESV, NIV, RSV), the word is based on an unused root צָהַר, possibly meaning "to shine" (Davidson). The noun צֹהַר can be a light or a window, and here in the dual form - a form that is neither singular or plural, but means exactly two - it is taken to mean "noon". *Targum Onkelos* opts to remove the time element altogether and substitutes בְּשֵׁירוּתָא, "the first meal"; Radak explains that this was because the mid-day meal was the first meal of princes and judges, who were earlier involved in public affairs. Rashi tries to point out that *Onkelos's* choice is unusual, for although the Aramaic word chosen is used many times for "meal" in the Talmud, all the other translations of צָהֳרָיִם in Scripture are translated using the Aramaic טִיהֲרָא, the formal word for "noon". Rashi feels that this must have been deliberate; the sense of the meal and which one it was, was more important than the exact time at which it took place. Pondering the use of the dual form, Hirsch comments that, "Mid-day is just a point in time. No man dines at mid-day. But until mid-day, light overcomes night; from there onwards, night progressively conquers light. צָהֳרָיִם is the hour, half of which is filled with the growing and the other half with the waning light."

To sum up, then, the commentators are talking about an event that certainly happened, that had importance because of which meal it was, which in turn was dependent on the people involved - in particular, Yosef at whose house and on whose schedule it was held - and for which the exact time was less important than as one of the indications of the significance of the meal itself. A similar time precision and yet obvious imprecision can be seen in the account of the final plague - the death of the firstborn - when God brought our people out of Egypt: "Now it came about at midnight that the Lord struck all the first-born in the land of Egypt, from the first-born of Pharaoh who sat on his throne to the first-born of the captive who was in the dungeon, and all the first-born of cattle" (Shemot 12:29, NASB). This clearly took time, as the following verses show in their description of the Egyptian reaction to the calamity, but is an accurate fulfillment of God's words to Moshe earlier in the chapter: "For I will go through the land of Egypt on that night, and will strike down all the first-born in the land of Egypt, both man and beast; and against all the gods of Egypt I will execute judgments - I am the Lord" (v. 12, NASB). Midnight is here used for a indefinite pointer to some point during the middle hours of darkness; it was an event that certainly happened, the importance of which is emphasised by the use of a precise word without actually intending that the exact meaning of the word be taken literally.

Neatly side-stepping the issue of which words and contexts should be taken literally and which are meant to be interpreted figuratively, the Gospels talk of future events with similar certainty but imprecision. During the story of the giving of sight to the man who had been born blind, following His explanation that sin was not involved in this man's blindness, Yeshua throws the *talmidim* a theological puzzle: "We must work the works of Him who sent Me, as long as it is day; night is coming, when no man can work. While I am in the world, I am the light of the world" (John 9:4-5, NASB). The miracle that had just been performed was a part of the work that Yeshua was doing, at His Father's behest. As long as He was present in the world, it was still day-time, but night - when, although He made post-resurrection appearances and remains the King in heaven, He is not "in the world" in the same way as He was when He spoke to the disciples - was coming when He would not be working in the same face-to-face way. William Hendriksen comments that the word translated "'as long as' here, as in most other instances, refers to a rather indefinite time relationship; Yeshua is not saying just how long He will be in the world." His departure is certain, but the time - at least for the disciples - remains vague and hidden.

Similarly, when speaking about the Last Judgement and the resurrection, Yeshua says: "Truly, truly, I say to you, an hour is coming and now is, when the dead shall hear the voice of the Son of God; and those who hear shall live" (John 5:25, NASB). Those who are spiritually dead, both at the time that He spoke and in the years since that time, hear His words and in hearing and receiving them enter eternal life. But Yeshua's ministry on earth took place over several years; those who heard and believed Him at the first are no less alive than the thief on the cross who was one of the last to hear and believe during those years; the "hour" referred not to the 60 minute hour within which Yeshau spoke, but to the period in God's history. Barely a breath later, Yeshua added, "for an hour is coming, in which all who are in the tombs shall hear His voice, and shall come forth" (vv. 28-29, NASB), referring to the time of the resurrection when according to Daniel, "And many of those who sleep in the dust of the ground will awake, these to everlasting life, but the others to disgrace and everlasting contempt" (Daniel 12:2, NASB). Again, a certainty that is already scheduled exactly on God's calendar; it will take some physical time, but was indefinite to the disciples and remains so for us in this day.

In many parables, Yeshua urges His *talmidim* to be ready for the day of His return, without telling them when it will be except for generalities that serve to emphasise the importance of the event. His words, "But of that day and hour no one knows, not even the angels of heaven, nor the Son, but the Father alone. For the coming of the Son of Man will be just like the days of Noah" (Matthew 24:36-37, NASB), are an allusion to the Day of Trumpets (*Yom Teruah*), which as the only feast that falls on the first day of the month is impossible to know in advance exactly when the New Moon will appear. This has led some scholars to suggest that Yeshua's return will be at the time of year of the Autumn Feasts, but we really don't know. The virgins were urged to have their lamps filled with oil at all times; the stewards were urged to attend to their masters' business and make sure that all the servants were properly fed and ready for their return; other servants were given investments to maximise a return before their master returned - all very certain events that would definitely happen but couched in time-indefinite ways. We simply have to be ready at any hour to receive Him back!

What of specific instructions or indications that we have been given in the meantime? If we are to be ready all the time, how do we avoid the curse of the modern financial word - short-termism - and invest for a long-term yield for the Kingdom of God? Some feel that they have been called to missionary or teaching work overseas; this may take years of preparation and training from the point at which they first felt God's call until the point of execution, but the preparation must be done and done properly if they are to be equipped for that work - if the Lord should return before that point has arrived, then they will still have been faithful in working towards the goal they were given. One brother was told some years ago that he would have an opportunity to preach in China; this has not yet arrived, but he is ready to answer that call when the moment comes and in the meantime is continuing to faithfully preach and teach in the work where he is currently engaged. So it is for all of us - we are to be ready now and preparing always for the future; available for the Lord so that when He calls, we will be ready to eat with Him at noon!

Further Study: Habakkuk 2:3; Romans 13:11; 2 Peter 3:9-10

Application: Are you caught in either of the traps the enemy sets for our souls: simply getting on with life while not believing that Yeshua will ever return, or stuck like a rabbit in the headlights of a car unable to plan for or see a future because Yeshua might be back next week? Come back to Scripture and see the balance that is there between the certainty of His return and the deliberate hiding of the time. Ask the Holy Spirit to set you free to be ready and invest in the future at the same time.

מִקֵּץ ז׳

Mikketz - At the end - 7

B'resheet / Genesis 43:30 - 44:17

B'resheet/Genesis 43:30 And Yosef was quick, for his feelings were warmed towards his brother and he was about to weep

וַיְמַהֵר יוֹסֵף כִּי־נִכְמְרוּ רַחֲמָיו אֶל־אָחִיו

akhiyv   el   rakhamayv nich'm'ru kiy   Yoseyf vaymahar

וַיְבַקֵּשׁ לִבְכּוֹת

liv'kot   vayvakeysh

The Hebrew text contains two idioms here that we need to understand. The verb נִכְמְרוּ, a *Niphal* affix 3mp form from the root כָּמַר, is most often connected with warming or burning food although it can be used for plaiting or braiding. Rashi gives several examples of the way the word is used: in the Mishnah, the phrase עַל הַכּוֹמֶר שֶׁל זֵתִים - on the *komer* of olives - refers to a vessel where olives are heated to soften them for oil extraction (*b.* Bava Metzia 74*a*); the Talmud uses a related Aramaic word מִכְמַר בְּשָׂרָא - the meat becoming warm (*b.* Pesachim 58*a*); in the book of Lamentations, the verse עוֹרֵנוּ כְּתַנּוּר נִכְמָרוּ - "our skin, like an oven, was scorched" (Lamentations 5:10). Sarna points out that the two words נִכְמְרוּ רַחֲמָיו only occurs in one other place in the Tanakh during the story of King Solomon arbitrating between two mothers over the living child - "The woman whose son was alive was filled with compassion for her son" (1 Kings 3:26, NIV) - where they mean "to have compassion for".

Sarna also helps us out with the second idiom by explaining that וַיְבַקֵּשׁ - a 3ms *vav*-conversive *Pi'el* form of the root בָּקַשׁ, apparently only used in the *Pi'el* or *Pu'al* stems - should be translated "on the verge of". He adds, "The root בקש in post-biblical Hebrew (i.e. *m.* Yoma 1:7) and its Aramaic equivalent בעי (i.e. Daniel 2:13) often carry the meaning 'to be about to'.. So instead of the impression that Joseph wanted or needed to cry, the strength of his emotions was such that he was unable to prevent himself from weeping any longer.

Hirsch takes us one step further with כָּמַר by noting that a plural form of the word - הַכְּמָרִים - is used (in 2 Kings 23:5 and Zephaniah 1:14) to refer to idolatrous priests, that offered sacrifices to idols. Without any true spirituality, they have to rely on heating up the emotions to produce a religious feeling, while the true priests - הַכֹּהֲנִים - do not need to stir up emotional heat; they have the reality of covenant relationship with the One True God to inspire their worship and service.

The Gospels show us a number of occasions when Yeshua showed varying degrees of emotion and had compassion on the people around Him. Early in His ministry, He came ashore from a boat and "When He saw the crowds, He had compassion on them because they were harried and helpless, like sheep without a shepherd" (Matthew 9:36, CJB); on another occasion, "when there was a great multitude and they had nothing to eat, He called His disciples and said to them, 'I feel compassion for the multitude because they have remained with Me now three days, and have nothing to eat; and if I send them away hungry to their home, they will faint on the way; and some of them have come from a distance'" (Mark 8:1-3, NASB). Yeshua's compassion moved Him to raising the dead: "The next day Yeshua, accompanied by His talmidim and a large crowd, went to a town called Na'im. As He approached the town gate, a dead man was being carried out for burial. His mother was a widow, this had been her only son, and a sizeable crowd from the town was with her. When the Lord saw her, He felt compassion for her and said to her, 'Don't cry'" (Luke 7:11-13, CJB) and healing the people who cried out to Him: "And moved with compassion, Yeshua touched their eyes; and immediately they regained their sight and followed Him" (Matthew 20:34, NASB) even if that involved touching people, coming into contact with ritual impurity or sharing their emotions. When Lazarus, the brother of Marta and Miryam, the family in Bethany where He had stayed and taught several times, died, the text tells that - even though Yeshua knew that He was about to raise Lazarus back to life - He so identified with the weeping sisters that He wept (John 11:35). He also told stories where His characters displayed similar compassion, so that they helped others in the same way that He did: "But a man from Shomron who was traveling came upon him; and when he saw him, he was moved with compassion. So he went up to him, put oil and wine on his wounds and bandaged them. Then he set him on his own donkey, brought him to an inn and took care of him" (Luke 10:33-34, CJB).

Here there is no whipped up false emotion, but a moving or warming of Yeshua's spirit in mercy and compassion for the people with whom He interacts. Where there is a need, He is aware of it and moves to satisfy that need; where a supernatural touch is required, He does not shrink from providing it or withhold healing. In fact, on no less than three occasions

Matthew tells us that Yeshua healed everyone who had come to Him (4:24, 8:16, 12:15). Not allowing demons to speak or to create a fuss, He simply spoke with plain authority to cast them out and release the people whom they were oppressing. While clearly miraculous, so that people were amazed at His authority and power, there is no mention whatever of hysteria or wild uncontrolled displays of emotion; Yeshua's ministry was almost shockingly matter of fact and down to earth.

Our text from the *parasha* tells us that Yosef was quick - he hurried through the formalities - so that he could leave the room because his compassion had been aroused. Similarly, with the exception of a deliberate postponement before going to raise Lazarus, Yeshua never delayed ministering to people who cried out to Him or came to Him. He wasn't so concerned with formalities but directly asked people, "What do you want Me to do for you?" (Matthew 20:32); He spoke immediately into their need. He calls us to do the same and to be moved with compassion for those we see around us and who He places in our path.

Visiting Jerusalem, a high point for any Jew, Yeshua was struck by the needs of the city and moved by His prophetic vision of the destruction that was to be brought on the city in only 40 short years' time, He showed compassion by weeping. "When Yeshua had come closer and could see the city, He wept over it, saying, 'If you only knew today what is needed for shalom! But for now it is hidden from your sight. For the days are coming upon you when your enemies will set up a barricade around you, encircle you, hem you in on every side, and dash you to the ground, you and your children within your walls, leaving not one stone standing on another - and all because you did not recognize your opportunity when God offered it!'" (Luke 19:41-44, CJB). Jerusalem failed to act when it had the option to do so. Over generations, in spite of the prophets being sent to speak and warn the people of the city, they failed to act so that finally a time of judgement would come. We too are called to act, to seize the moment when it presents itself and make the Kingdom of God a reality in our day.

Further Study: Psalm 119:57-60; Daniel 9:24; Luke 13:34-35

Application: How can you overcome inertia in your life? Ask God to help you be warmed with His compassion and then to act or speak as the Spirit leads you to address the situations He shows you.

רַיִּגַּשׁ

Vayigash - And he approached

B'resheet / Genesis 44:18 - 47:27

רִאשׁוֹן	Aliyah One	B'resheet/Genesis 44:18 - 30
שֵׁנִי	Aliyah Two	B'resheet/Genesis 44:31 - 45:7
שְׁלִישִׁי	Aliyah Three	B'resheet/Genesis 45:8 - 18
רְבִיעִי	Aliyah Four	B'resheet/Genesis 45:19 - 27
חֲמִשִׁי	Aliyah Five	B'resheet/Genesis 45:28 - 46:27
שִׁשִׁי	Aliyah Six	B'resheet /Genesis 46:28 - 47:10
שְׁבִיעִי	Aliyah Seven	B'resheet/Genesis 47:11 - 27

וַיִּגַּשׁ א׳

Vayigash - And he approached - 1

B'resheet / Genesis 44:18 - 30

B'resheet/Genesis 44:18 Then Y'hudah approached Yosef and said, "Please my lord! Let your servant say something ..."

וַיִּגַּשׁ אֵלָיו יְהוּדָה וַיֹּאמֶר בִּי אֲדֹנִי

adoniy   biy   vayomer   Y'hudah   eylayv vayigash

יְדַבֶּר־נָא עַבְדְּךָ דָבָר

davar   av'd'cha   na y'dabeyr

The Vilna Gaon sees great significance in Y'hudah being the one who steps forward at this point in the story of Yosef and his brothers, although Y'hudah is only the fourth oldest in the family. He points out that in last week's *parasha*, Y'hudah said, "If I fail to bring [Binyamin] to you ... let me bear the blame forever" (B'resheet 43:9, CJB). The Gaon suggests that Y'hudah was pledging his place in the World to Come for his brother's safety to his father. When, therefore, Yosef confirms that he intends to keep Binyamin as his slave as punishment for stealing Yosef's cup [a frame], Y'hudah speaks up and asks to enter a mitigating plea - for Binyamin, for their father and for himself.

We can see a strong precedent here of one pledging himself for another and then speaking up in that other's defence in order to redeem or make good on the pledge, even offering himself as a forfeit against the failure of that other.

The Psalmist is quite clear when he says, "Who shall ascend to the hill of the Lord, and who shall stand in His holy place? He who has clean hands and a pure heart, who has not lifted up his soul to an idol nor sworn in vain" (Psalm 24:3-4), then prophetically describes God observing mankind, "all turn aside, all alike are corrupt, no-one does what is right, not a single one" (Psalm 14:3, CJB). Yet God Himself pledged for our souls when He said, "I will free you ... I will rescue you ... I will redeem you ... I will take you as My people, and I will be your God" (Shemot 6:6-7). With all our failures, how was this to be done?

Following the same precedent, having given His pledge, God offered

Himself in the person of Yeshua the Messiah as the forfeit for our sin: "We all, like sheep, went astray; we turned, each one, to his own way; yet Adonai laid on Him the guilt of all of us" (Isaiah 53:6, CJB). God effected what Derek Prince called 'the great exchange', "[God] made Him who knew no sin to be sin on our behalf, that we might become the righteousness of God in Him" (2 Corinthians 5:21, NASB). Yeshua spoke up for us, "Father, forgive them, for they know not what they do" (Luke 23:34, ESV), then redeemed His pledge, rising from death to proclaim His victory, "O Death, where is your victory? O Death, where is your sting?" (1 Corinthians 15:55, NASB).

Further Study: John 15:12-13; Romans 5:6-8

Application: Have you accepted the great exchange offered by God? Do you know forgiveness and peace with God because Yeshua has redeemed you Himself? Call out to Him and know His peace today.

וַיִּגַּשׁ ב׳

Vayigash - And he approached - 2

B'resheet / Genesis 44:31 - 45:7

B'resheet/Genesis 44:33 And now, your servant will stay, please, in place of the youth: the servant of my lord

וְעַתָּה יֵשֶׁב־נָא עַבְדְּךָ תַּחַת הַנַּעַר עָבֶד
eved   hana'ar takhat   av'd'cha na yeyshev v'atah

לַאדֹנִי
ladoniy

Nechama Leibowitz points out that the word - slave, servant or bondman - occurs thirteen times in Y'hudah's oration to Yosef and twice in this particular verse. It is "underlining their humble posture in front of the mighty ruler," she concludes. The Ramban comments that Y'hudah is telling Yosef that he would rather become a permanent servant than go back to his father without Binyamin; that since Y'hudah stood surety for Binyamin's safe return (v32), his 'punishment' should be that he will substitute now for Binyamin's 'punishment' and remain in Egypt while Binyamin goes home to his father.

Here is a clear case of penal substitution: one taking the place or punishment of another. God can be seen doing the same thing: "For I am the Lord your God, the Holy One of Israel, your Saviour; I have given Egypt as your ransom, Cush and Seba in your place. Since you are precious in My sight, since you are honoured and I love you, I will give other men in your place and other peoples in exchange for your life" (Isaiah 43:3-4, NASB). Later on, Isaiah prophesies of the ultimate substitution (or 'great exchange' as Derek Prince called it), "We're all like sheep who've wandered off and got lost. We've all done our own thing, gone our own way. And God has piled all our sins, everything we've done wrong, on Him, on Him," (Isaiah 53:6, The Message).

In Yeshua's own time, Caiaphas - the high priest - "had advised the Jews that it was expedient for one man to die on behalf of the people" (John 18:14, NASB). Better that an innocent - if, from the religious leaders' point of view, somewhat troublesome - man should die than that the Romans should crush a popular uprising and end up killing many people, or take away what little freedom the Jewish people still retained to govern their own affairs.

It is Rav Sha'ul, however, who pulls the issue into sharp focus. "For while we were still helpless, at the right time, the Messiah died on behalf of ungodly people. Now it is a rare event when someone gives up his life even for the sake of somebody righteous, although possibly for a truly good person one might have the courage to die. But God demonstrates His own love for us in that the Messiah died on our behalf while we were still sinners" (**Romans 5:6-8, CJB**). Although we have no excuse before God, all of us having sinned (Romans 3:23), yet Yeshua voluntarily laid His life that we might be free; He took our punishment, although He deserved none, so that we could be restored to relationship with God.

Further Study: Romans 8:31-36; 2 Corinthians 5:21

Application: Today is a day to rejoice in your freedom. Know not only that God loves you, but that He gave His Son as a ransom for your sin so that He might know you and you could call Him 'Father'.

וַיִּגַּשׁ 'ג

Vayigash - And he approached - 3

B'resheet / Genesis 45:8 - 18

B'resheet/Genesis 45:8 "And now, it was not you that sent me here ..."

וְעַתָּה לֹא־אַתֶּם שְׁלַחְתֶּם אֹתִי הֵנָּה
heynah   otiy   sh'lakh'tem   atem   lo   v'atah

Sforno comments, perhaps somewhat wryly, "Now that you realise the Divine plan and purpose behind all this, a design which could not have been achieved without the earlier conflicts." Putting those words into Yosef's mouth, he demonstrates how although we pray and ask God to do things, we often cannot recognise the hand of God at work until afterwards, looking back with hindsight. Was it reasonable - within a few moments of discovering that this mighty Egyptian official was their brother Yosef, whom they had sold into slavery some twenty or so years ago and almost certainly had given up for dead - to expect these bewildered brothers to recognise the providence of God? "Now that you recognise the Divine plan ..." - that's a pretty tall order.

Richard Bauckham speaks about the way in which God is both novel and consistent: "He may act in new and surprising ways, in which He proves to be the same God, consistent with His known identity, but in unexpected ways. He may be trusted to be consistent with Himself, but He may surprise us in the ways He proves consistent with Himself. The consistency can only be appreciated with hindsight." So here, no-one could have predicted the sequence of events that led Yosef through sibling rivalry, slavery and prison to the most exalted position in Egypt, wielding an enormous power that affected the whole of the Middle East region for decades. Yet, looking back, we can see how God started sowing the seeds and gave specific promises and commitments to Avraham, Yitz'khak and Ya'akov, not to mention Yosef himself, that to the original hearers must have sounded a little strange, yet to us who see the whole picture from the end are really quite obvious indications of what is about to happen.

Imagine the surprise felt by the crowd surrounding the stake when Yeshua cried out, "Father, forgive them; for they do not know what they are doing" (Luke 23;34, NASB). At that moment they were unable to really see what was happening; they certainly saw the physical events of the crucifixion - for many of the crowd or those there in an official capacity, yet another crucifixion, one of many the Romans used as a deterrent to the unhappy people of Judea - but they were too close to be able to see the big picture. The disciples couldn't see it in spite of having been warned beforehand: "We are now going up to Jerusalem, where the Son of Man will be handed over to the head cohanim and Torah-teachers. They will sentence Him to death and turn Him over to the Goyim, who will jeer at Him, beat Him and execute Him on a stake as a criminal" (Matthew 20:18-19, CJB). The centurion in charge of the execution squad nearly saw it when he said, "Truly this was the Son of God" (Matthew 27:54, NASB). But it takes the hindsight of Peter some 53 days later to be able to recognise that, "this man was arrested in accordance with God's predetermined plan and foreknowledge; and, through the agency of persons not bound by the Torah, you raised Him up on a stake and killed Him" (Acts 2:23, CJB).

Further Study: Isaiah 42:5-9; Ephesians 1:9-12

Application: When we are in the heat of the fire we are often too distracted by the flames to be able to see the plan of God being worked out. If this is so for you today, then take a few moments to ask God to pull your head back from the bricks so that you can see the whole wall and recognise what He is doing in your life.

וַיִּגַּשׁ ד'

Vayigash - And he approached - 4

B'resheet / Genesis 45:19 - 27

B'resheet/Genesis 45:19 And you, you are commanded, "Do this: take for yourselves ..."

... לָכֶם קְחוּ עֲשׂוּ זֹאת צֻוֵּיתָה וְאַתָּה

... lachem k'khu asu zot tzuveytah v'atah

Rashi jumps straight in with: "**and you are commanded** by my mouth - to say to them - 'Do this.' Thus you shall say them, that it is with my permission." Pharaoh is speaking and is making sure that Yosef knows that Pharaoh is not just giving his permission to fetch his family from Canaan, but is positively telling him to do it. Moreover, since the verbs in the command are in the plural, we can also deduce that Pharaoh is also telling Yosef to pass the command on to his brothers and ultimately to Ya'akov, so that he too may obey Pharaoh and come down to Egypt.

Hirsch comments that this is a "very fine touch by the Egyptian ruler", for although Yosef really had the power and authority to do this for himself, Pharaoh steps in to make sure that Yosef overcomes his scruples at not wanting to abuse his position. It is as if Pharaoh is saying, "I know that you could do this yourself, but you are hesitating because you don't want to be seen to be taking advantage of your position, so I will give you my authority and approval to go ahead and do it; then no-one will question your motives or integrity."

Sforno adds that Pharaoh is making sure that Yosef passes his command to his brothers and father "so that you realise this objective, and your father not refuse to come." Commenting to verse 16, Sforno has already adduced that Pharaoh thinks that it will be good for Egypt that Yosef's family should all be there so that Yosef should be settled and secure, not worrying about his father and wanting to go to Canaan to see him, but able to concentrate fully on the affairs of state that Pharaoh has entrusted to him. Pharaoh wants Ya'akov and all his sons to come and settle in Egypt; he doesn't want Yosef to get distracted, to settle for just sending food and supplies to Canaan - the command ensures that Yosef will stay focused and not lose sight of Pharaoh's (and God's) purpose: getting Ya'akov and his whole family down to Egypt.

So it is with us: God has plans and purposes that we need to work out in our lives, affecting not only ourselves but those that we are responsible for - parents, spouse, children - and those around us - work colleagues, friends, neighbours and acquaintances - and He doesn't want us to get distracted by other issues and concerns, but to stay focused on accomplishing what we need to do. Rav Sha'ul wrote to Timothy: "Don't let anyone look down on you ... pay attention to the public reading of the Scriptures. Do not neglect your gift ... be diligent about this work, throw yourself into it ... Pay attention to yourself and to the teaching" (1 Timothy 4:12-16, CJB). Surely, all these things would have been exactly what Timothy wanted to do, the way he would have been conducting his ministry? Yes, but Rav Sha'ul wants to encourage him so that Timothy doesn't get distracted from any of the key parts of his faith and work, that he doesn't lose sight of where he is going or the purpose of what he is doing. Rav Sha'ul finishes, "continue in it, for by so doing you will deliver both yourself and those who hear you" (1 Timothy 4:16b, CJB); the success of Timothy's impact on both himself and others depends on his determination to follow through on his instructions, calling and vision. Each of us, then, is also called and chosen - "for such a time as this" (Esther 4:14) - and we have to stay "on target" if we are to hit our mark.

Further Study: Isaiah 49:1-3; 1 John 3:23-24

Application: Is there something in your life that you know God has told you to do and - over time - you have lost sight of the objective or come to think that it can't be done - at least by you - or perhaps you wonder if you misheard in the first place? If so, then now is the time to refocus and recalibrate! Ask God to re-confirm what He said, to give you a fresh vision of where you are and where you need to be, and then make a firm commitment before God to get there. Why not share that with someone close to you as a means of both accountability and encouragement.

וַיִּגַּשׁ 'ה

Vayigash - And he approached - 5

B'resheet / Genesis 45:28 - 46:27

B'resheet/Genesis 45:28 And Israel said, "Great! My son Yosef is still alive!"

וַיֹּאמֶר יִשְׂרָאֵל רַב עוֹד־יוֹסֵף בְּנִי חָי

khay   b'niy Yoseyf   od   rav   Yisra'el   vayomer

Focusing on the pointing here, notice where the *maqqef* is positioned in this text. Without it, we might have been tempted to group the words רַב עוֹד together to translate as "Enough already", so having Israel commanding his sons to stop telling him any more about Yosef because he had already decided - as the rest of the verse goes on to tell us - to go to Egypt to visit and see his long-lost son. The *maqqef*, however, forces us to take רַב as a free-standing adjective or exclamation, translated perhaps a little flippantly here as "Great!", leaving the עוֹד to combine with יוֹסֵף and produce the sense "still-Yosef lives". Rashi implies a couple of words and comments: "רַב - There is much joy and gladness for me because 'my son Yosef still lives'." This follows nicely from the last words of the previous verse that tell us that when Ya'akov has heard the news of Yosef's life and position in Egypt and saw the wagons that had been sent to collect him, "the spirit of their father Ya'akov was revived" (v. 27). After twenty years of mourning for his son, Ya'akov's spirits rise and - almost - for the first time in all these years, he has something to look forward to.

In 1 Kings 17 we find the start of the ministry of Elijah. After he has stayed with the widow of Zerepath and they have experienced the miracle of the jar of flour and cruise of oil, the widow's son dies; Elijah prays and *Hashem* restores the boy to life. "Elijah said, 'See, your son is alive.' Then the woman said to Elijah, 'Now I know that you are a man of God, and that the word of the Lord in your mouth is truth'" (1 Kings 17:23-24, NASB). Even though they have survived the drought and famine by the supernatural provision of flour and oil, yet it takes this miracle of restoring the dead boy to life to elicit this confession of faith from the widow: "Now I know ..." Perhaps in the shock of her son dying she had forgotten the flour and oil; perhaps because that miracle happened every day it had become commonplace and so diminished in value or impact; the way she now speaks is strongly reminiscent of the blind man whose sight had been given to him who, when questioned about the way it had happened, simply replied, "One thing I do know, that, whereas I was blind, now I see" (John 9:25, NASB).

Sometimes it seems that only seeing is believing! How would another parent - Miryam, the mother of Yeshua - receive the news that her son, publicly crucified, pronounced dead and then buried only three days before, was now alive again? The account in Mark's gospel reads: "When Yeshua rose early Sunday, He appeared first to Miryam of Magdala ... she went and told those who had been with Him ... but when they heard that He was alive and that she had seen Him, they wouldn't believe it. After that, Yeshua appeared in another form to two of them as they were walking into the country. They went and told the others, but they didn't believe them either" (Mark 16:9-13, CJB). This was difficult to swallow: everyone had seen Yeshua die and knew that it had been three days; after all, Elijah prayed for the widow's son on the day he died, and although Ya'akov had to wait over twenty years, Yosef hadn't really died. They all of them forgot Lazarus, whom Yeshua had raised from the dead after three days only a week or so ago! Luke's account sums up the disciple's reaction: "The emissaries didn't believe them; in fact, they thought what they said was utter nonsense" (Luke 24:11, CJB). It took several reappearances over the next few days to convince all the *talmidim* and Yeshua spent the next 40 days with them, teaching and encouraging them before He ascended into heaven.

Yet barely two weeks later - on the day of *Shavuot* - three thousand people, many of whom had come into Jerusalem for the feast and so had at best only heard of Yeshua, became believers. Hearing and believing the eye-witness testimony of those disciples, they accepted the reality of the resurrection and witnessed not only *Ruach*-inspired preaching but an outpouring of signs and wonders in the same way as Yeshua Himself started His ministry in the Galil. Years later, another biblical author wrote, "This deliverance, which was first declared by the Lord, was confirmed to us by those who heard Him; while God also bore witness to it with various signs, wonders and miracles" (Hebrews 2:3-4, CJB). So we can have confidence to believe in a God who does miracles and whose Son was raised from the dead. Like Ya'akov, we too can say: Enough already, I believe! Like Job we can proclaim: "I know that my Redeemer lives!" (Job 19:25, CJB).

Further Study: 2 Kings 4:32-37; John 20:29

Application: Where do you stand? Are you one of these proof people who are holding out for the final verdict before casting your vote? Sometimes we have to go on the available evidence and the balance of probability - if God is speaking to you, then you need to answer His call - what more evidence do you need? Respond and you'll find out quick enough that you have all the evidence you need.

וַיִּגַּשׁ

Vayigash - And he approached - 6

B'resheet / Genesis 46:28 - 47:10

B'resheet/Genesis 46:28 And he sent Judah before him to Yosef to clear before him to Goshen.

וְאֶת־יְהוּדָה שָׁלַח לְפָנָיו אֶל־יוֹסֵף לְהוֹרֹת

l'horot   Yoseyf   el   l'fanayv shalakh Y'hudah   v'et

לְפָנָיו גֹּשְׁנָה

Gosh'nah l'fanayv

The verb לְהוֹרֹת, a *Hif'il* infinitive construct from the root יָרָה, has generated discussion among the commentators. The basic root meaning is "to throw, cast; to shoot, as an arrow" (Davidson), but can also cover laying a foundation or sprinkling with water. In the causitive - *Hif'il* - stem, the meanings "to point out, show; to teach, instruct" are added and from that sense the noun תּוֹרָה (*Torah*) is derived, really meaning "instruction, direction" but most often translated as "law". A measure of interpretation, therefore, is needed to understand how the word is used in this context.

Two suggestions are very close to the text. The first is adopted by *Targum Onkelos*, who replaces the word with לְפַנָּאָה - to clear - which is understood as clearing a place, clearing through any local bureaucracy, possibly even clearing the land of other buildings or tenants, so that Ya'akov and his family could settle there together. Perhaps this could be likened to the way that when a travelling circus comes to town the advance party locate the camp-site, work out the best arrangements for the Big Top and all the vehicles, make arrangements for local deliveries of food or other supplies, put up the posters for advertising and liaise with the press.

The second stream focuses on the physical preparation, rather than on cultural matters. This idea sees Judah being sent to reconnoitre among the local people, to discover their language and customs so that when Ya'akov and the family arrive they could integrate comfortably without causing unnecessary offence to the previous residents of the area. At the same time, since Ya'akov would be coming as the father of the Viceroy of Egypt,

Pharaoh's right-hand man, Judah would have to teach the local people who Ya'akov and the rest of the family were and explain their culture and lifestyle to the Egyptians so that everyone knew what was going to happen.

The *Midrash* extends this still further by suggesting that Ya'akov sent Judah ahead to establish a house of study in Goshen so that the family would be able to continue their *Torah* study uninterrupted by their journey and arrival in Egypt. "Said Rabbi Nehemiah: to prepare an academy for him there where he would teach *Torah* and where the tribal ancestors would read the *Torah*" (B'resheet Rabbah 95:3). Rashi adds, "to establish for him a house of study from which instruction shall go forth", in an allusion to "For the law will go forth from Zion, and the word of the Lord from Jerusalem" (Isaiah 2:3, NASB). The rabbis see Ya'akov and his sons teaching the Egyptians about the God of Israel and His ways as well as simply studying themselves.

The Sforno takes another interesting step. "**To show the way before him unto Goshen** ... so that Judah should prepare and establish a home in Goshen before the arrival of Ya'akov." This surely reminds us of Yeshua's words when He said to His followers, "I go to prepare a place for you" (John 14:2). They had been talking during the Passover meal; Judas had just gone out to arrange the time and place with the Temple leaders where he was to betray Yeshua to them; Yeshua reminded the *talmidim* - as He had told them before - that He was about to go away and they they could not come with Him. Yeshua tells the disciples not to be afraid and to focus on their belief in Him and the Father, then says, "In My Father's house are many dwelling places; if it were not so, I would have told you; for I go to prepare a place for you. And if I go and prepare a place for you, I will come again, and receive you to Myself; that where I am, there you may be also" (John 14:2-3, NASB). Yeshua was going ahead, to prepare a place - in some translations "mansion" or "house" - for the disciples so that they could be with Him. Just as Judah was sent out to make preparations and to return to Ya'akov to accompany him on his journey, so Yeshua promises that once the places are ready, He will return to collect the disciples and personally escort them to that place where He will be with them; they they may be where He is.

The Bible is very clear that things don't "just happen"; careful preparation is required before things come into being or occur. In fact, God always trails anything significant so that we don't miss it. In times of distress, He tells our people, "Do not call to mind the former things, or ponder things of the past. Behold, I will do something new, now it will spring forth; will you not be aware of it? I will even make a roadway in the wilderness, rivers in the desert" (Isaiah 43:18-19, NASB); they are told not to worry about things that have already happened but to open their eyes and be aware of what God is about to do - something new, something quite different, something supernatural such as a river flowing in the desert. "Behold, the former things have come to pass, now I declare new things; before they spring forth I proclaim them to you" (Isaiah 42:9, NASB); God tells us about the new and amazing things that He is about to do so that when they happen we will know that they have come from Him and not from any other source or natural phenomenon. In His preparations, God foreknew us - as Yeshua said: "My sheep hear My voice, and I know them, and they follow Me" (John 10:27, NASB) and Rav Sha'ul wrote: "For whom He foreknew, He also predestined to become conformed to the image of His Son, that He might be the first-born among many brethren; and whom He predestined, these He also called; and whom He called, these He also justified; and whom He justified, these He also glorified" (Romans 8:29-30, NASB) - and He prepared the things that we should do and the way that we should walk: "For we are of God's making, created in union with the Messiah Yeshua for a life of good actions already prepared by God for us to do" (Ephesians 2:10, CJB).

Our participation in preparation is needed to make the process work. Yeshua told His *talmidim* to "Go and prepare our Seder, so we can eat" (Luke 22:8, CJB); the Passover meal would not just happen of its own accord, they needed to go and physically make preparations: buy food, spices, drink, make arrangements for cooking and so on; they had to "get it ready", "do the work". We, with the disciples, are urged to be ready for Yeshua's return, we are instructed to provide for our families, we are told to work in order that we may eat. We partner with God in the work of the kingdom. Rav Sha'ul said, "For we are God's co-workers; you are God's field, God's building" (1 Corinthians 3:9, CJB). In these days, it is this generation of believers that has been sent ahead to prepare the way for the Lord, we are the voices that cry in the wilderness; we are the ones who establish the houses of study, who teach our neighbours about the Lord and His ways, if not formally then by our lives.

Further Study: Amos 3:7; 2 Corinthians 6:1

Application: Do you hear the call to prepare? Do you long for the King to return and for many to be ready to receive Him? There has never been a better time to roll up your sleeves and get stuck into the harvest. Ask the Lord of the Harvest what your assignment is today!

וַיִּגַּשׁ ז׳

Vayigash - And he approached - 7

B'resheet / Genesis 47:11 - 27

B'resheet/Genesis 47:13 And there was no bread in all the land for the famine was exceedingly heavy

וְלֶחֶם אֵין בְּכָל־הָאָרֶץ כִּי־כָבֵד הָרָעָב מְאֹד
m'od   hara'av chaveyd kiy ha'aretz b'chol   eyn   v'lechem

As the text moves away from describing the affairs of Yosef's family - now comfortably settled in Goshen with a land-grant from Pharaoh himself - it turns back to the main narrative thread of the famine and Yosef's official role as the Grand Vizier of Egypt. Notice the word order here, deliberately chosen by the narrator in the opening phrase for emphasis; a literal translation would read, "and-bread there-was-not in-all-the-land", rather than the more usual "and-there-was-not bread in-all-the-land". By bringing the subject לֶחֶם to the front, it makes "bread" the focus of the clause; other things might still be available, but bread - the principle staple of every diet and here also used as a collective synonym for 'food' - there was not. As the song from the nineteen twenties ran: Yes, we have no bananas. The word הָאָרֶץ, here translated "the land" is rendered "the world" by a number of translations to show the scope of the famine and the profile it had in the minds of those who were blighted by it; the famine was not localised to a particular area or region, it affected the whole world of the Egyptians, their own immediate land and their area of military or political influence. The rest of the verse demonstrates the limit of the Egyptian reach: "both the land of Egypt and the land of Canaan were wasted because of the famine".

The adjective כָבֵד - from the root כָּבֵד, to be heavy - has a range of meanings that describe how the famine impinged upon the land: heavy, grievous, difficult, arduous. The word is also amplified by the adverb מְאֹד, exceedingly. Rashi refers to this time as "the years of hunger" and - with *Targum Onkelos* - translates the second half of the verse to say that Egypt and Canaan "became weary" as if the land itself had become exhausted in fighting against the famine. Ibn Ezra and Radak speak of the "craziness" caused by hunger. Pharaoh's vision of the seven scrawny cows and seven blasted ears of wheat is being fulfilled to the last detail.

Many times the Hebrew Scriptures speak of famine in a way that makes it clear that it is seen as a tool that God uses to chasten or rebuke His people: "There was a famine during the reign of David, year after year for three years. David inquired of the Lord, and the Lord replied, 'It is because of the bloodguilt of Saul and his house, for he put some Gibeonites to death'" (2 Samuel 21:1, JPS). Sometimes it happens a result or consequence of some action or event, while at other times, it is the deliberate decree of *Adonai*: "Elisha had said to the woman whose son he revived, 'Leave immediately with your family and go sojourn somewhere else; for the Lord has decreed a seven-year famine upon the land, and it has already begun'" (2 Kings 8:1, JPS). The prophets revealed times of famine as God's punishment upon the people for their sins: "When they fast, I will not listen to their outcry; and when they present burnt offering and meal offering, I will not accept them. I will exterminate them by war, famine, and disease" (Jeremiah 14:12, JPS).

One particular instance of famine, announced by the prophet Amos to the northern kingdom of Israel, stands out from the rest. "A time is coming - declares my Lord God - when I will send a famine upon the land: not a hunger for bread or a thirst for water, but for hearing the words of the Lord. Men shall wander from sea to sea and from north to east to seek the word of the Lord, but they shall not find it. In that day, the beautiful maidens and the young men shall faint with thirst - those who swear by the guilt of Samaria, saying, "As your god lives, Dan," and "As the way to Beer-sheba lives" - they shall fall to rise no more" (Amos 8:11-14, JPS). The people were well acquainted with the physical effects of drought and famine, of being hungry and thirsty; they knew only too well how that felt and what would happen to even the fit and able-bodied members of society, let alone to the weak and vulnerable. Amos used those vivid images to predict a famine for God's words, for there is to be a famine of the word of God throughout Israel. Moshe had taught the people that "man does not live by bread alone, but man lives by everything that proceeds out of the mouth of the Lord" (D'varim 8:3, NASB) and the people were to see that principle worked out in their country. Israel had turned away from worshipping the God of Israel and successive kings had erected altars and images, idols and poles to the gods of the land and the gods of the surrounding nations who sought control over Israel. God responded by explaining that when His word is denied to the people there is no spiritual life in the nation and the land comes under the judgement of famine. Individuals may seek the word of the Lord, but it will not be found in the land; people may travel from one end of the country to the other, looking for somewhere that the word of God is taught or spoken, but will not find it. Even the strong will waste away for lack of God's word and those who swore by the false gods and idols will entirely fall.

Time and again, that effect has been worked out among the nations of the world, both in history and in our midst today. Wherever God's word is suppressed, there is a spiritual famine that eventually destroys the people and the countries involved. For decades, communist Russia sought to deny the existence of God and persecuted those few who tried to maintain faith and relationship with Him; yet the communist empire fell and although growing again today is still greatly weakened. Britain turned away from the word of God, both in specific commitments regarding Israel and in the downgrading and de-emphasising of Scripture and has lost its empire and place upon the world stage; successive governments continue to destroy the economy, trusting in the broken reed of Europe rather than in the word of God. America seems to be in the grip of the same process; gradually denying being "one nation under God" to become simply one of the nations, its military, social and economic policies becoming increasingly godless and self-destructive. Other nations follow suit as God is abandoned in favour of the new world order, as man comes into his own to rule the world in tolerance and equality.

At a personal level, we see the peoples of the world echoing Amos's words. There is a huge demand for spirituality as man desperately searches for something to quench his spiritual thirst. Created for relationship with God, man knows full well that something is missing and is striking out in every direction to try and find something that will satisfy. The gnawing inside, growing doubt in the abilities of governments to realise his dreams for him, are driving man in ever more wild efforts to find the truth. He is looking everywhere but under his own nose. Discredited and despised, God's word lies unwanted on the floor, while the new age, *kabbalah*, eastern religions and practices and other false hopes draw millions - of both people and money - flocking to their ranks.

How do we respond to famine? By immersing ourselves in God and His word; by plumbing the depths of our relationship with Him to mine treasures to share with others and water to quench their thirst. Yeshua said, "I am the bread which is life! Whoever comes to Me will never go hungry, and whoever trusts in Me will never be thirsty" (John 6:35, CJB). He said, "Whoever puts his trust in Me, as the Scripture says, rivers of living water will flow from his inmost being!" (John 7:38, CJB). As we take from what we have and share it with others - not in a preachy or judgemental way, but simply as one human being to another - our supply will not run out; as Elijah said to the widow: "The pot of meal will not get used up, nor will there fail to be oil in the jug, until the day Adonai sends rain down on the land" (1 Kings 17:14, CJB). God is waiting for us to call Him on this; He has given us His promise, laid out His plans, shown us what to do and how to answer the desperate need all around us. He is waiting for us to start sharing His life in us with our families, friends, work colleagues, people at bus stops and in supermarket checkout queues, with anyone and everyone that He brings across our path. We are just like the twelve disciples that Yeshua sent out in the towns and villages in the Galilee; although most if us are not in Israel, we need to hear Yeshua say, "Yes indeed; I tell you, you will not finish going through the towns of Isra'el before the Son of Man comes" (Matthew 10:23, CJB); we will not finish sharing Him with our neighbours before He comes.

Further Study: 1 Chronicles 16:11-12; Isaiah 55:6-7; 2 Corinthians 6:2

Application: If you feel a personal famine, then turn to God without delay and ask Him to satisfy your deepest desires in Messiah Yeshua. Then make sure that you start giving it away as fast as God pours it into your lap so that the supply won't be choked off.

וַיְחִי

Vayechi - And he lived

B'resheet / Genesis 47:28 - 50:26

רִאשׁוֹן	Aliyah One	B'resheet/Genesis 47:28 - 48:9
שֵׁנִי	Aliyah Two	B'resheet/Genesis 48:10 - 16
שְׁלִישִׁי	Aliyah Three	B'resheet/Genesis 48:17 - 22
רְבִיעִי	Aliyah Four	B'resheet/Genesis 49:1 - 18
חֲמִשִׁי	Aliyah Five	B'resheet/Genesis 49:19 - 26
שִׁשִׁי	Aliyah Six	B'resheet /Genesis 49:27 - 50:20
שְׁבִיעִי	Aliyah Seven	B'resheet/Genesis 50:21 - 26

וַיְחִי א׳

Vayechi - And he lived - 1

B'resheet / Genesis 47:28 - 48:9

B'resheet/Genesis 47:28 Ya'akov lived in the land of Egypt seventeen years

וַיְחִי יַעֲקֹב בְּאֶרֶץ מִצְרַיִם שְׁבַע עֶשְׂרֵה שָׁנָה

shana   es'reyh   sh'va   Mitzrayim   b'eretz   Ya'akov vay'khiy

It is traditional within the hand-written *Torah* scrolls to leave a significant gap, sometimes even starting a new line, at the start of each *parasha*. This portion, by contrast, has a very small gap between it and the closing phrases of the previous *parasha*, implying a close connection between the two *parashiot*. Rashi and other commentators ask why this should be and suggest a number of possible solutions. If we examine the closing verse of the previous *parasha*, we can see a possible explanation: "Isra'el lived in the land of Egypt seventeen years. They acquired possessions in it and were productive, and their numbers multiplied greatly" (B'resheet 47:27, CJB). As long as the father of the family, Ya'akov, lived the people prospered, but as soon as he died, although formal enslavement did not start until later, the atmosphere changed and the attitude of slavery began to build up (Rashi, Mizrachi).

What was it that enabled Job to endure the trials that the Lord had allowed Satan to put him through? It was his faith in God. In the midst of being attacked by his so-called comforters, Job responds, "I know that my Redeemer lives, that in the end ... I will see God ... I will see Him for myself" (Job 19:25-27, CJB). Job knew that his hope was in God, and that God lives - as long as God lives (and He lives for ever) then Job had a hope that was greater than anything that this life could throw at him.

Rav Sha'ul addresses this issue head on when he writes to the congregation at Corinth, where he had heard that some were denying the resurrection of the dead. "If there is no resurrection of the dead, then the Messiah has not been raised; ... also your trust is in vain ... if it is only for this life that we have put our faith in the Messiah, we are more pitiable than anyone" (1 Corinthians 15:13-14, 19, CJB). He then rushes on to assert the truth of the resurrection: "But now Messiah has been raised from the dead, the first fruits of those who are asleep" (1 Corinthians 15:20, NASB), because our faith is not in the work of a man who lived and died and is no more, our faith is in the One who lived and died and lives again, who demonstrated that death could not hold Him.

So let us live in the good of the resurrection, knowing that the head of our family, the family of believers, lives and will live for ever, and that we live in Him.

Further Study: Galatians 2:20; Ephesians 1:11-14

Application: It is easy to pick up an attitude of embattlement and live as if we are always helplessly waiting for the cavalry to come over the hill. Ask God to reveal the truth of resurrection life for you today.

וַיְחִי ׳ב

Vayechi - And he lived - 2

B'resheet / Genesis 48:10 - 16

B'resheet/Genesis 48:10 And the eyes of Israel were heavy from age, he was not able to see

וְעֵינֵי יִשְׂרָאֵל כָּבְדוּ מִזֹּקֶן לֹא יוּכַל לִרְאוֹת
lir'ot   yuchal   lo   mizoken kav'du   Yisra'el   v'eyney

At first reading, the natural meaning of the words in the text seems a sufficient explanation: Ya'akov was certainly a lot older than any of us are today; he had undeniably been through many of the life experiences which are now listed by doctors as major causes of stress (moving, bereavement, ill-health of family members, employment difficulties, etc.); old age and the rigours of life had taken its toll - his eyesight had deteriorated to the extent that he was nearly blind. On the other hand, two of the words used in the text might lead to a different conclusion. While the word כָּבֹד usually means 'heavy' and is often used to describe the weight of God's glory - the heaviness of His presence - it can also mean 'dull', rather like someone's behaviour when sedated. Similarly, the verb יַכֹל, used here in its *Hif'il* stem, can have the meaning of being caused not to do something, or not being permitted. There is a sense, therefore, that there was more than a natural sight deficiency here - that Ya'akov was being blocked from seeing something, either physically or spiritually.

When the prophet Isaiah was commissioned during his vision of *Adonai* in the Temple, he was told, "Make the heart of this people fat, stop up their ears and shut their eyes. Otherwise, seeing with their eyes, and hearing with their ears, then understanding with their hearts, they might repent and be healed!" (Isaiah 6:10, CJB) This is an astonishing thing: Isaiah is being told that his ministry is to be the exact opposite of what he might have been expecting - instead of many people coming back to the Lord, his words will cause their hearts to harden and their eyes and ears to be shut to the message of God. Whilst hearing, they shall not hear; whilst seeing, they shall not see. The following verses show how strange this seems to Isaiah as he asks *Adonai* how long this is to be for and the Lord replies that it will be until His purposes are fulfilled.

Rav Sha'ul explains that there is a time and a season for all things (cf. Ecclesiastes 3:1-8) when he writes, himself quoting from Isaiah: "For [God] says, 'At the acceptable time I listened to you, and on the day of salvation I helped you'; behold, now is the acceptable time; behold, now is the day of salvation" (2 Corinthians 6:2, quoting Isaiah 49:8, NASB). There is clearly a time when God speaks to us and encourages us to respond to His invitation. Similarly, there is a time when it is much harder for us to turn to God or to be aware of Him; we are, in a sense, hardened. So Yeshua, speaking not only to the disciples, but also to us, says, "He who has ears, let him hear" (Matthew 11:15, NASB).

Further Study: 1 Kings 19:9-18; Isaiah 55:6-7

Application: Are you really seeking and hearing from God at this time? Has the world made your ears dull and heavy? Now is the season to seek the Lord and His face, to spend time with Him and clear out the wax so that you can hear Him clearly.

וַיְחִי 'ג

Vayechi - And he lived - 3

B'resheet / Genesis 48:17 - 22

B'resheet/Genesis 48:17 Yosef saw that his father was setting his right hand on the head of Ephraim

וַיַּרְא יוֹסֵף כִּי־יָשִׁית אָבִיו יַד־יְמִינוֹ עַל־רֹאשׁ
rosh al y'miyno yad aviyv yashiyt kiy Yoseyf vayar

אֶפְרַיִם
Ef'rayim

The expression יַד־יְמִינוֹ, translated "his right hand", more literally means "hand of his right side", based upon the verb root יָמַן, to take, use or turn to the right. As today, the majority of people in ancient times were right-handed, so that the right hand was seen as the hand of strength and blessing. Here, Ya'akov places his right hand, the symbol of his authority, upon the head of the younger son to confer his blessing contrary to the natural birth order, and we see God again making His choice between older and younger as with Yitz'khak and Ishma'el, Ya'akov and Esav; now here again with Ephraim and Manasseh.

The Psalmist sees God's right hand as a source of blessing: "In Thy right hand there are pleasures forever" (Psalm 16:11, NASB), support: "Thy right hand upholds me" (Psalm 18:35, NASB) and victory: "His right hand and His holy arm have gained the victory for Him" (Psalm 98:1, NASB). Moshe speaks of the power of God's hand: "Your right hand, Adonai, is sublimely powerful; Your right hand, Adonai, shatters the foe" (Shemot 15:6, CJB). The prophet Micaiah "saw Adonai sitting on His throne with the whole army of heaven standing by Him on His right and on His left" (1 Kings 22:19, CJB), while the Lord speaks through Isaiah to say, "My hand laid the foundations of the earth, My right hand spread out the heavens" (Isaiah 48:13, CJB). Isaiah also sees *HaShem's* right hand as a standard of truth and proof of His faithfulness: "Adonai has sworn by His right hand and by His mighty arm: 'Never again will I give your grain to your enemies as food; nor will strangers drink your wine, for which you worked so hard'" (Isaiah 62:8, CJB) - the

235

authority and power of God's right hand guarantees the promise He is making.

All these images form the backdrop to a request put to Yeshua - depending on which gospel you read - by two of His *talmidim* or their mother: "Then Zavdai's sons came to Yeshua with their mother. She bowed down, begging for a favour from Him. He said to her, 'What do you want?' She replied, 'Promise that when you become king, these two sons of mine may sit, one on your right and the other on your left'" (Matthew 20:21-22, CJB). What sort of a request is that?! Perhaps she thought that it would be nice for for her boys to be recognised as important people in the kingdom, those who knew Yeshua and had the King's ear. Yeshua points out that "to sit on My right and My left is not Mine to give, it is for those for whom the Father has prepared it" (v23, CJB). The positions of power in the kingdom are positions of real power and authority and only the Father determines who shall occupy them, on the basis of obedience and servanthood. But each of us has the ear of the King at any time and access to His throne whenever we need it.

Further Study: Acts 7:55-56; Colossians 3:1-3

Application: Although the Scriptures use the images of God's right hand as a sign of His majestic power and authority - and it is so - via His Son Yeshua we not only have access to God, but can know His kingdom authority flowing through us as He places His right hand on our heads to commission us to serve Him. Do you know that power today?

וַיְחִי 'ד

Vayechi - And he lived - 4

B'resheet / Genesis 49:1 - 18

B'resheet/Genesis 49:1 ... And I will proclaim to you what will befall you in the Last Days.

וְאַגִּידָה לָכֶם אֵת אֲשֶׁר־יִקְרָא אֶתְכֶם
et'chem yikra asher eyt lachem v'agiydah

בְּאַחֲרִית הַיָּמִים:
hayamiym b'akhariyt

At first glance the verb יִקְרָא, although a normal *Qal* prefix 3ms form, is confusing. The root קָרָא has two related but distinct families of meanings: the first - and more common - group is "call, cry, shout" and extends to "proclaim, publish, summon, invite" and even "read" and "name"; the second - less frequent - use is "befall, happen". It is this second meaning that is being employed here: Ya'akov has gathered his sons for the last time, as he is about to die, to share with them some of the insights that he has about the times to come. The Jewish commentators are almost universal in claiming that Ya'akov is about to prophesy of the Messianic Age but that the Shechinah, not wanting this revealed yet, left him so that the following "blessings" or comments about his sons contain almost no reference to the End Times except the prophecy that the tribe of Judah would supply the kings of Israel until Messiah - who would Himself be from the tribe of Judah - came.

The Sforno makes quite a long comment to the phrase בְּאַחֲרִית הַיָּמִים, "in the last days", pointing out that this refers to the Messianic Era when those nations who are enemies of God will decline and fall (Jeremiah 46:28). After showing that Balaam also spoke of this time (B'Midbar 24:14), Sforno quotes from the prophet Micah: "In the end of days it shall come to pass that the mountain of God's house shall be established as the top of the mountains" (Micah 4:1). He concludes - as we would expect - that this is the same time that Ya'akov refers to when he says, "Until Shiloh comes and to Him the obedience of the people" (B'resheet 49:10). Sforno deduces that when Messiah comes the authority of Judah will be extended from the tribes of Israel to encompass all the peoples and nations of the earth.

The commentators speculate on what else Ya'akov could or would have said had not the *Ruach* left him at that moment. We know that there are many more things yet to know about the Last Days; this has generated an enormous literature in the Christian world with many great figures attempting to pull a consistent picture of the End Times from the pages of Scripture: J. C. Ryle, A. W. Pink, Tozer, Charles Spurgeon and Hendrickson to name but a few. In recent times, the 1970s saw the film "Left Behind" while the last few years have brought the best-selling series of books by Tim LaHaye and Jerry Jenkins of the same title. If truth be told, the Scriptures only tell us so much and the rest, however educated, is only guesswork and opinion. Daniel is told, "But you, Dani'el, keep these words secret, and seal up the book until the time of the end. Many will rush here and there as knowledge increases" (Daniel 12:4, CJB); while John hears, "Seal up the things the seven thunders said, do not write them down!" (Revelation 10:4, CJB).

We are told to always have an answer ready for those who ask us about our faith (1 Peter 3:15) - a word in season and out of season (2 Timothy 4:2) - but how do we know when to speak and how much to say? Like Ya'akov, we are dependent on the Holy Spirit, as Yeshua told us, "when the time comes, the Ruach HaKodesh will teach you what you need to say" (Luke 12:12, CJB). We almost have the opposite problem, knowing when not to speak, or when to stop talking. Just as there is a time to speak, there is also a time to refrain from speaking in order to let God do His work without our fingers poking or trying to stir the pot.

Further Study: Isaiah 2:1-4; D'varim 29:29; Acts 4:8-13

Application: Have you found yourself talking on past the point when you know God told you to stop, but somehow you kept going although you slightly lost the plot and perhaps were not even sure of what you were saying? Ask God to make you better at hearing His voice and give Him permission to interrupt you, even in mid-flow.

וַיְחִי 'ה

Vayechi - And he lived - 5

B'resheet / Genesis 49:19 - 26

B'resheet/Genesis 49:19 Gad - a troop will troop out and he, he will troop back on [his] tracks

גָּד גְּדוּד יְגוּדֶנּוּ וְהוּא יָגֻד עָקֵב:

akeyv yagud v'hu y'gudenu g'dud gad

Here we have a fairly impenetrable piece of Hebrew - a complex word play built around the root גָּדַד. Falling in with *Targum Onkelos*, Rashi goes for the idea of troops (גְּדוּד is a noun meaning a detached party of soldiers, operating out of their own territory) coming out of the territory of Gad, crossing over the Jordan with the other tribes to take part in the conquest of the Land, and then returning home without any casualties. In similar vein, Hirsch offers the proposal that this talks of Gad being a peaceful tribe, always staying within their own borders unless attacked and then hitting back lustily and pursuing their attackers back over their own boundaries to teach them a lesson.

Ramban, on the other hand, connects the word יְגוּדֶנּוּ with the verse "I must wait quietly for the day of distress, for the people to arise who will invade us" (Habakkuk 3:16, NASB), thus making the troop hostile: "a troop will always assail Gad, that he will have many wars, with enemy troops spreading out over his land, and that he will follow the enemy in his track and be victorious over him and pursue him." Our sages are even more positive: "a troop will come trooping upon him, but he shall troop on it" (*y.* Sotah 8:10), that is to say, Nachmanides continues, "bands will come to gather wealth and assail him, but he shall troop upon them and bring his troops into their land".

A lot of this, therefore, seems to depend on your point of view. Just after Peter has made his statement of faith in Yeshua as the Messiah and Son of God, Yeshua responds by telling him, "upon this rock I will build My church; and the gates of Hades shall not overpower it" (Matthew 16:18, NASB). Two different perspectives can come from this statement, depending on which way it is seen. One view - in some Christian circles quite the majority - is that the church is fixed in place, on a rock, and that all the forces of hell are attacking it, round about on every side, and that the church's job is to hang on - fighting it out, as it were, to the last man - until the trumpet plays the William Tell overture and the cavalry come streaming over the hill to relieve the siege; Yeshua and the angels coming to rescue the embattled church which although hard-pressed, has not been completely overpowered. The other view is the complete opposite: it is the gates of Hades that are fixed in position and no matter what they do, what forces they can muster, no matter what dirty tricks they play, they are completely unable to break out from their defensive position and overpower the righteous advance of the Kingdom of God. Two different interpretive traditions from the self-same text, seeing the situation in very different and contrasting ways.

Our whole lives can be altered by the way we see things and the lenses through which we view the world. Even basic assumptions that we acquire early in life, as children, can colour our reading of people and the events around us, not to mention the Scriptures, in a way that can distort or twist reality. People, for example, who have had an abusive father often find it very difficult to relate comfortably with God as their heavenly Father; their experience of what fathers can do means that they just can't connect with God in that way and often see Him instead as an aloof or distant figure, rather stern and judgmental, fickle and impossible to please. Those of us who see God from a different point of view may find that difficult to comprehend, but we too have our acuity bias that colours the way we are able to see God.

So how do we cut through the lenses and filters to see God as He is, to understand His word without the cultural or familial background that we all bring into our relationships with Him? Good and insightful commentaries can help, but the two most important keys are: asking questions and listening to the answers. We must always ask God to explain and reveal His word to us whenever we open the pages of the Bible; anything that we don't understand or connect with forms another question about its meaning and why we don't connect with it; then, when we think we understand, a final question: "is this it, have I got it it?" to confirm our study. And we should expect God to answer and help us not only to understand the words and see how to connect them to our lives, but also to get to know Him better and build an ever deepening relationship with Him. We must be prepared to put aside long-held impressions and misunderstandings - if necessary - and to allow God to touch the hidden and hurting pieces of our lives so that He can heal and repair, stripping away the layers of accumulation that block or colour our relationship. As Rav Shaul wrote: "Let the word of Messiah, in all its richness, live in you" (Colossians 3:16, CJB).

Further Study: D'varim 6:6-9; 2 Timothy 2:15

Application: Do you sometimes struggle with the words of Scripture, feeling that they might as well be in Martian for all the good they do you? Remember, firstly, that we all have days like that, when our brains don't seem to be working and we simply can't connect with the words; secondly, remember that God - who wrote the words - wants to talk to you about them and is just waiting for you to ask Him to explain them to you. Just ask, and He'll be there!

וַיְחִי

Vayechi - And he lived - 6

B'resheet / Genesis 49:27 - 50:20

B'resheet/Genesis 49:28 All these are the tribes of Israel: twelve

כָּל־אֵלֶּה שִׁבְטֵי יִשְׂרָאֵל שְׁנֵים עָשָׂר
asar sh'neym Yisra'el shivtey eyleh kol

Here, at the conclusion of Ya'akov blessing each of his twelve sons, the text sums up that these, all these, precisely twelve, no more and no less, are the twelve sons and so the twelve tribes of Israel. The tribes were as yet only in embryonic form, being simply the sons and perhaps grandsons of Ya'akov's sons, but these twelve sons of Ya'akov were the very ones whose offspring were to be the nation Israel. The phrase כָּל־אֵלֶּה - all these - is a formula used after a list of things or names to emphasise the unifying factor: the sons that Avraham had with his second wife, after Sarah died, are summarised in this way: "All these were the sons of Keturah" (B'resheet 25:4). Similarly, the five kings who conspired to rebel against Chedorlaomer, leading to Lot's capture and subsequent rescue by his uncle Avraham, are listed: "All these joined together as allies at the valley of Siddim" (B'resheet 14:3).

The words שִׁבְטֵי יִשְׂרָאֵל - the tribes of Israel - are taken by Sarna to express, "the consciousness of an overall national unity and common identity that is 'Israel', even though each tribe is separately treated" in the preceding list of blessings and the rest of the Hebrew Scriptures. Even though each of Ya'akov's sons receives very different and particular words of encouragement, censure or prophecy; even though the tribes were to have separate and distinct land-holdings and ancestral boundaries, yet they are one. The *Torah's* author sees the proto-nation of Israel already in form; despite petty squabbles and sibling rivalries, the Jewish people will survive and have survived all the ravages of time and history because - whether orthodox, reform or secular - a Jew is a Jew is a Jew and God's covenant is with the Jewish people. Sarna also points out that this is the first mention of the twelve tribes as tribes rather than sons. As Ya'akov is about to die and the baton is passed on to the next generation, so the form of Israel changes from the family of a patriarch to the tribes of a nation.

Lest there should be any confusion over Ephraim and Menasseh, the two sons of Joseph, and the issue of land-holdings in the division of *Eretz Yisrael*, the Sforno makes a lengthy comment to tie together later passages of Scripture. These twelve who are "blessed by Jacob are the twelve authentic tribes; they are written on the breastplate and Ephod; they were present at Mt. Gerizim and Mt. Ebal; for these twelve Moshe set up twelve pillars and Joshua twelve stones from the Jordan at Gilgal and Elijah when he built the altar" on Mt. Carmel (1 Kings 18). The Sforno explains that Ephraim and Menasseh are only considered tribes, or half-tribes, in the division of the land where Levi is excluded, so that there should still be twelve divisions.

The Talmud demonstrates the same overview of unity among differences in respect of the interpretation of Scripture. After three years of argument between the House of Shammai and the House of Hillel over a particular piece of *halacha*, the Talmud records that a *bat kol* - a voice from heaven - announced that "These and these are the words of the Living God" (*b*. Eiruvin 13*b*) but rendered a decision to follow the opinion of the House of Hillel. What is important here is to see that despite differences between scholars over the precise implementation of one particular *halacha*, the scholars were all working within the same framework and for the same objective - the correct interpretation of the Scriptures - so that the people would know what to do. Even though the opinions differed, the rabbis recognised that God would be pleased by His people who were sincerely seeking to know His will and were following through by putting their convictions into action.

Rav Sha'ul picks up the same idea and applies it to the body of Messiah. Just as the household of Israel is not altered in the least by particular religious affiliation or the absence thereof, so the body of Messiah is not affected by denominations: provided that a believer has truly believed in Yeshua as the Messiah, it matters not whether he belongs to a Baptist church, a Methodist church, a pentecostal church or any other church; he is still a believer and is in relationship with Yeshua. This is the essence of "there is neither Jew nor Gentile, neither slave nor freeman, neither male nor female; for in union with the Messiah Yeshua, you are all one" (Galatians 3:28, CJB); by using categories in which it is impossible for there to be a mixture, reversal or confusion, Sha'ul makes the point that all these people, regardless of their station, calling or gender, are equally members of the body of Messiah. He makes the same point again when writing to another congregation: "For indeed the body is not one part but many. If the foot says, 'I'm not a hand, so I'm not a part of the body,' that doesn't make it stop being a part of the body ... But as it is, God arranged each of the parts in the body exactly as He wanted them. Now if they were all just one part, where would the body be? But as it is, there are indeed many parts, yet just one body" (1 Corinthians 12:14-20, CJB). There are many different body parts, with different appearances, functions, behaviours and characteristics; yet all are part of the body and all are needed for the body as a whole to fulfill its function as designed by God. No one part can remove itself and say "I don't want to play" because all are essential to the correct operation of the whole. Sha'ul goes on: "So the eye cannot say to the hand, 'I don't need you'; or the head to the feet, 'I don't need you'" (v. 21, CJB); he is saying that no member of the body can send away or remove another member just because they are a different part of the body. More importantly, no group of members can discipline or disenfranchise another group because their function or calling is different - that would be like the hands of a body cutting off the feet because they couldn't play the piano!

The same theme appears in more specific terms in another of Sha'ul's letters: "Now if the hallah offered as firstfruits is holy, so is the whole loaf. And if the root is holy, so are the branches. But if some of the branches were broken off, and you - a wild olive - were grafted in among them and have become equal sharers in the rich root of the olive tree, then don't boast as if you were better than the branches! However, if you do boast, remember that you are not supporting the root, the root is supporting you. So you will say, 'Branches were broken off so that I might be grafted in.' True, but so what? They were broken off because of their lack of trust. However, you keep your place only because of your trust. So don't be arrogant; on the contrary, be terrified! For if God did not spare the natural branches, He certainly won't spare you!" (Romans 11:16-21, CJB). The Gentile church is not to be arrogant to Jewish believers, forcing them to "fit" their idea of what church should be or the lifestyle a "Christian" should live where there is a difference based upon calling. Jews and Gentiles are to stay as they are when they become believers (1 Corinthians 7:17-24) and are to accept each other's expressions of faith - provided, of course that they don't reject Yeshua - as valid within the body. Messianic Jews are a part both of the body of Messiah and the household of Israel. To borrow the phrases from the Talmud and the rabbis: These and these are sons of the Living God - all these are the children of Avraham!

Further Study: Proverbs 27:8; Romans 12:3-8

Application: Where do you find yourself with regard to the Jewish question in the body of Messiah? Are you a Messianic Jew struggling to find acceptance from the Gentile church world, or are you a Gentile struggling with allowing Jewish ideas and identity from Jewish believers in your church? Why not ask God - the Father of all men - to help you to see this from His point of view: all are one in Messiah Yeshua!

וַיְחִי ז'

Vayechi - And he lived - 7

B'resheet / Genesis 50:21 - 26

B'resheet/Genesis 50:21 And now, do not fear; I will provide for you and your little ones.

וְעַתָּה אַל־תִּירָאוּ אָנֹכִי אֲכַלְכֵּל אֶתְכֶם
et'chem achal'cheyl anochi tiyra'u al v'atah

וְאֶת־טַפְּכֶם
tapchem v'et

These words are spoken by Yosef to his brothers after their return to their home in Goshen after Ya'akov has been buried in the Machpelah cave in Hebron. The brothers were concerned, the text tells us, that now Ya'akov had died and the protection his presence afforded them has gone, Yosef will turn on them and exact some kind of revenge for their treatment of him in the past. "So they sent this message to Yosef, 'Before his death your father left this instruction: So shall you say to Yosef, "Forgive, I urge you, the offense and guilt of your brothers who treated you so harshly." Therefore, please forgive the offense of the servants of the God of your father'" (B'resheet 50:16-17, JPS). Yosef wept when he heard their message because it showed that although he had forgiven them, they had not really believed or accepted his forgiveness so that there was still fear in their minds.

Yosef's reply starts with the word וְעַתָּה - and now - a homonym[5] with וְאַתָּה - and you - a measure of both meanings could be intended; the pronoun perhaps to emphasise the verb that follows and contrast with the 'I' pronoun that accompanies the next verb, the adverb to make sure that they are listening this time: pay attention! The particle אַל is used with second person prefix form verbs to give the sense of a negative imperative, which

---

5. A homonym is a word that sounds exactly like another word, so that you cannot tell the difference between them when spoken, without the context. This is true for these words today in Hebrew, but may not have been so in the days when biblical Hebrew was written; scholars suggest that the *alef* and *ayin* letters did have slight but distinctive guttural sounds which have been lost since than time.

Hebrew does not otherwise have; תִּירָאוּ is the 2mp *Qal* prefix form from the root יָרֵא, to fear. The next two words are a 1cs personal pronoun and a *Pilpel* prefix form of the root כּוּל, to sustain, maintain, nourish. The *Pilpel* stem is so named because it repeats the first and third letters of the three-letter root; it is almost always used only with hollow verbs[6]. "Now don't you worry," Yosef replies, "I myself will sustain you; I will provide for you and your little ones. You can trust me, really." The verse goes on, "And he comforted them, speaking to their heart". Rashi comments, "words that are acceptable to the heart"; gentle and encouraging words that would be easily heard and accepted so that the brothers could be sure that Yosef really meant what he said.

Picking up on that idea, Richard Elliott Friedman makes an important point about what Yosef is doing, rather more than what he is saying: "We have seen that each act of deception since Ya'akov led to another deception that came as a recompense. Thus deception and hurts within a family can go on in a perpetual cycle. In order to bring it to an end, one member of the family who is entitled to retribution must stop the cycle and forgive instead. That is what Yosef is doing here." While Yosef still might have turned on his brothers in retaliation, he chooses not to; he chooses to end the cycle by returning more good for the old evil. By his action here, confirming not the brothers' worst fears but instead their best hopes - that the past really has been forgiven - Yosef brings to an end the pattern of deception that his father had started and that had been manifest in Yosef's own generation by the bickering and in-fighting between the twelve brothers.

A note on an altogether different line comes from Nahum Sarna, writing in the JPS Torah Commentary. Quite short, it simply says: "**I will sustain you**: This reassurance is puzzling since the famine is long over. Again there is a hint of deterioration in the Israelite situation." Sarna points to verse 5 - "My father made me swear, saying, 'I am about to die. Be sure to bury me in the grave which I made ready for myself in the land of Canaan.' Now, therefore, let me go up and bury my father; then I shall return" (JPS), Yosef's words to Pharaoh to obtain permission to leave Egypt in order to honour Ya'akov's funeral wishes - and the report of who was allowed to go Canaan on the burial trip in verse 8: "Joseph's household, his brothers, and his father's household; only their children, their flocks, and their herds were left in the region of Goshen" (JPS). With hindsight, of course, Sarna sees a gathering cloud of restrictions upon the family and descendants of Ya'akov: their wives, children and flocks (meaning, their wealth) have to be left behind as hostage against their return from the funeral. In that light, Yosef's reply to his brothers takes on a different tone. Is Yosef saying that although he is Grand

---

6. Hollow verbs are those with a *vav* or *yod* as their middle consonant.

Vizier and could easily turn his back on and break the connection with his brothers in Goshen, he will in fact maintain the family ties and protect them? Or is he closing ranks with the brothers and promising to use his waning power and influence for the good of the family as long as he still has it? Does Yosef see the writing on the wall and recognise that the tide of blessing and favour with their Egyptian hosts has already ebbed?

As believers, we know that the world has never shown the Kingdom of God any long-term favour. Although temporarily granted for ministries and initiatives that benefit society as a whole, such favour is short-lived and is soon attacked by the enemy of our souls who mobilises his forces to negate or defeat favourable public opinion. The post-modern age in which we live has allowed us a breathing space of tolerance and relativism - our beliefs and practices are tolerated because everyone is entitled to their own opinions and no-one can say that others are wrong - but even this veneer is paper-thin and will not last much longer. Yeshua warned the disciples, "If you belonged to the world, the world would have loved its own. But because you do not belong to the world - on the contrary, I have picked you out of the world - therefore the world hates you" (John 15:19, CJB). True believers throughout history have been persecuted for their faith by governments, by other religious or anti-religious groups and even, quite often, by others who call themselves Christians but either seem unable to obey Yeshua's words to "love one another: just as I have loved you, you also are to love one another" (John 13:34, ESV), or have no real relationship with Yeshua. In the western world today, although there are notable exceptions, persecution is often hidden and not openly expressed as direct opposition to our faith. That does not mean that the clouds are not gathering; on the contrary, they are. We all need to be aware of the political, social and media maneouvering that is taking place to marginalise and restrict believers in Yeshua. As Jews, we are no strangers to persecution - significantly from the organised church - and should be in the vanguard of those who are proclaiming the truth and fighting for freedom and liberty.

We must not lose hope in the face of the gathering storm. Just as Yosef spoke words of comfort to his brothers and promised to use his influence to protect and shield them from the worst of the Egyptian animosity, so Yeshua has promised to be with those who have chosen to follow Him: "Remember! I will be with you always, yes, even until the end of the age" (Matthew 28:20, CJB). Unlike Yosef, Yeshua's power is not waning; His influence and authority is not in decline; He is not affected by the government of the day, or in danger of losing his position "because He is Lord of lords and King of kings, and those who are called, chosen and faithful will overcome along with Him" (Revelation 17:14, CJB). Yeshua speaks words of encouragement into our hearts, words that we can accept and know come from Him. "Be strong, all you people of the land - says the Lord - and act! For I am with you - says the

Lord of Hosts. So I promised you when you came out of Egypt, and My Spirit is still in your midst. Fear not! For thus said the Lord of Hosts: In just a little while longer I will shake the heavens and the earth, the sea and the dry land; I will shake all the nations. And the precious things of all the nations shall come here, and I will fill this House with glory, said the Lord of Hosts" (Haggai 2:4-7, JPS). There will be a shaking, such as the nations have never seen; there will be trials and persecution for the true followers of Yeshua. But the Spirit of the Lord will rest upon His chosen ones and, like Stephen giving his testimony before the Sanhedrin, our faces will shine as we give Him the glory.

Further Study: 2 Chronicles 20:14-17; Shemot 14:13

Application: Are you feeling beaten up, cast down and defeated by the world around you? Do you shake your head in despair and disbelief at what the world is coming to? Lift up your head and look the enemy squarely in the eye, for "greater is He who is in you than he who is in the world" (1 John 4:4, NASB).

Biographies

Abravanel - Don Isaac Abravanel, 1437-1508, Statesman and biblical commentator; born in Lisbon, died in Venice; claimed descent from King David; wrote commentaries on the whole of the Hebrew Scriptures

Ba'al HaTurim - Rabbi Yaakov ben Asher, 1269-1343, born in Cologne, Germany; lived for 40 years in and around Toledo, Spain; died *en route* to Israel; his commentary to the Chumash is based upon an abridgement of the Ramban, including Rashi and Ibn Ezra; it includes many references to *gematria* and textual novelties

Chizkuni - Rabbi Hezekiah ben Manoah (13th century), French rabbi and exegete; his commentary on the *Torah* was written about 1240 in memory of his father, based principally on Rashi, but using about 20 other sources

Dubnah Maggid - Joseph ben Wolf Kranz, 1740-1804, Lithuanian-born preacher and story-teller; famous for his parables and stories.

Heschel - Rabbi Abraham Joshua Heschel, 1907-1972, born in Poland, educated in Germany and fled to England and the USA from the Holocaust; considered one of the most significant Jewish theologian of the 20th century; Professor of Jewish Ethics and Mysticism at the Jewish Theological Seminary for 26 years

Hirsch - Rabbi Samson Raphael Hirsch, 1808-1888, German rabbi of Frankfurt am Main, author and educator; staunch opponent of the Reform movement in Germany and one of the fathers of Orthodox Judaism

Ibn Ezra - Abraham Ibn Ezra, 1089-1167, born in Tudela, Spain; died in the South of France after wandering all around the shores of the Mediterranean and England; a philosopher, astronomer, doctor, poet and linguist; wrote a Hebrew grammar and a commentary on the Bible

Maharal - Judah Loew ben Bezalel, 1520-1609, known as the Maharal of Prague; a writer on Jewish philosophy mysticism and a super-commentary on Rashi

Nechama Leibowitz - 1905-1997, born in Riga, graduate of the University of Berlin, made *aliyah* in 1931; professor at Tel Aviv University; taught

Torah for over 50 years

Rabbi Gershon - Levi ben Gershon, 1288-1344, born in Languedoc, France; he was a philosopher, Talmudist, renowned mathematician and astronomer/astrologer; wrote a commentary on the *Torah* and other scientific works

Rabbi Akiva - Akiva ben Joseph, c.50-c.135; one of the third generation of the Mishnaic Sages, who were active between 70 and 135; although starting life as an ignorant shepherd, he became perhaps the most central authority quoted in the Mishnah; known by some as the "father of the Rabbinic Judaism"

Rabbi Jeremiah ben Eleazar - Haggadist of the third Amoraic generation (second half of the third century CE). Several of his *haggadot* are found in the Babylonian Talmud, while only one is recorded in the Yerushalmi (*y*. Shab. 6.10).

Radak - David Kimhi, 1160-1235, a medieval rabbi, biblical commentator, philosopher, and grammarian; best known for his commentary on the Prophets

Ramban - Rabbi Moshe ben Nachman of Gerona or Nachmanides, 1194-1270, Spanish rabbi, author and physician; defended Judaism in the Christian debates in Barcelona before making *aliyah* to *Eretz Yisrael*

Rashi - Rabbi Shlomo Yitzchaki, 1040-1105, French rabbi who wrote commentaries on the *Torah*, the Prophets and the *Talmud*, lived in Troyes where he founded a *yeshiva* in 1067; perhaps the best-known of all Jewish commentators; focuses on the plain meaning (*p'shat*) of the text, although sometimes quite cryptic in his brevity

Sfat Emet - Rabbi Yehudah Aryeh Leib Alter, 1847-1905, named after his major work - a set of *Torah* homilies - was a Hassidic rabbi who succeeded his grandfather, Rabbi Yitzchak Meir Alter, as Rav of Ger (Poland) and became the Rebbe of the Gerrer Hasidim.

Sforno - Rabbi Ovadiah Sforno, 1470-1550, Italian rabbi, philosopher and physician; born in Cesena, he went to Rome to study medicine; left in 1525 and after some years of travel, settled in Bologna where he founded a *yeshiva* which he conducted until his death

Vilna Gaon - Rabbi Elijah ben Solomon, 1720-1797, Lithuanian Talmudist, kabbalist, grammarian and mathematician; not yeshiva educated; strong opponent of the Hassidim

Bibliography

Books by Author

Benjamin Davidson, *The Analytical Hebrew and Chaldee Lexicon*, Samuel Bagster & Sons Ltd, London 1850

Derek Prince, *The Divine Exchange*, Derek Prince Ministries UK, 1997

Nahum Sarna, *The JPS Torah Commentary - Genesis*, Jewish Publication Society, Philadephia 1989

Richard Bauckham, *God Crucified*, Eerdmans, 1998

Richard Elliott Friedman, *Commentary on the Torah*, Harper Collins, San Francisco 2003

William Hendriksen, *New Testament Commentary - John*, Banner of Truth, Carlisle, PA, 1954

Books by Title

Be'er Yitzkhak - a book of commentary and response by Rabbi Yitzchak Elchanan Spector, 1817-1896, the Rabbi of Kovno

B'resheet Rabbah - one of the components of the *Midrash Rabbah* collection (the Great Midrash), probably compiled around 400-450 CE in *Eretz Yisrael* from the oral teachings of many of the early sages - some named, some anonymous - in the previous 400 years

Gur Aryeh - A commentary by the Maharal on Rashi's *Torah* commentary

Midrash Rabbah - a collection of *aggadic* commentaries upon the *Torah* and some other books of the Bible most used in worship; different volumes have been collated in written form between the 4th and 13th centuries CE; they contain both very early oral material from the sages of the 1st and 2nd centuries and glosses and inserts down to the 1200s

Midrash Tanchuma - A collection of *midrashim* on the *Torah* collected and published in the ninth century

Mishnah - the collection of Jewish Law and custom codified (collected and written down) under the auspices of Rabbi Judah the Prince around the year 200 CE

Mizrachi - a super-commentary on Rashi written by Elijah Mizrachi, 1455-1525, born in Constantinople, in 1495 became Grand Rabbi of the Ottoman empire

Or HaHayyim - a commentary on the *Torah* by Chaim ben Moses ibn Attar, 1696-1743, a Talmudist and kabbalist; born at Mequenez, Morocco, died in Jerusalem

Sifre - the earliest rabbinic commentary to the books of B'Midbar and D'varim; probably composed of two parts, one from the Schools of Rabbi Simeo and Rabbi Ishmael, the other from the School of Rabbi Akiva; the earliest material dates from 100-150 CE, but there are later additions until *Talmudic* times

Sim Shalom - named after the last stanza of the *Amidah*, the official prayer-book of Conservative Judaism: The Rabbinical Assembly, *Sim Shalom*, New York City 2001

Talmud - literally, instruction or learning; the distilled writings of the early sages, a composite of the Mishnah and the *Gemarah* - an extensive commentary to the Mishnah; two talmuds exist: the Jerusalem Talmud, from around 400-450 CE, compiled in the Land of Israel; and the Babylonian Talmud, from around 550-600 CE, compiled in the Jewish communities in Babylon

Tanakh - the Hebrew Scriptures: *Torah* (Instructions/Law), *Nevi'im* (Prophets) and *Ketuvim* (Writings)

Tosafot Yom Tov - A commentary on the Mishnah, by Yom-Tov Lipmann Heller, 1578-1654, Bohemian rabbi and disciple of the Maharal

Zohar - The foundational book of Jewish mysticism, the *Kaballah*. Written in Aramaic, as if by Shimon bar Yochai, a second century rabbi, it was first published in the thirteenth century in Spain by a Jewish writer named Moses de Leon

Glossary

acharit hayamim - the Last Days

Adonai - literally, "My Lord" or "My Master"; although appearing in the Hebrew text as a word in its own right, it is widely used as a elusive synonym to avoid pronouncing the tetragrammaton - יהוה - the ineffable or covenant name of God; where the latter appears in a text, and is being read in a worship context, it will be pronounced as *Adonai*

aliyah (pl. *aliyot*) - literally "going up"; used as the name for one (or more) of the seven sections in which the *Torah* portion is read on *Shabbat*; so named because (1) the reader ascends physically to the *bimah* or platform in the synagogue to read and (2) the reader ascends spiritually by reading from the *Torah*

Amidah - The Standing Prayer, see *Shemoneh Esrei*

Chazal - an acronym: "Ch" stands for "Chachameinu", Our Sages, and the "z" and "l" correspond to the expression "Zichronam Livrocho", "of blessed memory"; this is a catch-all that often refers to the authoritative opinion in the *Talmud*, sometimes just the collected wisdom of the Sages in years past

chutzpah - the original Hebrew word means "insolence, audacity or impertinence"; colloquially, "nerve" or "gall"

cohen (pl. *cohanim*) - priest, so *cohen gadol* or *Cohen HaGadol*, the High Priest

Diaspora - from a Greek word meaning to scatter or disperse, this is the name given to the Jewish people scattered in exile throughout the world, as opposed to the part of the Jewish people that live in *Eretz Yisrael*

Eretz Yisrael - the Land of Israel

gematria - a system of assigning a numerical value to a Hebrew word or phrase (using the numerical values of the letters) in order to connect it to other words and phases having the same numerical value; produces some interesting results but can be abused to generate spurious connections

Goyim - the nations

Haftarah - literally, "leave taking"; the reading from the Prophets or Writings that follows the reading from the *Torah*; thematically linked to the *Torah* reading, some of these have been set since the Babylonian exile

halacha - literally "the walking"; the detailed case law of implementing Torah

HaShem - literally, "The Name"; widely used as a elusive synonym to avoid pronouncing the tetragrammaton - יהוה - the ineffable or covenant name of God; where this appears in a text, and is not being read in a worship context, if will be pronounced as *HaShem*

Hif'il and *Hof'al* - the causitive voices (active and passive, respectively) of a Hebrew verb

Itpa'al - a passive and reflexive voice of an Aramaic voice

kabbalah - literally, "receiving", teaching and school of thought concerned with the mystical aspect of Judaism. Emerged 11th - 13th century CE in Spain, recast in *\Eretz Yisrael* in the 16th century

komer - a unit of volume, equal to about 10 ephahs

Kotel - literally, "wall"; the Western Wall - the part of the western reatining wall of the Temple platform in Jerusalem that is exposed and visited by thousands of Jews each week; one of the closest accessible places to the Holy of Holies of the Second Temple

kvetching - Yiddish for "complain"; implies in a consistent or whiney way

Malach Adonai - literally "The Messenger of the Lord" or "Angel of the Lord"; thought by some scholars to be a pre-incarnation appearance of Yeshua

malkhut ha'shamayim - literally, the

masorete - The Masoretes were groups of scribes and scholars in Tiberias and Jerusalem - *masorete* meaning guardian or keeper of tradition - in the 8th - 9th centuries CE; they preserved the traditional pronunciation, chanting and breathing of the Hebrew Bible text, lest it should be lost and future generations unable to read and interpret the consonantal text

Masoretic Text - the standard Jewish text of the Hebrew Bible, as annotated with vowels and trope marks by the *Masoretes* in the 9th century CE; devised by Aaron ben Moses ben Asher in Tiberias, these pointed texts are preserved in the Aleppo Codex (~930 CE) and the Leningrad Codex (1008 CE)

Midrash (pl. *midrashim*) - literally, study or investigation; the technique of *Midrash* is to interpret or study texts based on textual issues, links to other verses and narratives; as a class it includes both *halachic* (law-based) and *aggadic* (story or narrative) material which often fills in many gaps in the biblical material

mikvah - pool with naturally running water for ritual washing

mitzvah (pl. *mitzvot*) - literally, command or commandments

Niphal - the passive voice of a Hebrew verb

parasha (pl. *parashiyot*) - one of the traditional names for the divisions into weekly portions of the Hebrew Bible; the *Torah* contains 54 portions, each with its own name taken from one of the first few words in the text

Parochet - the thick curtain that hung in the Temple as a division between the Holy Place - which was accessible to all priests throughout the year - and the Holy of Holies, where only the High Priest could go, once a year; described as being a cubit or more in thickness and decorated in rich colours and designs

Pi'el and *Pu'al* - the emphatic or stressed voices (active and passive, respectively) of a Hebrew verb

Pilpel - an alternative form of the *Pi'el* voice for hollow verbs

P'rushim - Pharisees

Qal - literally, light; the unmodified or unenhanced version of a Hebrew verb; the simplest meaning of a Hebrew verb root

Qohelet - the Hebrew name for the book of Ecclesiastes

Rosh Chodesh - literally, "head of the month"; the day of the New Moon feast, to be marked by the blowing of silver trumpets; declared by the *Sanhedrin* in Jerusalem after having received reliable testimony from two witnesses that the new moon has been sighted

Ruach HaKodesh - literally, "Spirit or Breath, the Holy"; most common Hebrew name for the Holy Spirit

Sanhedrin - the most senior court in biblical Israel, with seventy one members; recently re-founded in the modern state of Israel

Shabbat - the 24 hours from sunset Friday to sunset Saturday, the seventh day of the week; literally, "the ceasing" because as Jews we cease any kind of work during those hours

Shabbat Sheckalim - the day each year when the half-shekel tax for the upkeep of the Temple was collected; now set as the *shabbat* before the first of Adar (Adar II in a leap year); the *Torah* portion Shemot 30:11-16 is read

Shabbat Shuva - the *shabbat* that falls between *Yom Teruah (Rosh HaShana)* and *Yom Kippur* each year; so called from the Haftarah portion which is read: Hosea 14:2-10, starting with the imperative verb *Shuva*, Return!

shabbaton - loosely translated 'sabbatical' and may be used for a year, a month or an arbitrary time period; also used for 'sabbath' as a class rather than one particular *shabbat*

shaliach (pl. *shluchim*) - emissary or apostle

Shavuot - literally "weeks"; the name of the biblical Feast of Weeks at the end of the fifty days of counting the *Omer* (sheaf) from *Pesach* (Passover)

Shemoneh Esrei - literally, "The Eighteen" because it originally contained eighteen stanzas or blessings; the central prayer of the three daily prayer services. Also known as the *Amidah* - "standing" or simply "the prayer", the rabbis determined that this prayer was the act of service that replaced the sacrifices in worship after the destruction of the 2nd Temple

Sh'ma - the first word of D'varim 6:4; an imperative verb: Hear!; the name of the primary Jewish statement of faith: Hear O Israel, the Lord, our God, the Lord is One

Siddur - the standard Jewish prayer book or order of daily prayers; extant in many oral and traditional forms before 800 CE, first codified by Sa'adia Gaon around 850 CE, first printed 1486 CE in Italy; contains the basic fixed contents of the prayer services

sidra - another name for the portions of the *Torah*, from a root verb meaning "to order"; see *parasha*

talmid (pl. *talmidim*) - student or disciple

Targum - literally, translation or interpretation; two principle *targums* are known: *Targum Onkelos*, a translation with some paraphrase of the *Torah* into Aramaic; *Targum Jonathan*, a translation with rather more paraphrase of the Prophets into Aramaic. They were probably made between 200-400 and were used in the reading and study of the Hebrew scriptures: one line or verse in Hebrew, followed by the same line or verse from the *Targum*. Important early witnesses to the text and translation into a closely connected cognate language

tetragrammaton - the four letter covenant name of God: יהוה yod-hay-vav-hay; never pronounced as written within the Jewish tradition and never vowelised with a correct set of vowels to prevent pronunciation

tikkun - literally, "repair", "fixing up" or "restoration"; often linked in the phrase *tikkun olam*, "fixing up the world"

t'shuvah - repentance; from the Hebrew root to turn, so not "saying sorry", but "turning around"

Torah - the first in the three parts of the Hebrew Bible (with Prophets and Writings); from the root יָרָה, to throw or teach; often translated 'law' but probably better 'instruction'; used at a minimum to describe the five books of Moshe, often expanded to include the whole of the Hebrew Bible, the *Talmud* and the Jewish writings, so that it can be used as a totally encompassing term

tsuris - Yiddish word meaning trouble or aggravation

Author Biography

Although professionally trained and qualified as a software engineer, Jonathan's calling to the Messianic Jewish ministry started in the mid-90s after a season of serving as a local preacher in the churches of North Devon. He was ordained "Messianic Rabbi" by Dr Daniel Juster and Tikkun Ministries, and has served as a Tikkun network congregational leader in England for some years. Now the founder and director of Messianic Education Trust - an educational charity and ministry that works to share the riches of the Jewish background of our faith in Messiah with the church, while teaching Yeshua as the Jewish messiah - he lives in the south-west of England with his wife, Belinda, and three of his four daughters. There he contributes to the local body of believers by being involved in the Exeter Street Pastors project.

You can follow the work of Messianic Education Trust and read the weekly commentaries as they are produced each week, on the MET website at:

http://www.messianictrust.org

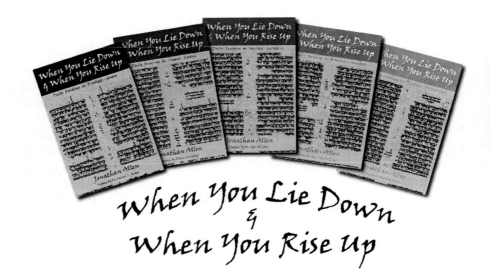

When You Lie Down & When You Rise Up

Daily Readings Following The Weekly Torah Portions

Rabbi Jonathan Allen

Daily Readings in B'resheet - Genesis - 1-901917-09-6

Daily Readings in Shemot - Exodus - 1-901917-10-X

Daily Readings in Vayikra - Leviticus - 1-901917-11-8

Daily Readings in B'Midbar - Numbers - 1-901917-12-6

Daily Readings in Devarim - Deuteronomy - 1-901917-13-4

Elisheva Publishing

www.elishevapublishing.co.uk

Lightning Source UK Ltd.
Milton Keynes UK
173505UK00001B/100/P